ELEMENTS
OF
FAMILY LAW

AUSTRALIA AND NEW ZEALAND
The Law Book Company Ltd.
Sydney : Melbourne : Perth

CANADA AND U.S.A.
The Carswell Company Ltd.
Agincourt, Ontario

INDIA
N. M. Tripathi Private Ltd.
Bombay
and
Eastern Law House Private Ltd.
Calcutta and Delhi
M.P.P. House
Bangalore

ISRAEL
Steimatzky's Agency Ltd.
Jerusalem : Tel Aviv : Haifa

MALAYSIA : SINGAPORE : BRUNEI
Malayan Law Journal (Pte.) Ltd.
Singapore and Kuala Lumpur

PAKISTAN
Pakistan Law House
Karachi

ELEMENTS
OF
FAMILY LAW

by

STEPHEN M. CRETNEY, MA, DCL, FBA,

Solicitor, Professor and Dean of the
Faculty of Law, University of Bristol

LONDON
SWEET & MAXWELL
1987

Published in 1987 by
Sweet & Maxwell Limited of
11 New Fetter Lane, London.
Computerset by
Burgess & Son (Abingdon) Limited,
Abingdon, Oxfordshire.
Printed in Great Britain by
Richard Clay (The Chaucer Press) Limited,
Bungay, Suffolk.

British Library Cataloguing in Publication Data

Cretney, S.M.
    Elements of family law.
    1. Domestic relations—England
    I. Title
    344.2061'5   KD750
    ISBN 0-421-35230-2
    ISBN 0-421-35240-X Pbk

PREFACE

The first edition of my textbook *Principles of Family Law* was published in 1974. It was specifically intended as a students' text book, and was 382 pages long. The fourth edition, published 10 years later, had grown to 1018 pages.

The present text is not intended as a substitute for *Principles of Family Law* which will, I hope, continue in successive editions to be found of value by students, teachers, practitioners and others who need a full account, supported by the conventional apparatus of scholarship, of the law in its social and historical context. Rather, this book is intended to meet the needs of those students who feel the need for a clear and concise guide to the basic principles or central core of English family law; and who are prepared to accept that such a guide can only be provided at the cost of some selectivity in the range and scope of the coverage.

Although some parts of the text—particularly in the earlier chapters— follow the pattern of *Principles* and incorporate abbreviated sections of the text of that work, much is entirely new. In particular, I have tried wherever possible to illustrate the operation of the law by summarising the facts of decided cases.

I hope that I have accurately stated the law on the basis of the materials available on January 5, 1987; but I have been able to incorporate brief references to some subsequent developments—notably the Government's proposals for sweeping changes in child care law. The last chapter of the book (Chapter 19, The Child of the Family Outside Marriage) contains an account of the likely general effect of the Family Law Reform Bill—described in the text as the Family Law Reform Act 1987—which is currently before Parliament. That chapter must obviously not be relied on as a statement of the law, but it seemed sensible in a work of this character to summarise the new provisions notwithstanding the fact that it will inevitably be some time before the legislation is brought into force.

I am grateful to my colleague Gillian Douglas whose expert scrutiny of the text both in typescript and proof has saved me from many errors and infelicities. I have benefited from discussions with Mr. Registrar Roger Bird, and parts of Chapter 11 have been influenced by his contributions to a Continuing Education course organised by the University of Bristol in which we both participated. I am also grateful to Mr. Registrar David Price who has kindly permitted me to reproduce the pro-forma calculators set out in the Appendix.

As always, I am deeply indebted to my wife, Antonia, and to my children Matthew and Edward. Without their support I could achieve little.

S.M. CRETNEY
St. Valentine's Day 1987

v

CONTENTS

TABLE OF CASES

TABLE OF CASES

TABLE OF STATUTES

United Kingdom Statutes

TABLE OF STATUTES

TABLE OF STATUTES

OTHER STATUTES

PART I—MARRIAGE AND ITS TERMINATION

The traditional view of English family law is that it is essentially about marriage and its consequences. Marriage was and is important for the lawyer because it creates a status in the sense defined by Lord Simon of Glaisdale in *The Ampthill Peerage* [1977] AC 547, 577: "the condition of belonging to a class in society to which the law ascribes peculiar rights and duties, capacities and incapacities." If a couple are married they automatically have certain rights and duties. In principle, the nature and quality of their relationship is quite irrelevant. A wife who has not lived with her husband for more than 40 years (as in *re Rowlands, dec'd* [1984] FLR 813) is nonetheless still in principle entitled, for example, to succeed to her husband's property on his intestacy.

Conversely, if a couple are not legally married, neither of them is automatically entitled to the legal rights which attach to the status of marriage. It makes no difference that their actual relationship is that of a happily married couple or that they have been living together for many years and that they have for long been regarded as a married couple by all their friends and relatives.

It is true that legislation now sometimes gives rights to those who have lived together as husband and wife; but marriage is still legally the most important relationship in family law. The first part of this book therefore deals with the creation and dissolution of marriage, as follows:

Chapter 1   *Formation of marriage*

Chapter 2   *Capacity to marry—annulment*

Chapter 3   *The modern law of divorce—introduction*

Chapter 4   *The modern law of divorce—the substantive law*

Chapter 5   *The modern law of divorce—further reform needed?*

Chapter 6   *Judicial separation and marital violence*

Chapter 1

FORMATION OF MARRIAGE

Introduction

The basic questions

All legal systems have ground rules about marriage. Is marriage to be   **1-01**
(as it is in English legal theory) the voluntary union for life of one man
and one woman to the exclusion of all others? Or is a man to be allowed to
have several wives? If so, how many wives may he have at the same time?
And what do we mean by "a man" and "a woman"? Can a 15-year-old
marry? Can a transsexual marry? What formalities have to be completed
to create a marriage?

Many different answers

Not surprisingly, the answers to such questions differ from country to   **1-02**
country. They also differ from time to time. For example:

(a) *Formalities*

Until the enactment of Lord Hardwicke's Marriage Act in 1753 English   **1-03**
law required virtually no formal procedures at all for the creation of a
marriage—the couple simply had to agree between themselves that they
were married. That sufficed to create what is correctly called a "common
law marriage,"—*i.e.* a marriage which was as valid as if it had been
celebrated by the Archbishop of Canterbury in Westminster Abbey in the
presence of a congregation of hundreds. This state of affairs lingered on in
Scotland (a fact which originally accounted for the popularity of Gretna
Green as a place for runaway marriages) until as recently as 1940, and still
exists in some parts of the world.

(b) *Who can marry whom?*

It was only in 1929 that Parliament decided that in this country a 15-   **1-04**
year-old child was not to be allowed to marry; whilst the rules about
marriages between relatives have been changed as recently as 1986 by the
Marriage (Prohibited Degrees of Relationship) Act which, as we shall see
(para. 2–09 below) even allows a man in certain circumstances to marry
his mother-in-law.

The basic rule

The basic rule of English law is that a marriage can be created between   **1-05**
any two people who have the necessary legal capacity and comply with

3

the stipulated formal requirements. Legal capacity is dealt with in Chapter 2; but first a little must be said about formalities.

FORMALITIES—THE MARRIAGE CEREMONY

1-06   One thing which can be said with absolute certainty about the English law is that it is astonishingly complex—so much so that the Law Commission said that it was "not understood by members of the public or even by all those who have to administer it": Law Com. No 53, Annex, para. 6. It is pointless to try to explain the details of the law contained in the Marriage Acts 1949 to 1986 in an elementary textbook: reference may be made to *Principles*, Chapter 1 for a fuller account. Here we simply state some of the main characteristics of the law.

(1) Parental consent sometimes required
1-07   If either party to an intended marriage is under 18 the consent of that person's parents is normally required. If the necessary consent is withheld, application may be made to the court for consent.

If a marriage is solemnised without the necessary consent it will nonetheless almost always be valid. The sanction is that one or both of the parties may be liable to prosecution for making a false statement.

(2) Requirements for banns, licence or certificate
1-08   The law stipulates certain preliminaries to the actual wedding. The objective is to publicise the parties' intentions, and give an opportunity for objection on the ground that there is, in the language of the Book of Common Prayer, some "just cause or impediment." The formalities required depend on whether the marriage is to take place according to the Rites of the Church of England or not.

(a) *Anglican marriages*
1-09   If there is to be an Anglican ceremony, Banns will usually be called. But the parties may alternatively obtain a Common Licence from the Church Authorities, or a Special Licence issued on behalf of the Archbishop of Canterbury. Banns are the cheapest preliminary, but involve the lengthiest delay. A Special Licence is at the other extreme. It can authorise a marriage at any time, without any delay and in any place. At one time the cost was such as to make it available only to the affluent, but the fees charged have not kept pace with changes in the value of money.

(b) *Other forms*
1-10   If there is to be a civil ceremony, or a non-Anglican religious ceremony, the parties must either obtain a Superintendent Registrar's Certificate —which is in some ways the equivalent of banns, being the cheapest of

the available procedures but requiring the longest waiting time, or a Superintendent Registrar's Certificate and Licence—often (incorrectly) called a "special licence"—which costs rather more but permits marriage after the expiration of one whole day from the giving of the notice. In either case, prescribed information has to be given and recorded in a marriage notice book which is open to public inspection.

Special cases

There are special provisions for the marriage of the terminally ill, the   1-11
housebound, and persons detained in prison or under the Mental Health legislation.

(3) The marriage ceremony

The legislation permits four types of ceremony. First, marriage   1-12
according to the rites of the Church of England. Secondly, a secular ceremony in a register office. Thirdly, marriages according to the rites of the religion concerned in a registered place of religious worship; and, finally, Quaker and Jewish Marriages.

(a) *The Church of England*

The marriage must be celebrated by a clergyman in the presence of two   1-13
or more witnesses. The clergyman will use the rite laid down in the Book of Common Prayer or authorised alternative form of service.

(b) *Register Office wedding*

The ceremony is simple in the extreme. The parties declare that they   1-14
know of no lawful impediment to the marriage, and "call upon these persons here present to witness that I, AB, do take thee, CD, to be my lawful wedded wife (or husband)." This must be done in the register office, "with open doors" and in the presence of two or more witnesses.

(c) *Marriages in a registered place of religious worship*

These provisions were originally intended to allow Roman Catholic   1-15
churches and non-conformist chapels to be used for marriages; but they can be used for marriages in Sikh or Hindu Temples, Mosques, or any other place of "religious worship"—an expression which has been held not to extend to the practices of scientologists: *ex parte Segerdal* [1970] 2 QB 697. The building has to be registered by the Registrar-General; but the form of the ceremony—which will usually be conducted by a minister of the religion concerned—is almost entirely a matter for the parties and the body controlling the building. At some stage in the proceedings the parties must make the statements set out in para. 1–14 above.

(d) *Jewish and Quaker Weddings*

The celebration of such marriages has, ever since Lord Hardwicke's Act,   1-16
been entirely a matter for the religions concerned. There is no requirement that the marriage take place in a registered building, in public, or that they be performed by an authorised person. The state's role is limited to

requiring that one of the stipulated preliminaries take place, and providing for the registration of such marriages.

(4) Registration

1–17   All marriages celebrated in this country must be registered. Registration provides proof that the ceremony took place, and also facilitates the collection of demographic information.

Chapter 2

CAPACITY TO MARRY—ANNULMENT

INTRODUCTION

This chapter outlines the rules which answer the question: "who can **2-01** marry whom?" But the law also has to deal with a separate question: what is to happen if someone goes through a marriage ceremony when the rules say that he cannot marry—suppose for example that a man (perhaps wrongly believing that his wife is dead) goes through a marriage ceremony with another woman, notwithstanding the fact that in English law a married person cannot contract another marriage?

The simplest answer to this question would be to say that in such circumstances the rules prevent any marriage from coming into existence, and hence that neither party could have any legal rights and duties as a result of having gone through the ceremony. There would no doubt be a procedure whereby those affected could get a document from a court or other agency in effect certifying that the apparent marriage was "null and void to all intents and purposes whatsoever" to avoid any trouble for the future. And this is indeed precisely how the law worked for many years in this country.

But things are now rather different. This is because of the development of the law of nullity (or annulment) of marriage, which we must now try to explain. It is rather curious that the law governing the rules about who can marry whom is part of a code of laws which effectively attaches many of the legal consequences of valid marriage to relationships which the same law declares to be invalid; but that is one of the many strange features of family law which are explained by historical factors.

VOID AND VOIDABLE MARRIAGES

The distinction and its consequences
A confusing feature of English law is that (as a result of the historical **2-02** relationship between the common law courts and the ecclesiastical courts) English law treats some marriages affected by irregularity as being voidable rather than void. The main differences between the two categories are:

(a) A decree of nullity can be pronounced in relation to a void marriage at any time, even after the death of the parties. Voidable marriages can only be attacked during the lifetime of both parties.
(b) If the marriage is void, then no valid marriage ever existed. If it is voidable, the marriage is perfectly valid unless and until it is annulled.

(c) If the marriage is void, any interested person may take proceedings; whereas only the parties to a voidable marriage can take proceedings to have it annulled.

BUT EVEN VOID MARRIAGES MAY HAVE LEGAL CONSEQUENCES

2-03 This basic distinction between the voidable marriage (which is perfectly valid unless and until it is annulled) and the void marriage (which does not exist and requires no decree to bring it to an end) is comprehensible enough. However, the distinction has become blurred because in recent years, in order to avoid hardship, many of the legal consequences of a valid marriage have been attached even to void marriages, provided that a decree of nullity is obtained. Hence, although it is never necessary to obtain a decree annulling a void marriage, it may be very much in a petitioner's interest to do so.

The essence of the matter can be illustrated by considering the case of an innocent woman who has been tricked into a bigamous marriage. Unless and until she gets a decree she has none of the rights of a wife since she is not married. However, once a decree has been granted, she will be entitled to apply for financial relief in the same way as a wife whose perfectly valid marriage has been dissolved by divorce.

THE SIGNIFICANCE OF NULLITY

2-04 At one time the law of nullity was important as a legal technique for dealing with the breakdown of a matrimonial relationship—until 1857 there was no judicial divorce, and nullity was the only way (short of an Act of Parliament) of getting a legal release from an unhappy relationship. Moreover, until the coming into force of the Divorce Reform Act 1969, the "guilty" party to a marriage could not divorce his "innocent" partner. Hence in some cases (for example of sexual incompatibility) a man who was anxious to remarry might petition for nullity if his partner refused to divorce him. But today nullity is of little importance in this context, since if a marriage has irretrievably broken down one party will, sooner or later, be able to get a divorce: para. 4–45 below. Indeed, in 1985 there were only 589 nullity decrees, compared with 161,409 decrees of divorce. However, the law of nullity remains of fundamental conceptual importance since it indirectly determines who may marry whom. A brief account of the modern law therefore follows.

THE MODERN LAW OF NULLITY

Law now statutory

2-05 The law governing nullity was for long derived from the practice of the ecclesiastical courts which exercised jurisdiction over marriage cases before the creation of the divorce court in 1857. In 1971 the law was comprehensively reformed by the Nullity of Marriage Act. The Act, which has now been consolidated in the Matrimonial Causes Act 1973, ("MCA 1973" hereafter) still preserves the conceptual framework of the old law derived from the canon law. But it constitutes an exhaustive codification of English law on the subject. The doctrines and procedures of the ecclesiastical courts no longer constitute a source of law, although they may be relevant in interpreting the concepts derived from the old law, *e.g.* what is meant by consummation of a marriage.

Structure of Chapter

The law is discussed under three heads:

(a) The grounds on which a nullity petition may be presented (paras. 2–06 to 2–37);
(b) the bars to the making of nullity decrees (paras. 2–38 to 2–43);
(c) the effects of a nullity decree (paras. 2–44 to 2–48).

THE STATUTORY GROUNDS

Void Marriages

The modern law preserves the distinction between void and voidable   **2-06** marriages resulting from the historical development of the law referred to above. The grounds on which a marriage is void are (i) parties within prohibited degrees; (ii) either party under 16; (iii) non-compliance with formalities; (iv) marriage bigamous; (v) parties not male and female: MCA 1973, s.11.

Voidable marriages

The grounds on which a marriage is voidable are (i) incapacity to   **2-07** consummate; (ii) wilful refusal to consummate; (iii) lack of consent; (iv) venereal disease, pregnancy by third party, and mental illness: MCA 1973, s.12.

VOID MARRIAGES

1. Prohibited Degrees

Consanguinity and affinity

In order to understand the law and the policy to which it gives effect,   **2-08** the distinction between rules dealing with relationships of consanguinity (that is to say, those which would be created by a marriage between blood relations, such as parent and child and brother and sister) and those based on affinity must be made clear. Relationship by affinity is a relationship created by marriage. Relatives by affinity are called "affines," and consist of the spouse (or former spouse) of one's own relatives, and relatives of one's spouse (or former spouse). The term thus extends to in-laws and to step relations.

Prohibitions on marriage between relations

2-09   English law prohibits marriage between a person and his parent, child, grandparent, brother or sister, uncle or aunt, and nephew or niece. (Unlike some other Western systems of law it has no restriction on marriage between cousins).

There are sound genetic reasons for forbidding marriage between close blood relations, since there is higher chance of mutant genes being present in common in two persons with a close common ancestor. But the issue is not altogether clear cut since the characteristics which appear in the offspring of a union between blood relatives may be either favourable or unfavourable—this is after all the secret of breeding successful racehorses.

The Problem of Affinity

Biological objections of this kind cannot apply to prohibitions between affines. Historically the objections to marriage between affines originate in the traditional doctrine of the church whereby marriage makes man and woman one flesh. If it is wrong to marry my sister it must be equally wrong to marry my wife's sister. Since my sister is within the prohibited degrees of consanguinity, my sister-in-law (that is to say, my wife's sister) was for the church within the (correspondingly prohibited) degrees of affinity. More recently objections have been based on broader considerations of social policy, and in particular the argument that it is important to exclude disturbing sexual relationships from the home circle.

This issue is more difficult than it might appear. For example, should a man be allowed to marry his step-daughter? At first glance, this might seem to many to be repugnant. Surely the law should protect girls from the danger of sexual exploitation by those in authority over them, and not allow a man to look on a young girl as a potential bride when his true role has been that of a father? But suppose that the facts are that a man has married a widow whose daughter is an adult living away from home; and that he meets (and falls in love with) the daughter only after her mother's death? Is there any justification for not allowing such a couple to marry?

The increase in divorce and remarriage much increased the risk that a couple who have never in fact been members of the same family unit would be debarred from marriage by reason of a relationship through marriage; and the law was changed by the Marriage (Prohibited Degrees of Relationship) Act 1986.

2-10   The basic principle of the legislation is that marriage with relatives by affinity is now permitted; but in two cases marriage is only permitted subject to conditions:

(i) *Marriage to a step-daughter.* A man may only marry his step-daughter if two conditions are satisfied. First, at the time of the marriage both parties must be 21 or over. Secondly, the intended wife must not have been a child of the man's family (see para. 16–03 below) at any time whilst she was under 18.

(ii) *Marriage to a daughter-in-law*. A man may only marry his daughter-in-law if both he and the daughter-in-law are 21 or over; and both his son (i.e. the daughter-in-law's husband) and the son's mother are dead.

The drafting of the legislation is complex; and the above summary is incomplete (for example, there are of course comparable restrictions on marriage between a woman and her step-son and son-in-law). Moreover, although the policy underlying the conditions is clear enough, the legislation does not always ensure that effect is given to it. Thus, the policy is clearly that a man may not marry his step-daughter if he has had a parental relationship with her, but that he should be permitted to do so in other cases, and a man should not be allowed to marry his daughter-in-law if he has been responsible for breaking up her marriage to his son. But the Act would, it seems, permit a marriage between a man whose present marriage (to a woman who was not the son's mother) was ended by divorce founded on adultery with the daughter-in-law which so over-whelmed the son that he committed suicide.

Adoption
An adopted child remains within the same prohibited degrees in   **2–11**
relation to his natural parents and other relatives as if he had not been adopted. Hence, a marriage between a man and a woman who is in fact his natural sister will be void even though he did not know and had no reasonable way of finding out about the relationship. It is also provided that an adopter and the adopted child are deemed to be within the prohibited degrees, and they continue to be so notwithstanding that the child is subsequently adopted by someone else. But there is no other prohibition arising by reason of adoption. Hence, a man is allowed to marry his adoptive sister provided she does not fall into any other of the prohibited relationships.

2. Minimum age

No marriage under sixteen
A marriage is void if either party is under 16. This simple rule (which   **2–12**
applies whether or not either or both parties knew the facts) should be distinguished from the rule which requires parental consent if either party is under 18. If a 17 year old gets married without bothering to get his parents' consent, the marriage will be perfectly valid. This is because failure to comply with the parental consent rule has no effect on the validity of the marriage. In contrast a marriage between a boy of 17 and a girl who everyone thinks to be 16 is void if it is subsequently shown that in fact she was one day short of her sixteenth birthday—and of course it makes no difference that both sets of parents consented to the marriage.

Although few people would now support a return to the pre-1929 position when marriages of 12-year-old girls were permitted, it is not quite so plain that an underage marriage should be void (as distinct from voidable). If a couple marry genuinely believing that they are both of marriageable age, it is hard on them if subsequently—perhaps many years later—they discover that their marriage is void. Moreover if a couple have lived together for many years believing their marriage to be valid, it would seem to be quite wrong to let a third party challenge it—perhaps to get a financial benefit under the succession laws—particularly in cases where the wife was an immigrant with no birth certificate and no-one realised that she had been under 16 at marriage.

3. Defective formalities

General Principle

2-13   In general only deliberate disregard of the marriage formalities will invalidate a marriage; and the Marriage Act 1949 provides that if the parties "knowingly and wilfully" disregard certain requirements (for example, that banns be called) the marriage shall be void. It has never been determined whether it is sufficient if the parties know that in fact the formality has not been observed, or whether they must also know that the defect will in law invalidate the marriage.

In contrast the Act stipulates that evidence of certain irregularities (for example, failure to obtain parental consent) is not to be given in proceedings touching the validity of the marriage; so that such defects cannot invalidate the marriage.

The Act is silent as to the consequences of certain irregularities—for example, the requirement that the marriage be celebrated with open doors, and that certain prescribed words be used. It seems probable that such irregularities would not affect the validity of the marriage.

4. Bigamy

2-14   A purported marriage is void if it is proved that at the time of the ceremony either party was already lawfully married to a third party. The fact that the parties believe on reasonable grounds that the third party is dead makes no difference. The question whether a marriage is void for bigamy is answered once and for all by reference to the facts as they existed at the date of the ceremony. A marriage which was void because at that time one of the parties was already lawfully married remains void even if the lawful spouse dies the day after the ceremony.

5. Parties of same sex

General Principle

2-15   The Act provides (s.11(c)) that a marriage is void if the parties are not respectively male and female.

In *Talbot* v. *Talbot* (1967) 111 SJ 213 a widow went through a marriage ceremony with a "bachelor" who was (it transpired) a woman. It was held that the marriage was void.

The interpretation of this apparently simple provision can however give rise to difficulties.

Transsexuals

Transsexuals are people who have the physical attributes of one sex (for 2–16 example, male genitalia) but nevertheless feel themselves to be members of the other. Can such a person marry as a woman if he undergoes a "sex-change" involving hormone treatment, the surgical removal of the male genitalia, and the construction of an artificial vagina?

The orthodox view in English law is that marriage is not permitted in such cases. A person's sex is fixed for all time at birth; and the only relevant tests of sexual identity are biological. A person born with male genitalia and a male chromosomal structure is in this view a man for the purpose of the marriage laws, even if he considers himself to be a woman, lives and has been accepted as a woman, has most of the external attributes of a woman and has in most ways become philosophically, psychologically and socially a woman.

The April Ashley Case

The leading case on the subject is *Corbett* v. *Corbett* [1971] P 83:

April Ashley had undergone a sex change operation, lived as a woman, and indeed worked successfully as a female model; she had also been recognised as a woman for national insurance and passport purposes. It was nevertheless held, applying the principles stated above, that she remained a man and her marriage to the petitioner was accordingly void.

Is the April Ashley case still law?

The decision in *Corbett* was based on the pre-1971 law (under which 2–17 the question was whether the parties were properly described as a "man" and a "woman"). The Matrimonial Causes Act 1973, however, uses the words "male" and "female"; and it may be possible to argue that these terms refer to a person's gender (that is to say, the sex to which he psychically belongs), and that accordingly the question whether a person is "male" or "female" is no longer to be resolved solely by reference to tests of biological sexuality.

Transsexuals feel that English law prevents their forming any legally recognised marital relationship; but the European Court of Human Rights has unanimously rejected the argument that the law constitutes a violation of the right to marry guaranteed by Article 12 of the European Convention on Human Rights: *Rees* v. *United Kingdom, The Times*, October 21, 1986. The Court considered that the right which was protected was a traditional marriage between persons of opposite biological sex. The Court also, by a majority, held that the Registrar-General's refusal to alter the birth register to reflect the applicant's change of sexual identity did not constitute a breach of the right guaranteed by Article 8 to respect for his private life.

Nullity decrees for homosexual "marriages"?

2-18   The statute states that a "marriage" is void if the parties are not respectively male and female. It may, therefore, only be in cases where there is "something which looks like a marriage" and where there is some reasonable doubt as to the sex of the parties that a decree would be granted on this ground. The matter is important since, if the court were to grant a decree of nullity in respect of a union between a couple who were undoubtedly of the same sex it would also have power to make orders for financial provision and property adjustment: see Chapter 11, below.

6. Polygamous marriages

2-19   MCA 1973, s.11(*d*) provides that an actually or potentially polygamous marriage entered into after July 31, 1971 is void if either party to the marriage was at the time domiciled in England and Wales. The interpretation of this provision is complex and outside the scope of this book. Reference should be made to works on Private International Law, and to the Report of the Law Commissions (Law Com. No 146, 1985) which recommends the modification of the rule.

VOIDABLE MARRIAGES

1. Incapacity to consummate

2-20   MCA 1973, s.13(1) provides that a marriage shall be voidable if it has not been consummated owing to the incapacity of either party to consummate it. This is a statutory codification of a basic principle of the canon law. Although marriage was formed simply by consent it was an implied term of the contract that the parties had the capacity to consummate it; and physical capacity was thus as much a basic requirement of marriage as the intellectual capacity to consent. The law is still influenced by its origins in the canon law.

Salient features of the law

2-21   The main principles of the law can be summarised:

(i) *What is "consummation"?* Consummation means sexual intercourse which is "ordinary and complete": there must be both erection and penetration for a reasonable length of time. It is not necessary for either party to have an orgasm; nor are sterility or barrenness relevant.

(ii) *May be psychological.* Although some cases of incapacity are based on physical abnormality, many arise from psychological impotence. The reason for the incapacity is not material; and it follows that it is equally immaterial that the impotence is only *quoad hunc* or *hanc, i.e.* that the respondent is capable of having intercourse with other partners. It also follows that a spouse who suffers from invincible repugnance to the act of intercourse with the other will, for this purpose, be regarded as incapable

14

of consummating the marriage. But it would seem that some element of psychiatric or sexual aversion is necessary and that a rational decision not to permit intercourse is insufficient.

(iii) *Pre-marital intercourse irrelevant.* The fact that the parties have had normal intercourse prior to the marriage ceremony is irrelevant because what is in issue is whether *the marriage* has been consummated.

(iv) *Permanent and incurable.* The incapacity must be permanent and incurable. It will be deemed to be incurable if any remedial operation is dangerous, or if the respondent refuses to undergo an operation.

(v) *Evidence required.* It is for the petitioner to prove that the incapacity exists. The court has power to order a medical examination, and may draw adverse inferences against a party who refuses to be examined.

(vi) *Either party can petition.* Before the enactment of the Nullity of Marriage Act 1971 a spouse who relied on his or her own incapacity would fail if, at the time of the marriage, he knew of his incapacity, or if it would, in all the circumstances, have been unjust to allow him to succeed. But there is nothing in the Act to suggest that this particular rule survives; and it seems that a petitioner who knew of his own incapacity will be entitled to a decree unless the respondent can establish the modern statutory bar of approbation as laid down in the MCA 1973: see para. 2–41 below.

(vii) *Must have existed at time of marriage?* It was a basic requirement of the canon law that the incapacity exist at the date of the marriage. This was because there is a vast theoretical difference between, on the one hand, recognising that the marriage was a nullity in those cases where incapacity existing at the time of the marriage could be proved, and on the other, dissolving a valid marriage by a divorce decree because of some supervening cause. Has this been changed by the modern legislation, which does not in terms require that the incapacity should have existed "at the time of the celebration of the marriage"? Does it mean—for example—that a wife whose husband is made impotent as a result of a car accident on the way from the church to the honeymoon could now petition successfully for nullity? It seems clear that the statutory codification of the law was not intended to effect any change; and the courts might well interpret the statutory provision in the light of the classical distinction between nullity and divorce, and thus refuse a decree in such a case.

2. Wilful refusal to consummate

Anomalous but useful

MCA 1973, s.12(*b*) provides that a marriage is voidable if it has not been consummated owing to the wilful refusal of the respondent to consummate it. Conceptually, wilful refusal (which is something which occurs after marriage) should not be a ground for nullity; and it was only

2-22

introduced into English law in 1937. However, in practice it is found very useful, and in fact constitutes the main ground on which nullity decrees are granted: in 1975, 360 out of a total of 470 decrees annulling voidable marriages were granted on the ground.

The main features of the law

(i) *Must be refusal*

2-23 A decree will only be granted if an examination of the whole history of the marriage reveals "a settled and definite decision" on the part of the respondent, "come to without just excuse." A husband (it has been held) must use appropriate tact, persuasion and encouragement:

> In *Potter* v. *Potter* (1975) 5 Fam Law 16, CA a wife was refused a decree because the husband's failure to consummate resulted from a natural and not deliberate "loss of ardour" after a prolonged history of sexual difficulties.

(ii) *Without excuse*

2-24 If the respondent can show a "just excuse" for his refusal to consummate he is not guilty of wilful refusal. For example, if the parties have agreed that a civil marriage would be followed by a religious ceremony, the fact that the religious ceremony has not taken place is a "just excuse" for refusing to consummate the marriage. The courts have gone even further:

> In *Kaur* v. *Singh* [1972] 1 WLR 105 a marriage was arranged between two Sikhs. A civil ceremony took place, but (as the parties well knew) by Sikh religion and practice a religious ceremony was necessary in order fully to marry. The husband refused to make the arrangements, notwithstanding the fact that it was his duty to do so. The court held that the wife was entitled to a decree on the grounds of his wilful refusal to consummate: one party's refusal to go through the religious ceremony is a failure to implement the agreement and itself amounts to wilful refusal to consummate the marriage. The result would apparently be the same if he had tried to have intercourse but the wife refused.

(iii) *What is intercourse?*

2-25 The House of Lords has said that this word must be interpreted as understood in common parlance, and in the light of social circumstances known to exist when the legislation was passed:

> In *Baxter* v. *Baxter* [1948] AC 274 it was held that a wife's refusal to allow intercourse unless her husband used a contraceptive sheath was not a refusal on her part to consummate the marriage.

There are conflicting decisions as to whether a marriage is consummated by *coitus interruptus*; but the issue is probably now irrelevant since an insistence by one party in this practice would almost certainly found a divorce petition based on "behaviour": MCA 1973, s.1(2)(*b*); para. 4–15 below.

3. Lack of consent: duress, mistake, insanity, etc.

No marriage without consent

For the Canon Law, marriage was created by the consent of the parties.   2–26
In the absence of true consent there could be no marriage, and until the
Nullity of Marriage Act 1971, lack of consent made a marriage void. As a
result of a somewhat controversial provision in the 1971 Act, a marriage
celebrated after July 31, 1971 is voidable if either party did not validly
consent to it, whether in consequence of duress, mistake, unsoundness of
mind or otherwise: MCA 1973, s.12(c).

The mental element in marriage—the dilemma

Cases alleging lack of consent usually involve situations in which there   2–27
has been an apparent expression of consent, but it is subsequently alleged
that this was not accompanied by the necessary mental intention. For
example, a man may say that he only spoke the words of consent because
his bride's father was standing behind him with a shotgun. In such cases it
can be argued that the apparent consent is not real, and that there should
in principle be no marriage; but it would obviously give rise to great
uncertainty if an apparently valid marriage could be avoided simply by
proving the existence of a state of mind or belief which was not evident at
the time of the ceremony.

The solution

English law seeks to resolve this juristic dilemma. On the one hand, it   2–28
refuses to allow private reservations or motives to vitiate an ostensibly
valid marriage; on the other hand it accepts that there may be cases in
which there has been no consent at all. In the result the law is somewhat
complex; and the cases can best be considered under the three heads
specifically referred to in the legislation: (a) insanity; (b) duress and fear;
(c) mistake.

(a) *Insanity*

Marriage (according to a nineteenth century judge) is a very simple   2–29
contract, which it does not require a high degree of intelligence to
understand: Sir James Hannen P. in *Durham* v. *Durham* (1885) 10 PD 80,
81. Mental illness or deficiency will only affect the validity of consent if
either spouse was, at the time of the ceremony incapable of understanding
the nature of marriage and the duties and responsibilities it creates. Such
incapacity is hard to establish; and it is difficult to believe that petitions
will ever again be brought on this ground. This is because such marriages
are now only voidable; and it is thus no longer possible for relatives
whose succession rights have been prejudiced by a marriage to attack it
after the death of one of the parties. If either party to the marriage wants
to terminate it, he will usually be able to rely on the alternative "mental
illness" ground introduced in 1937 precisely because it was so difficult to
establish lack of consent: see para. 2–37, below.

(b) *Duress and fear*

2-30 The question is whether there has been a real consent. Hence (it has been said) "where a formal consent is brought about by force, menace or duress—a yielding of the lips, not of the mind—it is of no legal effect." The main conditions seem to be as follows:

(i) *Must be overriding fear.* This principle is most clearly illustrated by an American "shotgun" marriage case: the marriage was void because (said the judge) "if there had not been a wedding, there would have been a funeral" (*Lee* v. *Lee* (1928) 3 SW 2d 672). In contrast if the marriage was deliberately contracted out of a sense of obligation to family or religious tradition; then it cannot be annulled on this ground:

> In *Singh* v. *Singh* [1971] P 226, the bride had never seen her husband before the marriage, and only went through the ceremony out of a "proper respect" for her parents and Sikh traditions. The court refused to annul the marriage because there was no evidence of fear.

2-32 (ii) *Test subjective.* Although it is sometimes suggested that it is only a threat of immediate danger to life, limb or liberty which suffices to override a person's will, the reality is that a weak-minded person's will may be overcome by threats which would have no impact on a stronger character. Accordingly, the recent decision of the Court of Appeal in *Hirani* v. *Hirani* (1982) 4 FLR 232 that the test is simply whether the threat or pressure is such as to destroy the reality of the consent and to overbear the will of the individual is much to be welcomed, even though it is difficult to reconcile it with earlier cases which were influenced by the now outdated view that a marriage should not be legally terminated save in the most exceptional circumstances.

2-33 (iii) *Fear must arise from external circumstances, but not necessarily from acts of the other party.* In *Szechter* v. *Szechter* [1971] P 286 threats to life and liberty arising from the policies of a totalitarian regime were held to suffice: the parties married so that they would be allowed to leave the country and thus avoid imprisonment. This seems to be a very doubtful decision, however, since, although the parties were no doubt frightened, their decision to marry was a conscious and indeed a rational one. The parties wanted to be married so that they could enjoy the legal consequences of matrimony.

2-34 (iv) *Does it make any difference if the threats are justly imposed?* Suppose that a man is told he will be prosecuted for defilement unless he marries the girl (as in *Buckland* v. *Buckland* [1968] P 296)? On one view such a petition will fail if the petitioner is guilty; a decree may be obtained only if the accusation is false, or if the petitioner was threatened with a more severe penalty than the courts could have imposed (as in an American case where the man was told that having sexual intercourse with a minor was a hanging matter). But it is submitted that this view of the law is both illogical and contrary to principle—illogical because the justice of the threat has nothing to do with the subjective question of consent, and contrary to principle because the canon law held a marriage void even if the petitioner was subjected to a just fear through his own fault.

(c) *Mistake and fraud*

Generally neither mistake nor fraud avoids a marriage. The maxim "caveat emptor" (let the buyer beware) applies, it has been said, just as much to marriage as it does to the purchase of a horse (or motor car). Even fraud is not a vitiating factor if it induces consent, but only if it procures the appearance without the reality of consent. Hence, a marriage into which a woman tricked a man by concealing the fact that she was pregnant by a third party was valid at common law. (Since 1937 it has been possible, subject to certain conditions, to have a marriage annulled on the ground that the respondent was pregnant by a third party: see para. 2-37 below).   **2-35**

Mistake is only relevant if vitiates consent. The cases fall into three groups: **2-36**

(i) *Mistake as to the person as distinct from his attributes.* If I marry A under the belief that she is B this is sufficient to found a petition; but if I marry A erroneously believing her to be a chaste virgin of good family and possessed of ample wealth the marriage will be unimpeachable.

(ii) *Mistake as to the nature of the ceremony.* It has been held to suffice that one party thought he was appearing in a police court, or that the ceremony was a betrothal or religious conversion ceremony (*Mehta* v. *Mehta* [1945] 2 All ER 690) or that one of the parties was so drunk (or under the influence of drugs) that he did not know what he was doing at the time: *Sullivan* v. *Sullivan* (1812) 2 Hag Con 238, 246.

(iii) *But mistake about legal consequences of marriage insufficient.* In *Way* v. *Way* [1950] P 71 a petition failed where H assumed that his Russian wife would be allowed to leave the Soviet Union and live with him.

In *Messina* v. *Smith* [1971] P 322 W went through a marriage ceremony, knowing that it was such a ceremony, and that the purpose of it was to enable her to obtain British nationality and a British passport and thereby protect herself against the risk of deportation for offences incidental to her carrying on her trade of prostitution. A petition to annul the marriage failed. The parties did intend to acquire the status of married persons, and it was immaterial that one or both of them may have been mistaken about, or unaware of, some of the incidents of that status.

4. Venereal disease, pregnancy by another and mental illness

The remaining three grounds on which a marriage may be voidable were originally introduced by the Matrimonial Causes Act 1937 because of the absence of any matrimonial relief for fraudulent or wilful concealment of material facts. For instance, a man who discovered that his wife was   **2-37** carrying another man's child had until 1937 no ground of matrimonial relief: deceit was not a ground for annulment, and the pregnancy did not establish that she had, since the marriage, committed adultery.

The grounds (which were amended in some minor respects in 1971) are now:

(i) that at the time of the marriage the respondent was suffering from *venereal disease* in a communicable form;

(ii) that at the time of the marriage the respondent was *pregnant* by some person other than the petitioner; and

(iii) that at the time of the marriage either party, though capable of giving a valid consent, was suffering (whether continuously or intermittently) from *mental disorder* within the meaning of the Mental Health Act 1983, of such a kind or to such an extent as to be unfitted for marriage. This subsection is intended to cover the case where, although the afflicted party is capable of giving a valid consent to the marriage, his mental disorder makes him incapable of carrying on a normal married life. A petitioner may rely on his own mental disorder for the purposes of a petition on this ground.

BARS

2-38   If one of the grounds set out above is established, the petitioner will usually be entitled to a decree. However, if the marriage is voidable, he may still fail if one of three bars contained in MCA 1973, s.13 is established. (There are now no bars to the granting of a decree where the marriage is alleged to be void). The three bars are:

(1) Time

2-39   In the case of proceedings on the ground of (a) lack of consent, (b) venereal disease, (c) pregnancy by a third party, it is an absolute bar that proceedings were not instituted within three years of the marriage. (The court may however allow a petitioner who has during the three year period suffered from mental disorder to start proceedings after that period if it is in all the circumstances just to do so).

(2) Knowledge of defect

2-40   A petition founded on (a) venereal disease or (b) pregnancy by a third party will fail unless the petitioner can satisfy the court that, at the time of the marriage he was ignorant of the facts alleged. It is not sufficient that the husband knew that the wife was pregnant, he must also have known that she was pregnant by another man.

(3) Approbation

2-41   MCA 1973, s.13(1) provides that the court shall not grant a decree of nullity on the ground that a marriage is voidable if the respondent satisfies the court:

"(a) that the petitioner, with knowledge that it was open to him to have the marriage avoided, so conducted himself in relation to the respondent as to lead the respondent reasonably to believe that he would not seek to do so; and

(b) that it would be unjust to the respondent to grant the decree."

This bar replaces the complex and uncertain bar of approbation which was inherited from the ecclesiastical courts. Three separate matters must be proved:

(i) conduct by the petitioner in relation to the respondent which resulted in the respondent reasonably believing that the petitioner would not try to have the marriage annulled;

(ii) knowledge by the petitioner, at the time of the conduct relied on, that he could have the marriage annulled; and

(iii) injustice to the respondent if a decree were to be granted.

The case of companionship marriages

Suppose that an elderly widower marries a spinster on the frank   **2–42** understanding that they are not to have sexual relations—that their marriage is to be "for companionship only." After living with her for some years, the husband changes his mind and seeks to have sexual relations. The wife (who had on the marriage at the husband's request given up a job carrying pension rights) refuses. Will she be able successfully to defend a nullity petition alleging wilful refusal? If the wife can prove that the husband knew that nullity was available it would seem that she might do so, since in this case the loss of pension rights could probably constitute injustice to her which the courts' powers are insufficiently extensive to overcome (*cf. Scott* v. *Scott* [1959] 1 All ER 531).

Not a public interest bar

The law is now only concerned with the conduct of the parties towards   **2–43** each other, and injustice to the respondent; it is not concerned with representations which have been made to third parties, or with considerations of public policy:

In *D* v. *D (Nullity: Statutory Bar)* [1979] Fam 70 it was held that the fact that a couple adopted a child (and thus represented to the court considering the application that they were husband and wife) did not debar one of them from subsequently petitioning on the ground of wilful refusal. It is no longer relevant that it might be contrary to public policy to allow either subsequently to assert that the marriage was a nullity.

Effects of a Decree

Historical position

At one time a void marriage had no legal consequences. Hence, for   **2–44** example, any children born to the parties would necessarily be illegitimate. Neither party to the relationship would be entitled to acquire the other's British citizenship or to inherit on the other's intestacy. A man could not be required to maintain a woman who had been living with him in the belief that they were married. In the eyes of the law, such people were not, and never had been, more than a man and mistress.

The same consequences followed even if the marriage was only voidable. This was because, although the marriage was valid until annulled the decree when made operated retrospectively and the marriage became void ab initio.

Modern law
2-45   Over the years the law has been reformed, and the position is now radically different:

(a) *Voidable marriages—decrees not retroactive*
2-46   Under the old law, the parties to a voidable marriage were validly married until annulment, but once a decree absolute had been pronounced they were deemed never to have been married:

> In *Re Rodwell* [1970] Ch 726 the deceased's daughter could only qualify as a "dependant" within the meaning of the Inheritance (Family Provision) Act 1938 if she had "not been married." The daughter's voidable marriage had in fact been annulled; and Pennycuick J. held that because of the retrospective effect of the decree she qualified as a person who had not been married.

This anomalous, inconvenient and uncertain rule was abolished in 1971; and a voidable marriage which is annulled is now treated as if it had existed up to the decree.

(b) *Legitimacy of children*
2-47   Children of voidable marriages are legitimate because the marriage is treated as valid. Even the child of a void marriage will be "treated as" the legitimate child of his parents provided that at the time of the act of intercourse resulting in his birth (or at the time of the celebration of the marriage if later) both or either of the parties reasonably believed that the marriage was valid.

(c) *Financial provision for parties*
2-48   If the marriage is voidable, the parties' financial rights are the same before annulment as they would have been under a wholly valid marriage. The court has the same financial powers on granting a decree of nullity as it has on divorce: see Chapter 11 below.

If the marriage is void the parties are not married; and they have no legal rights as husband and wife. But if a decree of nullity is obtained, the court will have exactly the same powers to order one party to make financial provision for the other as it would have if a valid marriage had been dissolved. Similarly, a "wife" or "husband" who has obtained such a decree can apply to the court for reasonable provision out of the other's estate after his death. It is the decree which gives the right; and this fact could cause hardship to a woman who, for example, only discovered that her "marriage" was void for bigamy after her "husband's" death. Such a woman could have no right to succeed as his widow on the "husband's" intestacy; and it would be too late for her to obtain a decree. To deal with this problem a person who has in good faith entered into a void marriage with a person now deceased has been given a right to apply to the court for reasonable provision out of the deceased's estate, exactly as if the applicant were his widow, or had obtained a decree of nullity carrying with it the right to be considered for financial provision: Inheritance (Provision for Family and Dependants) Act 1975, s.25(4); see further 8–30 below.

CONCLUSION—DO WE NEED THE LAW OF NULLITY?

The law of nullity has lost much of its practical importance partly because **2-49** many of the legal consequences of marriage have now been attached to even a void marriage, and partly because virtually all marriages can sooner or later be dissolved by divorce if either party wishes it. This is in sharp contrast to the position before the Divorce Reform Act 1969. Then a divorce could be obtained only if one party could prove that the other had committed a matrimonial offence; and if he could not do so, the only way of escape was by obtaining a decree of nullity. Now a man separated from his wife for many years will be able to divorce her whether she wants a divorce or not, save in the most exceptional circumstances. Thus, in 1985 there were only 589 nullity decrees (of which 120 were because the marriage was bigamous, and 420 were based on non consummation) as against 161,409 divorces.

In view of the inevitable unpleasantness of nullity proceedings (sometimes involving medical examination) it is often suggested that the concept of the voidable marriage might be abolished; instead the parties should be left to obtain a divorce based on the breakdown of their marriage. This has been done in Australia; but the Law Commission, for reasons which not all have found convincing, rejected such a solution for this country. However, the number of nullity petitions has fallen dramatically in recent years: the number filed in 1985 was only half the number filed in 1984. This may have been because it is now less difficult to obtain a divorce in the early years of marriage: see para. 4–01 below.

Chapter 3

THE MODERN LAW OF DIVORCE—INTRODUCTION

DEVELOPMENT OF THE LAW

3-01 The modern law of divorce cannot be understood without some knowledge of its historical development. Until the Reformation, English law followed the canon law of the Catholic Church in not permitting divorce (in the sense in which that word is used today). By the 18th century, however, a procedure for divorce by private Act of Parliament had been developed.

Divorce for matrimonial offence

3-02 The Matrimonial Causes Act 1857 created the Court for Divorce and Matrimonial Causes, and gave it power to dissolve marriages if the petitioner could prove adultery, that he was free of any matrimonial guilt, and that there was no connivance or collusion between the parties. Divorce was thus a legal remedy only available to an injured and legally guiltless spouse. The grounds for divorce were somewhat widened in 1937; but it was still (in theory at least) not possible to obtain a divorce by consent. More important, it was not possible to obtain a divorce against an "innocent" spouse. Hence a man might have left his wife twenty or thirty years ago and committed himself to another woman by whom he had children, but he would not be able to marry her so long as his first wife refused to divorce him and herself abstained from committing any matrimonial offence.

Pressures for reform

3-03 The administration of the law also involved much unpleasantness—for example a petitioner who had himself committed adultery was not guiltless, and could thus only obtain a divorce if he could persuade the court to exercise its discretion in his favour. This involved the petitioner filing a so-called "discretion statement" containing full details of his transgressions; and as recently as 1969 the Court of Appeal held that a solicitor not only had to make sure his client understood the meaning of "adultery" but had also to warn him of the need to disclose adultery committed at any time before the case was heard: *Pearson* v. *Pearson* [1971] P 16. Not surprisingly, therefore, there was strong pressure for change not only from those who wished to be able to remarry, but also from within the legal profession. Bills designed to allow divorce on proof of seven years separation attracted considerable support, and the crucial breakthrough came with the publication in 1966 of *Putting Asunder*, the report of a Committee set up by the Archbishop of Canterbury.

Putting Asunder was effectively the catalyst for the divorce reforms   **3-04**
effected by the Divorce Reform Act 1969. It favoured as the lesser of two
evils the substitution of the doctrine of breakdown for that of the ⓘ
matrimonial offence; but the Archbishop's Committee thought that in
order to answer the question whether the marriage had indeed broken
down the court should carry out a detailed inquest into "the alleged fact ⓥ
and causes of the 'death' of a marriage relationship." The Committee
also proposed that the court should be obliged to refuse a decree ⓥ
(notwithstanding proof of breakdown) if to grant it would be contrary
to the public interest in justice and in protecting the institution of
marriage.

The Field of Choice

The Lord Chancellor immediately referred the report to the newly   **3-05**
established Law Commission. The Commission took as its starting point
that a good divorce law should seek "(i) To buttress, rather than to
undermine, the stability of marriage; and (ii) When, regrettably, a
marriage has irretrievably broken down, to enable the empty legal shell to
be destroyed with the maximum fairness, and the minimum bitterness,
distress and humiliation." The Commission rejected the view that a
divorce law, which is directed essentially towards dissolving the marriage ⓥ
bond, could do nothing towards upholding the status of marriage: the law
could "and should ensure that divorce is not so easy that the parties are
under no inducement to make a success of their marriage and, in
particular, to overcome temporary difficulties. It can also ensure that
every encouragement is afforded to a reconciliation and that the ⓥ
procedure is not such as to inhibit or discourage approaches to that
end."

Inquisitorial approach rejected

The Commission favoured reform; but it did not accept the proposal   **3-06**
made by the Archbishop's group that divorce should be available only
after the breakdown of the marriage had been established by a full inquest
into the marriage. The Commission thought that such an inquiry into
causes might be humiliating and distressing to the parties. Moreover,
without a vast increase in expenditure of money and human resources it
would be impracticable to have an inquest in all cases. Possible
alternatives were discussed; and agreement was reached between the
Commission and the Archbishop's group on the principle ultimately
embodied in the Divorce Reform Act 1969. This principle is that
breakdown should be the sole ground for divorce; but breakdown is not to
be the subject of a detailed inquest by the court. Instead it is to be inferred,
either from proof of certain facts akin to the old matrimonial offences or (i)
two years' separation if the respondent consents, or (ii) five years'
separation if he does not consent.

SOURCES OF MODERN LAW

3-07 The Divorce Reform Act 1969 (which came into force on January 1, 1971) radically reformed the law. That Act was subsequently consolidated in the Matrimonial Causes Act 1973 which made no substantial change in the law. The Matrimonial and Family Proceedings Act 1984 made a number of significant procedural and other amendments, but it did not change the law governing the ground for divorce itself.

OUTLINE OF SUBSTANCE OF THE MODERN LAW

3-08 A person who wants a divorce must present a petition to the court, which he is not permitted to do before the expiration of one year from the date of the marriage. That petition must allege that the marriage has irretrievably broken down; and the petitioner must satisfy the court of one or more of five specified facts from which the court is empowered to infer such breakdown. Unless the other spouse (called "the respondent") satisfies the court that the marriage has not irretrievably broken down, or successfully opposes the grant of the decree on the ground that the dissolution of the marriage would cause the respondent grave financial or other hardship the court will grant a decree of divorce. This will in the first instance be a decree nisi; and the marriage is not finally dissolved until the court grants a decree absolute, which it will normally do on the petitioner's application six weeks or more after decree nisi.

DIVORCE NOW DOMINATED BY PROCEDURE

The Special Procedure

3-09 Until 1973 all divorce cases were heard in open court; and the court could not grant a decree without hearing the oral testimony of the petitioner; but under the so-called "special procedure" which was first introduced in that year with a view to achieving simplicity, speed and economy (Latey J., *R v. Nottingham County Court, ex parte Byers* [1985] 1 WLR 403) there will usually be no oral proceedings at all unless the respondent takes steps to defend the proceedings.

In outline, the "special procedure" is as follows. The petitioner completes a standard form of petition, which he lodges together with an affidavit verifying the truth of his answers to a standard form of questionnaire. These documents are then considered by a Registrar in private; and if the Registrar is satisfied that the petitioner has sufficiently proved the contents of the petition and is entitled to a decree he will make and file a certificate to that effect. (As the Booth Committee—set up in 1982 to investigate procedure: see para. 5–06 below— said, in reality the Registrar can do no more than read the few documents before him; and Registrars have been urged not to take an over-meticulous or over-technical approach: *ex parte Byers*, above.) The decree is then pronounced by a judge in open court, usually in the form "I pronounce decree nisi in cases 1 to 50."

The great majority of divorce cases (some 97%) are dealt with in this way. Very few cases are actually fought out—in 1985, for example, only 464 were disposed of after trial, and no doubt in some of those cases the trial became a formality because the parties came to an agreement at the door of the court. There are a number of reasons for the very small number of contested cases. First, if either party wants a divorce he will today in practice sooner or later be able to obtain one; and a solicitor is therefore likely to advise a client not to oppose the grant of the decree, but perhaps rather to bargain for satisfactory financial and other arrangements as the price for not putting the petitioner to the trouble and expense of dealing with a defended case. Secondly (as the Booth Committee put it, para. 2.16) the cost of litigation usually makes it "unrealistic, if not impossible", for most couples to pursue their suits to a fully contested hearing. (If it is clear that the marriage has irretrievably broken down, legal aid is not usually available to a respondent to enable him or her to defend, although the Court of Appeal has recently said that legal aid should be granted if there are serious allegations which the respondent should be allowed to meet: *McCarney* v. *McCarney* [1986] 1 FLR 312.) Finally, the court itself "discourages defended divorce not only because of the futility of trying a contention by one party that the marriage has not broken down despite the other party's conviction that it has, but also because of the emotional and financial demands that it makes upon the parties themselves and the possible harmful consequences for the children of the family."

Hence, as a result of the widespread use of the "special procedure," divorce, although in legal theory still judicial, has in uncontested cases more of the attributes of an administrative act. This has profound consequences for the administration of the law: many of the problems which case law had exposed on the working of the legislation do not in practice arise, and it is therefore possible to deal with the law comparatively briefly. Nevertheless, the reader must resist the temptation to regard the substantive law as irrelevant: there are still some defended cases in which the law will be applied in the usual way; and even in undefended cases under the "special procedure" the petitioner may encounter difficulties if he (or his advisers) are ignorant of the underlying legal rules.

Chapter 4

THE MODERN LAW OF DIVORCE—SUBSTANTIVE LAW

Bar on Petitions Within One Year of Marriage

4-01   Between 1937 and 1984 no petition for divorce could be presented before the expiration of the period of three years from the date of the marriage, unless it was shown that the case was one of exceptional hardship suffered by the petitioner or one of exceptional depravity on the part of the respondent. In 1984 Parliament accepted the advice of the Law Commission that the 1937 provision was unsatisfactory not least because it involved the making of distressing and humiliating allegations in a substantial number of cases (1,604 in 1983). But it was also thought desirable to impose some restriction on the availability of divorce early in marriage so as symbolically to assert the state's interest in upholding the stability and dignity of marriage, and to prevent divorce being apparently available within days of the marriage ceremony.

It is therefore now provided (MCA 1973, s.3) that no petition for divorce shall be presented to the court before the expiration of the period of one year from the date of the marriage. This rule simply prevents divorce proceedings being started within one year of the marriage; it does not affect the ground upon which divorce may be obtained. It is specifically provided that the rule does not prevent the presentation of a petition based on matters (such as, for example, the respondent's adultery or his behaviour) which occurred before the expiration of that period. Conversely, the mere fact that a year has elapsed since the celebration of the marriage does not entitle the petitioner to a decree of divorce. In order to obtain such a decree he must establish the ground for divorce, as explained below.

Other remedies dealt with later in this book—such as judicial separation or ouster orders under the Domestic Violence and Matrimonial Proceedings Act—can be used to provide legal redress in the first year of the marriage.

There has never been any comparable bar under the law of Scotland; and statistical comparisons suggest that this omission has had little effect on the divorce rate. The reality is that a time restriction was originally introduced in 1937 as part of the price which had to be paid to get the substantive law of divorce reformed; and considerations of political expediency seem to have influenced the decision taken in 1984 to retain an, albeit short, time restriction.

28

IRRETRIEVABLE BREAKDOWN MISLEADINGLY DESCRIBED AS THE GROUND FOR
DIVORCE

In legal theory, there is now one ground, and one ground only, on which   **4-02**
the court has power to dissolve a marriage, and that is that the marriage
has broken down irretrievably: MCA 1973, s.1(1). But the statement that
breakdown is the sole ground for divorce is for two reasons misleading:

(i) The court may not dissolve a marriage, however, clear it may be that it   **4-03**
has broken down irretrievably, unless the petitioner satisfies the court of
one or more of five "facts," (three of which are similar to the old
matrimonial offences of adultery, cruelty and desertion).

> In *Richards* v. *Richards* [1972] 1 WLR 1073 for example the husband (who
> suffered from mental illness) assaulted the wife, and was moody and taciturn. In
> the end, the wife left and the judge found that the marriage had irretrievably
> broken down. In spite of this a decree was refused: the Court held that the wife
> had not established that, given the husband's mental illness, she could not
> reasonably be expected to live with him: see para. 4–15.

(ii) The statement that breakdown is the sole ground for divorce might   **4-04**
lead one to think that the court would investigate whether or not there
had been such a breakdown. In practice, however, it does not do
so—notwithstanding the fact that it is (by reason of a provision originally
enacted as long ago as 1857) obliged "to inquire, so far as it reasonably
can, into the facts alleged" by the parties: MCA 1973, s.1(3). This is
because:
  (a) Although the specified facts in theory merely provide the necessary
evidence from which the court may infer breakdown, proof of any one of
them will raise a strong presumption that there has been a breakdown
which is irretrievable. The Act in practice puts the burden of proving that
there has not been an irretrievable breakdown on the respondent; and
there has in fact been only a single reported case (and that was wholly
exceptional) in which the court has refused a decree because it was not
satisfied that the marriage had irretrievably broken down: *Biggs* v. *Biggs*
[1977] Fam 1. Cases such as *Le Marchant* v. *Le Marchant* [1977] 1 WLR 559
(in which a decree was granted notwithstanding the wife's denial that the
marriage had broken down irretrievably and her protestations that she
still loved her husband) are much more typical. In the rare cases in which
there is doubt as to whether or not the marriage has irretrievably broken
down even though a "fact" has been established the only practical
solution will be for the court to adjourn the proceedings to enable
attempts to be made to effect a reconciliation.
  (b) The second reason why the court will rarely be in a position to
consider the question of irretrievable breakdown stems from the almost
universal use of the "special procedure" explained above: para. 3–09. It is
true that a respondent may in theory defend the case simply on the issue
of whether the marriage has in truth irretrievably broken down; but in

practice it will be difficult for him to get legal aid for this purpose: see para. 3–09 above. If the special procedure does apply all that is in practice required is a statement by the petitioner in his affidavit; and (as the Booth Committee, para. 2.17 put it) the "ability of the court to carry out its statutory duty to inquire is "greatly circumscribed."

THE FIVE FACTS

4–05   One or more of the "facts" specified in section 1(2) MCA 1973 must be proved. They are: (i) adultery; (ii) behaviour; (iii) desertion; (iv) two years' separation and consent to divorce; (v) five years' separation.

1. Adultery

Simple adultery insufficient

4–06   To establish this fact it is necessary to satisfy the court not only (i) that the respondent has in fact committed adultery, but also (ii) that the petitioner finds it intolerable to live with the respondent.

(a) *The fact of the respondent's adultery*

4–07   Adultery involves voluntary or consensual sexual intercourse between a married person and a person (whether married or unmarried) of the opposite sex, not being the other's spouse.

4–08   *Sexual intercourse.* This has for this purpose the same meaning as in the crime of rape—there must be some penetration of the female genitalia by the male member, however brief. Thus, a woman who has herself artificially inseminated without her husband's consent is not guilty of adultery; and it seems that a married man who has sexual relations with a partner who had undergone a sex-change operation involving the construction of an artificial vagina would probably not be guilty of adultery. It is clear that mere indecent familiarities (such as mutual masturbation) cannot suffice to establish adultery; but in such cases a petition based on "behaviour" (see para. 4–15 below) might be considered.

4–09   *Intercourse must be voluntary or consensual.* This means that a wife who is raped, or who has insufficient mental capacity to consent to intercourse either because she is too young or because she is mentally handicapped cannot be guilty of adultery. Drunkenness may, it seems, negative consent if it is excusable, *e.g.* where a woman has been given a laced drink against her will.

Proof of adultery

4–10   This used to cause many difficulties; and the standard of proof was said to be high. Today it is common to find that the petitioner alleges adultery against a person whose identity is not known; and if the case is undefended there will in practice be no further enquiry. But it is wrong to deceive the court; and if the adulterer's identity is known it must be revealed: see *Bradley* v. *Bradley* [1986] 1 FLR 128.

(b) *The petitioner finds it intolerable to live with the respondent*
The policy of the Divorce Reform Act was that adultery was relevant   **4–11**
only in so far as it was a symptom of marital breakdown; and the Act was influenced by the philosophy that adultery should "not in itself . . . be regarded as demonstrating breakdown unless the petitioner can in addition satisfy the court that the act of adultery is so offensive and deeply wounding to him or her that any further married life with the respondent is unthinkable."
    In practice the Act does not achieve this objective. In *Cleary* v. *Cleary* [1974] 1 WLR 73 the Court of Appeal held that the "fact" is established if, for whatever reason, the petitioner genuinely finds it intolerable to live with the respondent, even if the adultery has not played any significant part in the breakdown of the marriage. The court refused to construe the section as if it required proof "that the respondent has committed adultery by reason of which the petitioner finds it intolerable to live with the respondent". Moreover, it is clear that the test of whether the petitioner finds it intolerable to live with the respondent is subjective, not objective. It is sufficient if the petitioner does in fact find it intolerable to live with the respondent; it is immaterial that a reasonable person might not find it so.

No link between requirements
The view that no link between the two requirements need be shown   **4–12**
can in theory lead to some apparently bizarre results. (In *Roper* v. *Roper* [1972] 1 WLR 1314, 1317 Faulks J. suggested that a wife might even divorce a husband who had committed a single act of adultery because he blew his nose more than she liked.) But even so this interpretation seems correct. It gives effect to the plain words of the section; and it is consistent with the aim of the legislation that breakdown of marriage should be the sole ground for divorce. Breakdown is not, but adultery is, a justiciable issue. Once adultery has been established, the court draws the inference of irretrievable breakdown unless there is evidence to the contrary. The only reason why a literal construction of the Act seems strange is that it produces results unjust to a party who wishes to preserve the existence of the marital status. But the law is not now concerned with such considerations. The fact that the divorced spouse is "wholly innocent" and the petitioner "wholly responsible" for the breakdown is not a reason for keeping in existence the empty legal shell of a marriage which has in fact broken down.

Six months living together a bar
If one spouse knows the other has committed adultery, but has   **4–13**
continued to live with the other for six months or more, he cannot base a divorce petition on that act of adultery: MCA 1973, s.2(1). Conversely, if they have lived together for less than six months that fact is to be

disregarded "in determining . . . whether the petitioner finds it intolerable to live with the respondent." The object of this rule is to make it clear that a couple can seek a reconciliation without running the risk which existed under the old matrimonial offence doctrine that by living together the innocent party would be held to have forgiven (or condoned) the offence of adultery.

Reasons why adultery popular

4-14   A petitioner seeking to establish the "adultery" fact may simply state in the petition that the respondent has committed adultery with a person or persons unknown. In his affidavit in support of the petition he will be asked to state his reasons for believing that the respondent has committed the adultery alleged, to give the date on which it first became known to him that the respondent had committed that adultery, and whether husband and wife have thereafter lived in the same household (these latter questions being relevant to the six month provision referred to above). The petitioner is also asked whether he finds it intolerable to live with the respondent. The reality is (as the Booth Committee recognised: para. 4.9) that under the special procedure the court does not have the means to investigate whether uncontested allegations of adultery are true; and that in "the absence of any obvious discrepancy the court will invariably accept the respondent's admission as conclusive." (para. 4.13.) In reality, therefore, the adultery "fact" permits immediate divorce by consent; and this may be one of the reasons why it is so much used—in 1985 there were 53,330 petitions (28 per cent. of the total).

2. Respondent's behaviour

4-15   MCA 1973, s.1(2)(b) allows the court to infer breakdown on proof of the "fact" that "the respondent has behaved in such a way that the petitioner cannot reasonably be expected to live with him."

Most commonly used fact

4-16   This fact is more often than any other: in 1985 as many as 81,220 divorce petitions (out of a total of 190,481) were based on it. This is regrettable, since the need to prove such behaviour is inconsistent with the policy of enabling marriages which have irretrievably broken down to be dissolved with the "minimum bitterness, distress and humiliation." The Booth Committee (para. 4.17) concluded that petitions based on this fact "give rise to difficulties more often than petitions under other . . .-facts. We are in no doubt that part of the reason for this is that such petitions frequently contain a catalogue of incidents relied on by the petitioner in support of his allegation".

Allegations sometimes trivial

4-17   Sometimes these allegations may be of extreme triviality:

In *Livingstone-Stallard* v. *Livingstone-Stallard* [1974] Fam 47 the court had to consider the parties' methods of washing their underwear.

In *Richards* v. *Richards* [1984] AC 174 the petition alleged that the husband never remembered the wife's birthday or wedding anniversary, did not buy her Christmas presents, failed to give her flowers on the birth of their child and failed to notify her parents of the event, refused to take her to the cinema, and refused to dispose of a dog which caused considerable damage to the matrimonial home.

But even such allegations may cause great distress—particularly if the respondent believes he is innocent, and all the more so if he believes that the petitioner has been the more culpable.

But often serious

Physical violence (for example, blacking wife's eye on two occasions   **4-18** and striking her in the face on another: *Bergin* v. *Bergin* [1983] 1 WLR 279) is a common complaint. Sometimes it is coupled with other delinquencies (such as drunkenness and alcoholism: *Ash* v. *Ash* [1972] Fam 135, or making unjustifiable remarks to the husband's superiors with results potentially damaging to his career: *Bateman* v. *Bateman* [1979] Fam 250.) The courts also find themselves considering details of the parties' sexual behaviour:

In *Mason* v. *Mason* (1980) 11 Fam Law 143 it was held that a wife's refusal to permit intercourse more than once a week did not, in all the circumstances, amount to behaviour from which the irretrievable breakdown of the marriage could be inferred.

Petitions frequently allege such matters as the practice of perversions, and the making of excessive sexual demands. Often there is a lengthy catalogue of alleged misbehaviour:

In *Stevens* v. *Stevens* [1981] 1 WLR 885 it was said that the husband deliberately attempted to make life so unpleasant for wife that she would leave the house. He deprived her of lighting, and cooking facilities, invaded her bedroom to search through her belongings, sought to humiliate her by calling her a "slut," reminded her of a suicide in her family, and told her she was insane.

Sometimes there is an element of mental unbalance on the part of the respondent:

In *O'Neill* v. *O'Neill* [1975] 1 WLR 1118 the husband, a retired airline pilot, had a withdrawn personality and the marriage had never been entirely satisfactory, but the "last straw" for the wife was that for two years the husband carried out a prolonged renovation programme in their flat which involved mixing cement on the living room floor, having no door on the lavatory for eight months, and so on.

Problems of interpretation

The interpretation of this provision has caused some difficulties; and it   **4-19** cannot be said that discussion of them is entirely academic since it seems that petitions based on this "fact" are more likely than others to be defended. It is true that for some time it was the practice of the legal aid authorities to refuse legal aid to defend if they considered that the marriage has irretrievably broken down, and that the grant of the decree on that basis would not prejudice the respondent in financial and other matters. However, if the suggestion made by the Court of Appeal that a respondent should be entitled to legal aid to refute any sufficiently serious allegations (*McCarney* v. *McCarney* [1986] 1 FLR 312) is acted on, there may be a dramatic increase in the number of defended petitions. It is necessary for this reason to set out, albeit in summary form, the more important doctrinal points which emerge from the case law:

(a) *Two distinct requirements*
4-20   The petitioner must establish, first, that the respondent has behaved in a certain way; and secondly, that on the basis of such facts as are proved about the respondent's behaviour, the petitioner cannot reasonably be expected to live with him or her.

(b) *"Unreasonable behaviour" incorrect*
4-21   This abbreviation is often used; but it is wrong to do so. In Eekelaar's words, it "is not the behaviour that needs to be unreasonable, but the expectation of cohabitation." For example:

> In *Bannister* v. *Bannister* (1980) 10 Fam Law 240 the wife's undefended petition alleged that the husband had not taken her out for two years, did not speak to her except when it was unavoidable, stayed away for nights giving her no idea where he was going, and had been living an entirely independent life ignoring her completely. She failed at first instance on the ground that these facts did not constitute "unreasonable behaviour"; but the Court of Appeal allowed the wife's appeal because the husband's behaviour made it unreasonable to expect the wife to live with him.

(c) *Test objective*
4-22   The question is: can the petitioner "reasonably be expected" to live with the respondent?; not "has the respondent behaved reasonably?" It must follow that the court will consider all the circumstances, including any provocation by one spouse of the other:

> In *Stevens* v. *Stevens* [1979] 1 WLR 885 a wife's petition based on her husband's behaviour had been dismissed because the court found that (although the marriage had irretrievably broken down) it was not his, but her, behaviour which was the cause of the trouble. The parties thereafter continued to live under the same roof; and the husband coldly and deliberately set about attempting to make life so unpleasant for her that she would have to leave: see para. 4–18 above. The wife started fresh proceedings, which were successful: she could not have complained if the husband's behaviour to her was no more antagonistic or inconsiderate than might be expected from the situation for which she had been held to be responsible, but on the facts his behaviour since the first action went beyond what might have been expected, so that she ought not to be called upon to endure it.

(d) *Reasonableness judged through eyes of parties*

The court must consider the particular parties to the suit before it, not   **4-23**
"ordinary reasonable spouses." It seems to follow that a violent petitioner
may reasonably be expected to live with a violent respondent; a petitioner
who is addicted to drink can reasonably be expected to live with a
respondent similarly addicted; a taciturn and morose spouse can
reasonably be expected to live with a taciturn and morose partner; a
flirtatious husband can reasonably be expected to live with a wife who is
equally susceptible to the attractions of the other sex; and if each is
equally bad, at any rate in similar respects, each can reasonably be
expected to live with the other:

> In *Ash* v. *Ash* [1972] Fam 135 the husband accepted that he had been violent and
> had tendencies to alcoholism and to drunkenness (which he attributed to the
> availability of an expense account, to the demands of his work, and to his wife's
> lack of understanding); but the court concluded that she could not reasonably
> be expected to live with her husband.

On the other hand:

> In *Pheasant* v. *Pheasant* [1972] Fam. 202 the husband's complaint was simply
> that the wife was not able to give him the spontaneous, demonstrative affection
> which he said his nature demanded and for which he craved; and he said this
> made it impossible for him to live with her. It was held that he had failed to
> establish the behaviour "fact," since the wife had been guilty of no breach of
> any of the obligations of marriage. The couple had simply (it would seem)
> become incompatible, and that—perhaps strangely if the sole ground for
> divorce is really that the marriage has irretrievably broken down—does not
> suffice.

(e) *Right-thinking person test*

Value judgments about the nature of marriage are obviously involved   **4-24**
in making such assessments; and the Court of Appeal (*O'Neill* v. *O'Neill*
[1975] 1 WLR 1118) has favoured an approach which puts the issue in
terms of a direction to a jury:

> "Would any right-thinking person come to the conclusion that this
> husband has behaved in such a way that this wife cannot reasonably
> be expected to live with him, taking into account the whole of the
> circumstances and the characters and personalities of the parties?"

This will necessarily involve the court taking a view about the
obligations and standards of behaviour implicit in marriage—a task for
which some may think the courts are not altogether well-suited.

(f) *Respondent need not be morally culpable*

This point may be particularly relevant where the behaviour in question   **4-25**
results from mental illness; and there are some cases in which it is clear
that, whatever the excuse, the petitioner cannot reasonably be expected to
live with the other:

> In *White* v. *White* [1983] Fam 54 it was alleged that the husband was, by his own

account, intending to kill himself by jumping from a balcony when he heard a message from God telling him not to kill himself but to kill his wife instead; he told the wife that he would obtain a shotgun and would blow her head off and play football with it thereafter. On such facts a decree would be granted notwithstanding the fact that the husband was affected by mental illness to such an extent as not to be responsible for his actions.

In *Katz* v. *Katz* [1972] 1 WLR 955 the husband was a manic depressive who had been an in-patient at a mental hospital. He constantly criticised the wife and this coupled with other abnormal behaviour resulted in her suffering acute anxiety which culminated in a suicide attempt. She was granted a decree.

But the cases provide no clear answer to the question of principle: what is it reasonable to expect a spouse to tolerate?

In *Thurlow* v. *Thurlow* [1976] Fam 32 where a husband was granted a decree against his epileptic and bed-ridden wife, it was said that the court would take full account of the obligations of married life, including "the normal duty to accept and share the burdens imposed upon the family as a result of the mental or physical ill-health of one member."

But the task is a balancing one, and the fact that the health of the petitioner or that of the family as a whole is likely to suffer is a powerful factor influencing the court in favour of granting a decree. Similar considerations would presumably apply if the respondent's behaviour is caused by physical disease such as disseminated sclerosis, or cerebral thrombosis. The courts (see for example *O'Neill* v. *O'Neill* [1975] 1 WLR 1118) have deprecated reference to the wording of the marriage service in the Book of Common Prayer (which includes an undertaking to take the other "for better or for worse, in sickness and in health"); but it is not clear that the test of "reasonableness" can be applied without some view as to the nature of the obligations of marriage.

(g) *Behaviour may be either positive or negative*

4-26   However, in practice, the fact may be more readily established in cases where the behaviour is positive. Rees J. said in *Thurlow* (above) that spouses may often be expected to tolerate more in the way of prolonged silences and total inactivity than of violent language or violent activity. Just as unjustified refusal of sexual intercourse, and incorrigible or inexcusable laziness which led to financial stress affecting the wife's health were held to constitute the matrimonial offence of cruelty under the old law, so they would constitute "behaviour" for the purpose of the present "fact." Nevertheless, there must be something which can properly be described as "behaviour." This again may be relevant in cases of illness: in *Thurlow* v. *Thurlow* the court referred to a hypothetical case of a spouse reduced to a human vegetable as the result of a road accident, and removed at once to hospital to remain there for life. In such a case the petitioner could face "very considerable difficulties in establishing that there was any, or any sufficient behaviour towards him."

(h) *Living together after conduct in question*

Can the respondent say that the fact that the wife has gone on living **4–27**
with him proves that she has shown that she *can* live with him? The Act
contains a provision (s.2(3)) which is intended to facilitate reconciliation
by enabling the parties to live together for a short period without losing
the right to sue for divorce if the attempt is unsuccessful. In deciding
whether the petitioner can reasonably be expected to live with the
respondent the court must disregard cohabitation for up to six months.
Longer periods do not constitute an absolute bar; and the longer the
period the more difficult it will be to show that the petitioner cannot
reasonably be expected to live with the respondent. But the petitioner is
entitled to rebut such an inference:

> In *Bradley* v. *Bradley* [1973] 1 WLR 1291 the trial judge refused to grant a decree
> to a wife who was still living in a four-bedroomed council house with the
> husband and seven children; but the Court of Appeal held that she should be
> allowed to prove that, although she was in fact living with her husband, it was
> unreasonable to expect her to continue to do so. As Scarman L.J. pointed out,
> there could be reasons (particularly concern for the interests of the children)
> which might explain her continued residence with him.

The dilemma of the behaviour fact

The existence of the behaviour "fact" presents something of a problem. **4–28**
On the one hand its existence is difficult to reconcile with the policy of the
law in minimising the bitterness, distress and humiliation incidental to the
breakdown of a marriage; on the other hand, so long as it exists, it seems
wrong that those who are confronted by a behaviour petition which,
under the traditional practice of the legal aid authorities, they are often
unable to defend should be "publicly maligned and with no effective
means of reply". The Booth Committee (para. 4.26) has put forward a
radical proposal to deal with this problem, namely that a petition founded
on "behaviour" should no longer give any particulars of the behaviour
alleged; and the nature of the allegations would never be known unless
the respondent sought details of them. No doubt this change in practice
would (as the Committee put it) "shift the emphasis away from the
particulars of behaviour and guilt to the fact of the breakdown of
marriage" and it would thus "be wholly in accordance with the spirit of
the reformed legislation." (para. 4.25) However, it may also bring into
prominence the question whether the legislature was right in adopting the
structure now embodied in the law. If a decree is to be granted merely
because one party says that the marriage has broken down and the other
does not dissent, why should it be necessary to state in addition that one
party has behaved in such a way that the other cannot reasonably be
expected to live with him or her?

3. Desertion

To make out the desertion "fact" (MCA 1973, s.1(2)(*c*)) two things must **4–29**
be proved. First, that the respondent has deserted the petitioner; and

secondly that he has done so for a continuous period of two years, which immediately preceded the presentation of the petition.

Unimportant in practice

4–30   The desertion fact is relied on in less than 5 per cent. of divorce petitions (8,000 out of 190,480 in 1985); and desertion will rarely be found relevant in practice. This is because if a couple have lived apart for two years and both consent to a divorce that is sufficient to establish a "fact" evidencing breakdown; if they have lived apart for five years that is also of itself a "fact." In consequence it will only be necessary to rely on the desertion "fact" in two cases: first, where the couple have lived apart for at least two (but not five) years and the respondent is unwilling to agree to a divorce; secondly, where they have lived apart for five years, but the petitioner fears that the grant of a decree based on that fact might be opposed on the ground considered at para. 4–58 below.

Law disproportionately complex

4–31   Desertion is one of the traditional matrimonial offences; and the divorce courts for long adopted a restrictive attitude to the concept, for fear that too wide a definition would lead to what statute now in fact (if not strict legal theory) permits, *i.e.* divorce by consent after a period of separation. The effect of the courts' struggles with changing policy considerations over the years was to introduce what Lord Diplock (*Hall* v. *Hall* [1962] 1 WLR 1246, 1254) called "metaphysical niceties" into the law; and in consequence it is difficult to make clear statements of principle without over-simplification. Nevertheless, the attempt must be made.

First requirement: the respondent has deserted the petitioner

4–32   The main elements of desertion are: (a) the fact of separation; (b) the intention to desert. The intention to desert involves (i) lack of consent to the separation on the part of the petitioner; (ii) lack of any justification for the separation; and (iii) the respondent having the mental capacity to form the intent.

(a) *The fact of separation*

4–33   Factual separation is an absolute prerequisite to desertion; and the typical case of desertion is where one spouse leaves the matrimonial home. However "desertion is not the withdrawal from a place, but from a state of things," as Lord Merrivale put it in *Pulford* v. *Pulford* [1923] P 18, 21. What is required is a separation of households, not a separation of houses. This has two important consequences:

4–34   (i) *Factual separation can be established even if the parties are living under same roof.* The question has been reduced to whether or not there has been any sharing (however minimal) of a common life. Sharing a common living room, or taking meals at a common table, would be fatal to establishing the necessary degree of separation:

In *Le Brocq* v. *Le Brocq* [1964] 1 WLR 1085 the wife excluded her husband from the matrimonial bedroom by putting a bolt on the inside of the door. There was no avoidable communication between them, but the wife continued to cook the husband's meals, and he paid her a weekly sum for housekeeping. Hence he failed to establish the factum of desertion: there was, as Harman L.J. put it, "separation of bedrooms, separation of hearts, separation of speaking: but one household was carried on. . . . "

(ii) *Existence of matrimonial home not essential.* A husband's failure **4–35** without good cause, to establish a matrimonial home may by itself lead to the inference of desertion; and if husband and wife cannot agree on where the matrimonial home should be—for example, the husband wishes to take a job in Penzance whereas his wife wishes to continue living in Newcastle—the court will have to decide whether one of them is being unreasonable. The husband no longer has any absolute right to decide where he and his wife should live: *Dunn v. Dunn* [1949] P 98.

(b) *The intention to desert—animus deserendi*
The mental element required is an intention, inferred from the words **4–36** and conduct of the spouse alleged to be in desertion, to bring the matrimonial union permanently to an end: *Lang v. Lang* [1955] AC 402, PC. It follows that not every separation will constitute desertion, since (a) the separation may be consensual; (b) there may be good cause for the separation; or (c) the respondent may lack the mental capacity necessary to form the intention to desert. It is necessary to say a few words about each of these requirements.

(i) *Separation consensual.* Desertion is a matrimonial offence; and one **4–37** party cannot complain if he freely agrees to the separation. However, the fact that one spouse is glad that the other has gone does not mean that he has consented to the separation; and in this respect allowance is made for the emotional realities of the situation—

A wife who said: "Go if you like, and when you are sick of her, come back to me" was held not to have consented to the separation: *Haviland v. Haviland* (1863) LJPM & A 65.

The significance of consent as negativing desertion is much reduced by the "living apart" provisions of the modern divorce legislation. It seems likely to be relevant only in those cases where the parties have been separated for two (but not five) years, and the respondent refuses to consent to a decree. In those circumstances a petitioner may hope to establish the desertion "fact" but such a petition will fail if the *separation* was consensual.

(ii) *Good cause.* The respondent may be justified in leaving the petitioner **4–38** against the latter's will, either (i) by necessity; or (ii) because of the petitioner's behaviour. The question is really whether the respondent has a "reasonable excuse." Thus, in *G v. G* [1964] P 133 where the husband's behaviour terrified the children, it was held that the wife was justified in not allowing him into the matrimonial home even though by reason of mental illness he was not morally responsible for his actions. Again "grave and weighty" behaviour (for example adultery, cruelty, or unjustifiable refusal of sexual intercourse by the petitioning spouse) justifies the respondent in leaving:

> In *Quoraishi* v. *Quoraishi* (1985) FLR 780 the Court of Appeal held that a husband's conduct in taking a second wife (as he was permitted to do by his personal law) in the circumstances justified his first wife in leaving him. His petition for divorce was rejected, and a marriage which had evidently irretrievably broken down was kept legally in existence.

4–39   (iii) *Mental incapacity.* Mental illness may prevent the formation of the intention to desert. It is a question of fact (the onus of proof being on the petitioner) whether it has done so. If by reason of insanity one spouse has deluded beliefs about the conduct of the other, the rights of the parties in relation to the charge of desertion are to be adjudicated on as if that belief were true.

> In *Perry* v. *Perry* [1964] 1 WLR 91 the wife believed that her husband was trying to murder her. She left him. If the deluded belief had been true she would have been justified in doing so. Hence she was not in desertion.

Constructive desertion—driving spouse out

4–40   It is necessary to mention the doctrine of constructive desertion since it may still have some limited relevance. Under the old law (as the Privy Council explained in *Lang* v. *Lang* [1955] AC 402, 417) it was recognised that:

> "the party truly guilty of disrupting the home is not necessarily or in all cases the party who first leaves it. The party who stays behind (their Lordships will assume this to be the husband) may be by reason of conduct on his part making it unbearable for a wife with reasonable self-respect, or powers of endurance, to stay with him, so that he is the party really responsible for the breakdown of the marriage. He has deserted her by expelling her: by driving her out."

4–41   Under the modern law, the party who has left in such circumstances will be able to prove the "behaviour" fact (para. 4–15 above) and will thus not need to wait for two years before petitioning. Constructive desertion will accordingly no longer be relevant in such cases. But suppose that the husband simply orders the wife to leave—as in *Khan (Sajid)* v. *Khan (Sajid)* [1980] 1 WLR 355 where the husband was alleged to have said "I am telling you in front of your father, you are not to come back again"? It has been held in *Morgan* v. *Morgan* (1973) 117 SJ 223 that such cases should continue to be dealt with as cases of constructive desertion (rather than "behaviour"); and the practical consequence will be that no decree can be obtained for two years from the date of the separation. Of course if there is expulsive behaviour (such as violence) a decree based on the "behaviour" fact could be granted immediately.

Second requirement: respondent has deserted petitioner for a continuous period of two years immediately preceding the presentation of the petition

Two main points have to be noted about calculating the necessary   **4–42**
period of desertion:

(a) *Desertion an inchoate offence*

Desertion can be terminated (for example, by the party in desertion   **4–43**
making an offer to return and thus demonstrating that he no longer has
the necessary intention to desert) at any time before the filing of the
petition. If it is, the desertion "fact" has not been established. Again
desertion will be terminated if it becomes consensual (for example by the
parties making a separation agreement) or if supervening events remove
the duty to cohabit (for example, if a decree of judicial separation is made.)

(b) *Continuous does not mean continuous*

Although the Act stipulates that the respondent must be shown to have   **4–44**
deserted the petitioner for a continuous period of two years, it also
provides that in deciding this issue "no account shall be taken of any one
period (not exceeding six months) or of any two or more periods (not
exceeding six months in all) during which the parties resumed living with
each other, but no period during which the parties lived with each other
shall count as part of the period of desertion . . . ." (MCA 1973, s.2(5))
However, it is still necessary to prove an aggregate of two years'
desertion; and any period or periods of resumed living together is
deducted in calculating the overall period: for example, if H deserted W in
January 1986, W could petition in July 1988 even if they had resumed
living together for six months. But she could not petition in January 1988.

4. Living Apart

The real breakdown facts

The provisions of MCA 1973, s.1(2)(*d*) and s.1(2)(*e*) constitute the real   **4–45**
novelty of the reformed divorce law. Section 1(2)(*d*) requires proof that
the parties have lived apart for a continuous period of at least two years
immediately preceding the presentation of the petition and that the
respondent consents to a decree being granted. Section 1(2)(*e*) merely
requires proof that the parties have lived apart for a continuous period of
at least five years immediately preceding the presentation of the petition.
In effect, therefore, these provisions permit divorce by consent, and
divorce of a blameless spouse by repudiation. It is these "facts" which
best justify the claim that the law is now based on the irretrievable
breakdown of marriage. As Ormrod L.J. said in *Pheasant* v. *Pheasant*
[1972] Fam 202, 207, "separation is undoubtedly the best evidence of
breakdown, and the passing of time, the most reliable indication that it is
irretrievable." Moreover, it is only in cases based on the living apart facts
that the spouses are (as the Booth Committee put it, para. 2.9) no longer
required at the outset of proceedings to "think in terms of wrongdoing

and blameworthiness." It may be thought by some to be an indictment of the Act that comparatively little use is made of these morally neutral "facts" in practice—in 1985 some 19 per cent. of petitions (36,460 out of 190,480) were founded on two years' separation, and 6 per cent. (10,210 petitions) on five years' separation.

The period required

4-46 In both cases the Act requires that the separation be "continuous;" but in pursuance of the policy of encouraging reconciliation no account is to be taken of any period or periods (not exceeding six months in all) during which the parties resumed living with each other. However, no period during which the parties lived with each other is to count as part of the period for which they lived apart.

Meaning of "living apart"

4-47 The courts have held that living apart involves both (a) a physical and (b) a mental element:

(a) *Physical separation*

4-48 As with desertion, a couple can be treated as living apart even if they are still living under the same roof. The Act provides (s.2(6)) that "a husband and wife shall be treated as living apart unless they are living with each other in the same household, and references in this section to the parties to a marriage living with each other shall be construed as references to their living with each other in the same household."

4-49 *One household test.* The result of this provision is that husband and wife are to be treated as living apart, even if they are living under the same roof, unless it can be said that they are still living in the same household. The question to be asked is whether there is any community of life between them, which in practical terms means: does one party continue to provide matrimonial services for the other, and is there any sharing of domestic life? If the parties still share the same living room, eat at the same table and sit by the same fire (or perhaps watch television together) they are still to be regarded as living in the same household:

> In *Mouncer* v. *Mouncer* [1972] 1 WLR 321 the parties had for some time been on bad terms—to the extent that the wife petitioned for divorce on the ground of cruelty in 1969. An attempt at reconciliation was made, but this was not wholly successful. Nevertheless the divorce suit did not go ahead, the parties continued to live under the same roof (although in separate bedrooms), they usually took their meals together, and the wife did most of the household cleaning. In 1971 the husband left the house, and petitioned for divorce. The wife consented; but it was nonetheless held that living apart for two years had not been made out. The spouses had continued to live as a single household "from the wholly admirable motive of caring properly for their children", but this could not affect the fact that there had been no sufficient separation of households.

4-50 *As husband and wife.* There may be exceptional cases in which the parties live under the same roof and the one provides services for the other, but in some capacity other than that of a spouse:

In *Fuller* v. *Fuller* [1973] 1 WLR 730 husband and wife separated in 1964, the wife living with a third party as his wife, and adopting his name. In 1968 the husband had a serious heart attack. The medical evidence was that he could not live on his own again. He therefore moved into the house in which the wife was living with her lover. He lived as a lodger, sleeping in a back bedroom, and was provided with food and laundry by the wife in return for a weekly payment. The Court of Appeal held that the parties were not living with each other in the same household. "Living with each other" connoted something more than living in the same household; the parties must also be living with each other as husband and wife, rather than as lodger and landlady.

(b) *The mental element in living apart*

In the case of *Santos* v. *Santos* [1972] Fam 247 the Court of Appeal held   **4-51**
that living apart for the purpose of these "facts" can only start when one party recognises that the marriage is at an end—that is to say, when he and his spouse are, in common parlance, "separated," rather than simply living apart by force of circumstances. Until that date (so the Court held) the spouses are not "living apart," although they may "be apart." This requirement of a mental element means that a decree would not be granted in cases such as the following:

> H is sentenced to 10 years' imprisonment. After he has been confined for five years, W (who until then has stood by him) falls in love with X and wishes immediately to marry him. H does not want a divorce. W cannot petition until five years after she decided the marriage was at an end.
> H, with W's agreement, took up employment abroad in 1984, and has not seen W since then. H has now met another woman whom he wishes to marry. W recognises that the marriage has irretrievably broken down, and is prepared to consent to a divorce. She cannot however petition under section 1(2)(*d*), although if H admits adultery she will be able to petition under section 1(2)(*a*).

But intention need not be communicated. How does a petitioner prove the   **4-52**
necessary intention? In *Santos* the Court of Appeal held that it was not necessary for one spouse to communicate his decision that the marriage was at an end to the other. For example:

> H has been a patient in a mental hospital for more than 10 years. W decided more than five years ago that she would not resume married life with H, but has never told him because the news would upset him, and also because at that time she did not wish to remarry. She has now met someone she does wish to marry. There is no hope of H ever recovering sufficiently to leave hospital. W can now petition for divorce under section 1(2)(*e*) although H has had no grounds to suspect that the marriage was in difficulties. She will of course have to prove her case; and it can be objected that the decision thus encourages the recording of a decision to terminate the marriage in all cases of anticipated long separation, contrary to the Act's professed object of facilitating reconciliation in matrimonial cases.

Approach inconsistent with special procedure. The Court of Appeal's   **4-53**
decision in *Santos* was based on the assumption that consensual divorces based on separation require close judicial scrutiny; but this reasoning has been completely undermined by the adoption of the special procedure. It

is true that the petitioner is required in his affidavit to "state the date when and the circumstances in which you came to the conclusion that the marriage was in fact at an end;" and the Registrar will thus have before him a sworn statement by which he can satisfy himself that the *Santos* principle has been observed. But it will not be possible for any probing of that evidence to take place; and in practice the only result of the decision is to complicate the law, and confuse some petitioners who do not have access to legal advice and thus do not realise the importance of stating that they had come to the conclusion the marriage was over more than two or five years ago.

Differences between two and five year periods

4-54   There are two main differences between the two living apart facts. First, where the petition is based on two years living apart the respondent must consent to a decree being granted; secondly, where the petition is founded solely on five years living apart the court may in certain circumstances withhold a decree if it is satisfied that the dissolution of the marriage would cause grave financial or other hardship to the respondent.

The respondent's consent

4-55   Rules of Court seek to ensure that the respondent is given such information as will enable him to understand the consequences, as they affect him, of his consenting to a decree being granted, *i.e.*:

- (i)   that his rights of intestate succession will cease on decree absolute;
- (ii) that rights to a pension which depend on the marriage continuing, the right to a State widow's pension, and rights of occupation under the Matrimonial Homes Act 1983 (unless the court otherwise orders) will all cease; and
- (iii) that there may be other consequences applicable in the respondent's particular circumstances on which the advice of a solicitor should be sought.

How consent is given

4-56   Consent will normally be given by the respondent answering the appropriate question in the form of acknowledgment of service, but since the relevant point of time is that of the pronouncement of decree nisi the respondent has until then an absolute right, for any or no reason, to withdraw consent. The proceedings will then be stayed. It follows that, in effect, a consent may be given conditionally—*e.g.* on terms that the petitioner will not seek an order for costs against the respondent.

Rescission of decree if respondent misled

4-57   MCA 1973, s.10(1) empowers the court to rescind the decree at any time before decree absolute if it is satisfied that the petitioner misled the respondent (whether intentionally or unintentionally) about any matter which the respondent took into account in deciding to give his consent. The question appears to be entirely subjective: did this particular respondent in fact take the matter into account (not, would a reasonable respondent have done so)? Thus, if H leads his wife to believe that he wants a divorce so that he can marry X (when in fact he does not intend to do so), or that if he is divorced he will marry not X but Y (when he intends to marry X), or that his mistress is pregnant (when she is not), or that she is not pregnant (when she is), application may be made to have the decree rescinded. It should, however, be noted that the petitioner must have misled the respondent. If the respondent without any representation by the petitioner forms a mistaken view on any matter the section's requirements are not satisfied. Furthermore, the court's power is discretionary. It might not be exercised if, for example, the change of mind were for trivial reasons. In practice there seem to be very few applications to rescind decrees under this provision.

Refusal of decree because of hardship

At the time of the 1969 reforms there was a lot of concern about the plight of the "innocent" wife who could not have been divorced under the old law. MCA 1973, s.5 is intended to provide some protection in such cases; but the legislation is restrictively drafted and has itself been given a restrictive interpretation by the courts.   **4-58**

When defence available

The Act provides that the court may dismiss a petition founded solely on the five year living apart "fact" if two distinct conditions are satisfied: (a) that dissolution will result in "grave financial or other hardship to the respondent" and (b) "that it would in all the circumstances be wrong to dissolve the marriage."   **4-59**

(a) *Hardship*

There are two elements: first, the hardship (whether financial or otherwise) must be "grave"; secondly it must result from the dissolution of the marriage (rather than from the fact that it has broken down.)   **4-60**

(i) *Must be grave.* In *Reiterbund* v. *Reiterbund* [1975] Fam 99 it was said that this word has its ordinary meaning; and the hardship must therefore be important, or very serious. It is not sufficient to show that a spouse will lose something; a wife is not entitled to be compensated pound for pound for what she will lose in consequence of the divorce: **4-61**

> Mrs Reiterbund, a 52 year old wife who would lose her entitlement to the state widow's pension if her 54 year old husband died before she reached the age of 60, failed to stop the divorce. First on the evidence the risk of the contingency occurring was not great. Secondly, even if it did she would receive exactly the same income under the supplementary benefit system..

(ii) *Need not be financial.* It is, in theory, open to a respondent to prove that he will suffer grave hardship other than financial hardship; but in fact there has been no reported case in which such a defence has succeeded. In particular the courts have taken a robust approach to pleas based on   **4-62** religious belief. It is not enough for the respondent to show that divorce is contrary to her religion, and that divorce will cause her unhappiness and a sense of shame. She must be able to point to some specific hardship flowing from the divorce:

> In *Rukat* v. *Rukat* [1975] Fam 63 the wife (a Sicilian) had married her husband in 1946. In 1947 she returned with their child to Sicily, where she had subsequently lived with her parents. Although there had been various unsuccessful attempts at reconciliation, the wife had then lived as a separated woman in Sicily for more than 25 years. She alleged that because of the social structure in Sicily a divorce would cause serious repercussions to her and her child, that she would not be accepted in her community, and that she would be unable to return to live where her property was and where her parents and child lived. A decree was nevertheless granted because the wife had failed to establish that anyone in Sicily would know there had been a divorce or that any adverse consequences would follow from the divorce (as distinct from the separation).

4-64   (iii) *Must result from divorce, not from breakdown.* The respondent must prove that her position as a divorced woman is worse than her position as a separated one. This is difficult to do. Many people involved in divorce suffer serious financial problems; but the divorce court has wide powers to make financial orders and the problems usually stem from the fact that the marriage has broken down, and that there is just not sufficient money to keep two households, rather than from the fact that the marriage has been legally dissolved by divorce.

4-65   (iv) *The problem of pensions.* Exceptionally, the divorce court has virtually no powers to reallocate contingent pension rights on divorce; and most of the cases in which the defence has been successfully raised involve the loss of such benefits—the Act defines "hardship" as "including" the loss of the chance of acquiring any benefit which the respondent might acquire if the marriage were not dissolved. For example, in *Parker* v. *Parker* [1972] Fam 116 a wife aged 47 was entitled, contingently on surviving her husband, to a pension under the police pension scheme; and it was held that this loss of possible future security after the death of her husband, was a grave hardship considered in the light of her probable financial stringency at that time. More generally, in *Le Marchant* v. *Le Marchant* [1977] 1 WLR 559 the Court of Appeal held that the loss of a contingent right to an index-linked pension (*i.e.* one which gives a high degree of protection against inflation) was prima facie grave financial hardship to a wife.

4-66   (v) *Burden on respondent to provide acceptable alternative.* In such cases, it will often in practice be possible for the husband to compensate the wife for the lost entitlement. For example:

> In *Le Marchant* v. *Le Marchant* (above) the husband agreed to make an outright transfer of the matrimonial home to the wife and a cash payment of £5,000 on his impending retirement; he also agreed to take out a life policy under which £5,000 would be payable to the wife if she survived the husband. That would

give her £10,000 if the husband predeceased her which she could invest in stocks and shares or in buying an annuity; and this was held adequately to compensate her for the loss of an index-linked pension of £1,300 per annum.

(b) "Wrong in all the circumstances"

If, but only if, the court is satisfied that such hardship will result, it will **4–67** proceed to the next stage, and consider whether it would "in all the circumstances" be wrong to dissolve the marriage. The Act specifically directs attention to a number of matters to be considered. These include the conduct of the parties to the marriage:

> In *Brickell* v. *Brickell* [1974] Fam 31 the court took into account the fact that the "innocent" wife had in the past deserted her husband and damaged his business, and allowed his petition even though the dissolution would cause the wife grave financial hardship.

The Act also directs attention to the interests of the parties to the marriage (so that it will usually be a material factor that the petitioner wishes to re-marry); the interests of any children (which would include the petitioner's children by the woman he intends to marry) and the interest of any other persons concerned—for example, the woman whom the husband will marry if he is freed to do so.

Balancing hardship against policy of law. Having considered these **4–68** circumstances, the court must then balance, on the one hand, the policy embodied in the modern divorce law—which (as Finer J. put it in *Reiterbund* v. *Reiterbund* [1974] 1 WLR 788, 798) "aims, in all other than exceptional circumstances, to crush the empty shells of dead marria-ges"—against, on the other hand, the "grave financial or other hardship" which will thereby be caused to the respondent. It is only if it is then of opinion that it would be wrong ("unjust" or "not right") in all the circumstances to dissolve the marriage, that it must dismiss the petition. It may well not be "wrong" to destroy the empty legal shell, even at the expense of grave hardship to the wife.

In the light of these factors it is not surprising that there have been few **4–69** cases in which a decree has been refused. *Julian* v. *Julian* (1972) 116 SJ 763 will serve as one of the rare examples:

> The husband was 61 and the wife 58. Neither was in good health. The wife was receiving periodical payments from the husband which could be increased to £946 per annum, but they would cease if the husband pre-deceased her. The wife would lose her right to a police widow's pension of £790 per annum. The only financial provision the husband could make for her after his death was an annuity of £215. It was held the potential loss of income from the periodical payments constituted grave financial hardship. The court also held that it would be wrong in all the circumstances to dissolve the marriage: it could not be said to be hard on the husband to deprive him of the chance to remarry given his age, health and circumstances.

Conclusion—scope of defence limited but perhaps adequate

4-70   In practice, the statutory hardship defence seems likely to be used primarily to protect middle-aged and elderly wives against the loss of pension rights, and then only very sparingly. The reality seems to be that the extent of the mischief at which the provision was aimed is narrower than was thought. The worry was that to permit divorce on the basis of five years' separation would be to establish a "Casanova's charter," under which husbands would "put away" their blameless wives for no other reason than a decline in their physical attractiveness. But this fear has been shown to have been exaggerated. In 1984, for example, of the 10,780 petitions based solely on this fact, more were presented by wives (5,810) than by husbands (4,970); and only 17 per cent. of all divorced women were 45 or over. In the circumstances the response given by section 5 to the problem might be thought to be adequate.

Other protection for respondents in separation cases

4-71   MCA 1973, s.10(2) contains a complex provision which is intended to secure the financial position of a spouse who is divorced on either of the two "living apart facts." It enables her to stop a decree nisi being made absolute unless and until the court has satisfied itself that the financial arrangements are "reasonable and fair" or "the best that can be made in the circumstances." It was originally enacted when the court had less extensive powers than it now enjoys; and is today comparatively rarely invoked.

Chapter 5

THE MODERN LAW OF DIVORCE—FURTHER REFORM NEEDED?

THE SUBSTANTIVE LAW

The divorce rate and its significance

The divorce rate in England and Wales is now one of the highest in   **5–01**
Europe, and it has increased more rapidly than in almost any other
country. In 1966 there were 3.2 divorces per thousand married persons, in
1971 there were 6.0; in 1981 11.9, whilst in 1984—the latest year for
which figures are available—there were 12. The divorce rate has thus
doubled since the introduction of the new divorce law and quadrupled
over the last 20 years. Is this a cause for concern? In 1986, Lord Simon of
Glaisdale, who was the President of the Family Division at the time of the
1969 reforms, described the 1969 Act as "disastrous," and asserted that it
had led to a "momentous break-up" in marriage: Hansard (HL) Vol. 471,
col. 889. Is he right?

Relationship between divorce and breakdown

It has for many years been part of the conventional wisdom that the   **5–02**
increased divorce rate does not necessarily indicate any increase in marital
breakdown: all divorces evidence breakdown of a marriage, but not all
breakdowns are evidenced by divorce. A man who leaves his wife and
establishes a "stable illicit union" with another partner has, in social
terms, achieved much the same result as a man who divorces one wife
and remarries; but it is only in the latter case that the breakdown will be
reflected in the divorce statistics. It has often been claimed that the
increase in divorce rates may thus be explained, at least in part, by what
Rheinstein has described as a shift from informal to formalised marriage
breakdown; and the rise in the rate may well reflect to some extent the fact
that divorce is increasingly seen as "more respectable than other
outcomes of a broken home." However, the latest demographic evidence
suggests that there has been some increase in the rate of marital
breakdowns, and that the increase is not solely in the proportion of
breakdowns which are formalised by divorce.

Increase in breakdown and the institution of marriage

It does not follow from these facts that there has been any decline in   **5–03**
respect for the institution of marriage. Many divorced persons remarry;
more than half of a sample of persons divorced in 1973 had remarried
within $4\frac{1}{2}$ years, and there is evidence of a considerable commitment to
the concept of the permanent marriage among persons remarrying after
divorce. It can therefore be argued that the statistics reflect "a modern
morality that is opposed to the idea of continuing with a marriage long
since dead but not to a rejection of the institution of marriage." Changes

49

in social, economic and demographic circumstances have led to the essence of marriage now being seen as a personal relationship which ceases to have any function if the spouses' emotional relationship is destroyed; it is no longer necessary (as perhaps it once was) to preserve the bond for economic reasons. Marriage should be a source of happiness; if it is not, fulfilment may legitimately be sought in a second union. Those who take this view (as Mary Ann Glendon has put it) look on easier divorce laws as almost a conservative measure: such laws encourage the legalisation of informal unions, discourage factual dissolution of marriage by simple desertion, and enable economic responsibility for dependants to be formally adjusted. In any event it is important to remember that divorce is a legal remedy which, as such, only severs the legal aspects of the marriage bond. As Wilkinson has put it, "divorce is not responsible for the emotional ills which its processes both highlight and exacerbate and neither can it offer any cure for them: *Children and Divorce*, 1981, p. 18."

Divorce and children
5-04   On the other hand, it can also be argued that knowledge of the easy availability of divorce may lead to a belief that it offers an appropriate remedy for the unhappily married; and in assessing whether divorce should be readily available a relevant factor must be the effect which divorce (as against the preservation of an unhappy but still to some extent functioning marriage) will have on the children. Some recent research findings (Eekelaar, 1982) have cast doubt on the conventional view amongst those favouring liberal divorce that children suffer more if the parents stay together than if they part.

Minimising bitterness
5-05   In any event, there seems today to be little support for seeking to make the divorce law more restrictive. There can be no doubt that the first of the objectives for a good divorce law set out by the Law Commission in *The Field of Choice* (para. 17) has been achieved: it is now, in all save the most exceptional cases "possible to dissolve the legal tie once that has become irretrievably broken in fact". Attention has now shifted to the second objective: does the law now enable marriages which have broken down to be dissolved "in a way that is just to all concerned, including the children as well as the spouses, and which causes them the minimum of embarrassment and humiliation." Does the law "take the heat out of the disputes between husband and wife and certainly not further embitter the relationships between them or between them and their children"? Does it not "merely bury the marriage, but do so with decency and dignity and in a way which will encourage harmonious relationships between the parties and their children in the future"?

Improving procedures sufficient?
5-06   In recent years the view has been increasingly expressed that the law does not achieve these objectives. In 1981 the Law Commission (Law Com. No 112, para. 13) reported that it was then widely thought that "the

inevitable unhappiness associated with most matrimonial proceedings" had apparently been "considerably magnified by the adversarial nature of the court proceedings and of the preliminaries thereto"; and in response the Lord Chancellor established a committee under the chairmanship of Booth J. "to examine procedures . . . and to recommend reforms which might be made—(a) to mitigate the intensity of disputes; (b) to encourage settlements; and (c) to provide further for the welfare of the children of the family . . . ".

The Booth Committee's view

The Booth Committee proposed a large number of procedural changes   5-07
but it also recorded its view that the substantive law was in part responsible. "On the evidence presented to us we are satisfied that the bitterness and unhappiness of divorcing couples is frequently exacerbated and prolonged by the fault element in divorce and that this is particularly so where the fact relied upon is behaviour, whether or not the suit is defended." (para. 2.10).

One year living apart as sole ground

The suggestion thus seems to be that it is the retention of the "offence"   5-08
based "facts" which are harmful; and The Law Society (*A Better Way Out*, and *A Better Way Out Reviewed*) and others have suggested that the law should be reformed on the pattern of the Australian Family Law Act 1975 under which breakdown proved by separation for not less than one year is the sole ground for divorce. There may, however, be difficulties in adopting this solution in England. How easy would it be, in practice, for a wife—and wives petition for divorce more often than husbands: 88 per cent. of "behaviour" petitions are by wives—to find herself somewhere else to live so that she could establish the necessary period of living apart? Would there be an increase in the (already large) number of cases in which wives seek injunctions from the court to oust their husbands from the matrimonial home? Would there be an increase in the number of cases in which a wife was advised to set up a separate household in the matrimonial home, so that after a year she could present a divorce petition? Would such separations—probably involving the couple having nothing to do with each other even for the sake of the children: *cf. Mouncer* v. *Mouncer* [1972] 1 WLR 321, discussed at para. 4–49 above—be potentially damaging not only to the parties but also to their children? These are questions which need to be answered.

A more radical approach?

There are those who think that the law should simply recognise that the   5-09
best evidence of breakdown is, in reality, a considered decision by one spouse that the marriage has indeed irretrievably broken down. In this view, to obtain a divorce it should only be necessary to file in court a notice of intention to seek dissolution of the marriage. A divorce would then be granted automatically after a prescribed period during which, perhaps, conciliation services would be made available to the parties to

help them to reach agreement about matters such as the arrangements to be made for the children.

Such a scheme clearly has strong logical attractions; but would it be likely to be acceptable to public opinion? Discussion of the provision in the Matrimonial and Family Proceedings Act 1984 whereby divorce was made available, on proof of the breakdown in the prescribed manner, after one year of marriage suggests that a divorce law which could, without undue exaggeration, be said to have similarities to the system of *talak* divorce (in which a husband can divorce his wife by uttering that word thrice) would be strongly opposed; and it is not clear that there is any popular pressure for change.

Prospects for reform of substantive law uncertain

5–10   It is thus difficult to evaluate the prospects for reform. The Law Commission announced as long ago as 1980 that it intended to undertake a review of the law, by analysing the operation of the present law and presenting a field of choice for reform; but it is not yet clear when this review is likely to be published.

ANOTHER WAY?—RECONCILIATION AND CONCILIATION

Reconciliation as an objective of the law

5–11   The Divorce Reform Act was described in its long title as an Act to (amongst other things) "facilitate reconciliation in matrimonial causes" and it introduced for the first time the notion of reconciliation as an institutionalised feature of matrimonial litigation. In practice, however, the provisions included to that end in the Act had an exceedingly limited effect and it increasingly came to be thought that reconciliation (in the sense of "reuniting persons who are estranged") had little chance of success once divorce proceedings had been started.

Conciliation

5–12   The emphasis then shifted to providing facilities for conciliation ("the process of engendering common sense, reasonableness and agreement in dealing with the consequences of estrangement"). Expert help might not save the marriage but it could often help the parties to a marriage to resolve issues relating to finance and child custody with the minimum possible anxiety to themselves or their children. Even if it failed to do this, it might be possible to identify the issues on which the parties remained seriously at variance, thus limiting the scope of any litigation. In brief, the short term objectives of conciliation have been stated to be "to help the parties reach a workable settlement which takes account of the needs of the children and adults involved." The longer term objective has been said to be "to help both parents: (a) maintain their relationship with their children, and (b) achieve a co-operative plan for their children's welfare." (Extended Code of Practice for Family Conciliation Services issued by the National Family Conciliation Council's Executive Committee: (1985) 15

Fam Law 274—and see also Appendix A to L. Parkinson, *Conciliation in Separation and Divorce* (1986) which gives a full account of the whole issue).

Putting the parties in control

In essence, therefore, the short term objective of conciliation is to   **5-13**
diminish the part played by contentious litigation and thereby to minimise the bitterness incidental to the break-up. It is, as the Booth Committee pointed out (para. 3.10), "of the essence" of conciliation that responsibility should remain at all times with the parties themselves; and that the role of the neutral conciliator is simply to assist the parties. In this view, contested legal proceedings are not to be seen as the norm, but are "only appropriate where parties have been unable to reach agreement after being given every assistance and encouragement to do so". The Committee, in strongly supporting the use of conciliation in matrimonial proceedings (para. 3.11), claimed that conciliation puts the responsibility for reaching agreement about the consequences of the breakdown onto the parties, who should not expect simply to leave matters to lawyers. The Committee also thought that conciliation encouraged the parties to face up to difficulties which might otherwise be suppressed, only to emerge at a later date as a source of conflict.

Different models of conciliation

Immense interest has been generated in the subject of conciliation; and   **5-14**
this is likely to be increased by the Booth Committee's recommendation (para. 3.11) that conciliation should become a recognised part of the legal procedure. However, there is a great deal of diversity in the different conciliation schemes; and it is possible in this book to give only the briefest outline of what are conveniently (if perhaps arbitrarily (Booth Committee, para. 3.12) described as "in court" and "out of court" services. For a full account reference should be made to Parkinson, 1986 (see para. 5-12 above).

In court conciliation

These developments have focussed primarily on the use of a "pre-trial   **5-15**
review" to encourage parties to realise that a settlement is preferable to a solution imposed by the court after a, perhaps bitterly fought, forensic contest. The pre-trial review (which is commonly used in other litigation in order to define the issues and expedite the trial process) was first specifically adapted to promoting conciliation, in the sense of achieving settlements, in cases where the petition was being defended. The Registrar would at the review seek to ascertain "the true state of the case" and to give such directions as were necessary for its "just, expeditious and economic disposal." Experience had (according to a *Practice Direction* [1979] 1 WLR 2) demonstrated that:

> "under the registrar's guidance, the parties are often able to compose their differences or to drop insubstantial charges and defences, and to concentrate on

the main issues in dispute. Experience has shown that, following the pre-trial review, many cases proceed undefended under the special procedure with consent orders as to financial provision or in respect of the custody of, or access to, the children. Where contested issues remain the registrar is able to give directions to facilitate their expeditious determination at their subsequent hearing before the judge."

5-16   Subsequent experience—particularly in an experimental scheme in Bristol—suggested that the summons for directions could be adapted, with encouraging results to many cases in which there appeared to be a conflict between the parties, and particularly to cases in which there was a conflict about the children. It is significant that in the Bristol Scheme a specialist team of Divorce Court Welfare Officers was made available to the court and the parties; and this enabled the registrar with the assistance of the Senior Welfare Officer not only to identify at any early stage those petitions in respect of which a welfare report was likely to be required, but also to offer the services of the team to conciliate over disputed issues.

The Principal Registry Scheme

5-17   Many courts now use the summons for directions to the same end; and in 1983 a pilot in-court conciliation scheme was introduced in the Principal Registry of the Family Division. At first, this applied to contested applications in matrimonial proceedings for custody, access and variation thereof, but it has subsequently been extended to a number of other applications involving children. Whenever a summons is issued, a conciliation appointment is made, which must be attended not only by the parties and their advisers but also by any child over the age of 8 who is living with either party and whose custody, etc., is in issue. The appointment takes place before a registrar, attended by a court welfare officer; and the nature of the application and the matters in dispute are outlined by the parties or their advisers. If the dispute continues, the parties and advisers will be given the opportunity of retiring to a private room together with the welfare officer to attempt to reach agreement. The *Practice Direction* [1982] 1 WLR 1420 states that if the conciliation appointment is successful "the registrar will make such orders as are agreed between the parties"—a striking acceptance of the principle that in reality it is for the parties to make their own arrangements about the upbringing of their children, which the court is scarcely in a position to investigate or question.

5-18   The *Practice Direction* also contains provisions to safeguard the parties' position if the appointment does not result in an agreement. It is, for example, provided that any subsequent hearing will normally be dealt with by a different Registrar and welfare officer; and that the discussions and statements made at the conciliation appointment will remain privileged, so that they cannot be relied on in any subsequent litigation. If the conciliation appointment is unsuccessful, the Registrar will also give directions on such matters as the obtaining of a welfare officer's report and the filing of evidence of the parties.

The dangers—pressurising the parties

A number of variants on this model of in court conciliation can be   5-19
found in experiments in different parts of the country, but most of the schemes have in common the involvement of both the registrar and a welfare officer. This may be an effective method of producing agreement, since the Registrar is invested with the symbolic authority of the court (albeit he has no power to impose a solution on the parties at the conciliation appointment itself, and that he will not personally adjudicate on the case should the appointment be unsuccessful). But the question whether the parties should be exposed to what they may—at the time or subsequently—regard as pressure to settle is controversial.

Another danger—confusing the role of the welfare officer

In-court conciliation involves some risk that the role of the welfare   5-20
officer will be misunderstood. Conciliation is a wholly different function from reporting (see para. 16–12 below), and it should be carried out by different people. But cases have been reported in which an officer who has failed to bring about a successful conciliation has nonetheless purported to write the welfare report—a practice which is wholly wrong: see *Re H (Conciliation: Welfare Reports)* [1986] 1 FLR 476; see also *Scott v. Scott* [1986] 2 FLR 320, CA. The clear principle is that a welfare officer who carries out conciliation has no authority over the parties at the conciliation appointment (or indeed subsequently); but, however careful the officer may be to observe the proper distinction, there is still an obvious danger that the parties will believe he has a power to influence the court in favour of the solution which appears best to him.

Out of court conciliation

The "in-court" conciliation schemes outlined above are only available   5-21
to parties who have started the litigation process; yet it is generally recognised that (in the words of the Booth Committee: para. 3.12) "early intervention can be a major factor in developing a positive and conciliatory approach", and that accordingly the prospects of success are highest at a very early stage in the breakdown. In recent years, a large number of schemes have been established largely by voluntary effort —one of the best known is the Bristol Courts Family Conciliation Service—to make conciliation available before relationships have been further soured by litigation. Referrals are received from solicitors, and other agencies (such as Citizens Advice Bureaux) and from the parties direct, frequently before a divorce petition is filed. Although there are considerable variations in the techniques used by the different services, the conciliator will usually be a trained social worker; and joint or separate meetings (sometimes including the children) may be held over many weeks.

The future of conciliation

5-22   Conciliation services have been plagued by lack of secure funding; and
in 1983 a committee of officials was asked to advise on the nature and
scope of conciliation services, and particularly whether such services
could produce "savings and other benefits to the individuals concerned
and public resources." This Committee concluded that, although there
was a role for conciliation in matrimonial disputes, this was best provided
as an adjunct to the Court system; and that out-of-court conciliation
schemes did not save money overall and appeared to be less cost-effective
than in-court schemes. Central Government funding of out-of-court
schemes was, in the Committee's view, not justified. But these conclusions were strongly criticised; and the Government funded an ambitious
research programme to be conducted by a team from the University of
Newcastle-upon-Tyne and completed by September 1988. This involves
the creation of an independent project unit to monitor and assess the costs
and effectiveness of different types of conciliation scheme.

REFORM OF PROCEDURES

5-23   In 1982, (as noted at para. 5–06 above) the Government set up the
Matrimonial Causes Procedure Committee, better known as the Booth
Committee. The Committee's Report (1985) envisages major changes in
procedure. Of these, one of the most important is the introduction of an
"initial hearing" in many cases. The initial hearing will be used to make
orders in respect of agreed matters, to refer the parties to conciliation
where appropriate, to define the issues remaining between them, and to
give directions: para. 3.5. This proposal reflects the Committee's view that
the emphasis should be shifted from adjudication to agreement; and also
that the court should retain control in cases where adjudication is
necessary. The committee envisaged that the parties would thereby be
given a stronger sense of participating in and controlling the litigation so
that they would be less willing subsequently to tolerate delay: para. 3.9.
      It is impossible in a book of this kind to give a full account of the
Committee's proposals, much less to seek to evaluate them. In some ways
however the most interesting proposals are those of detail designed to
minimise the bitterness often incidental to proceedings under the current
practice. For example, the Committee propose that joint applications
should be permitted in respect of all "facts" (even "behaviour"); that it
should not be necessary to give the name of the alleged adulterer if the
allegation is not contested (cf. para. 4–10 above); and that it should not be
necessary to give details of the specific acts relied on in "behaviour"
petitions. The Committee propose that the decree should be in a neutral
form, merely recording that the marriage has irretrievably broken down,
rather than (as at present) that the petitioner had established that the
other had, for example, behaved in such a way that the respondent could
not reasonably be expected to live with him.
      The Government is undertaking consultations on these proposals; and

at the date of going to press it is not known how many of them are likely to be implemented. Leaving considerations of cost on one side, there will undoubtedly be those who will say that the Committee is proposing increasing recourse to legal fiction, and that it is in effect seeking to change the substantive law without the approval of Parliament. For example, whilst in theory "behaviour" would remain the "fact," in reality the petitioner would merely need to recite that allegation, and the court would be unable to examine its truth, even cursorily. The result would in substance be divorce by the parties' consent, rather than by judicial process. On this view it would be better to recognise the fact by changing the substantive law of divorce. However to do so would require primary legislation which would undoubtedly be controversial.

Chapter 6

JUDICIAL SEPARATION AND PROTECTION AGAINST MARITAL VIOLENCE

JUDICIAL SEPARATION

6-01 Judicial separation is a somewhat misleadingly entitled form of relief. In theory, the principal effect of a decree is to remove the duty of one spouse to live with the other (MCA 1973, s.18(1)); but a decree does not require the parties to separate, much less does it mean that the court will compel them to separate—the court will not, for example, necessarily exclude a husband against whom a decree of judicial separation has been granted from the matrimonial home: see para. 9–06 below. But judicial separation was until very recently surprisingly often used: in 1984 6,098 petitions were presented, and 4,445 decrees pronounced.

What accounts for this popularity? So long as divorce was only available on proof of a matrimonial offence judicial separation was used by wives who wanted to invoke the court's powers to order the husband to make financial provision whilst denying him the right to remarry. Even after the introduction of the reformed divorce law, there were still special restrictions on starting divorce proceedings within the first three years of the marriage (see para. 4–01 above), and there is some evidence that judicial separation was widely used as a short-term alternative. In 1985—after the substitution of one year for three years as the period in which divorce is not available—the number of judicial separation petitions fell dramatically to 3,479; and it seems that judicial separation will in the future be primarily a form of short-term matrimonial relief: see futher para. 6–07 below.

The fact that judicial separation is one of the original "matrimonial causes" administered since 1857 by the Divorce Court along with divorce, nullity and some other forms of relief which have been abolished (such as the decrees of Restitution of Conjugal Rights and Jactitation of Marriage) explains why it is still easiest to consider this form of relief separately from the many other legal procedures now available to deal with family disputes.

JUDICIAL SEPARATION—THE GROUNDS

6-02 The Divorce Reform Act 1969 amended the law so as to be consistent with the new code of divorce: a petition for judicial separation may be presented to the court by either party to a marriage on the ground that any of the "facts" for divorce set out in MCA 1973, s.1(2) and discussed at paras. 4–05 to 4–57 above exists: MCA 1973, s.17(1). It is specifically provided that in the case of petitions for judicial separation, the court is not to be concerned with the question of whether or not the marriage has broken down irretrievably: MCA 1973, s.17(2). If one of the relevant facts—adultery, behaviour, desertion, or living apart—is proved, the court is bound to grant a decree.

EFFECTS OF A DECREE OF JUDICIAL SEPARATION

There are three main consequences of the grant of a decree of judicial separation: **6-03**

(1) Powers over money and children
The court's ancillary financial and custody powers may be invoked. The **6-04** court may also grant injunctions in the course of judicial separation proceedings; and at one time this may have accounted for the continued popularity of the procedure. However, the courts now have power under the Domestic Violence and Matrimonial Proceedings Act 1976 and under the Matrimonial Homes Act 1983 to grant injunctions without it being necessary to apply for any further relief: see paras. 6-13 to 6-21 below.

(2) Limited protection for wife
Once a decree has been pronounced, it ceases to be obligatory for the **6-05** petitioner to cohabit with the respondent: MCA 1973, s.18(1). As already pointed out, this obligation is not enforceable; but the removal of the duty does still have one—albeit now not usually important—legal consequence: neither party can thereafter be in desertion. More important is the fact that it has been held (*R. v. Clarke* [1949] 2 All ER 448) that the termination of the duty to cohabit revokes the consent to submit to sexual intercourse which is implied from the existence of marriage, and accordingly a man may be convicted of raping his wife if a decree of judicial separation was in force at the relevant time.

(3) Succession rights
For the purposes of intestate succession, a decree operates as a divorce; **6-06** and neither spouse has thereafter any right to succeed to the property of the other on intestacy: MCA 1973, s.18(2).

USE MADE OF JUDICIAL SEPARATION

Primarily short-term remedy?
The fact that divorce is now available on the basis of five years' **6-07** separation means that after a period a respondent spouse will almost invariably be able in effect to convert a decree of judicial separation obtained against him into a decree of divorce. Hence, judicial separation should now be primarily a short-term remedy which can be used in the following cases:

(i) where a decree of divorce cannot yet be obtained because one year has not elapsed since the celebration of the marriage;

(ii) where the petitioner wishes to take advantage of the court's ancillary powers to make financial orders, and its power to make orders for the custody of the children, but neither party wishes to remarry; and,

(iii) where the petitioner does not wish to obtain a divorce, but wants a formal recognition of the separation and the respondent is not yet in a position to establish one of the "facts" necessary for a decree of divorce—for example, a wife may obtain a decree of judicial separation on the basis of her husband's adultery or behaviour; he may want a divorce, but not be able to obtain one until he can establish the five year living apart "fact."

Long-term remedy

6-08   There are of course cases in which—for religious or other reasons—neither party to a broken marriage wishes to divorce; and judicial separation may be an appropriate technique in such cases to deal with the financial and other consequences of the breakdown.

MARITAL VIOLENCE

6-09   In recent years there has been great concern about domestic violence; and the legal procedures intended to provide a remedy to its victims have proliferated. The result is (to quote Lord Scarman in *Richards* v. *Richards* [1984] 1 AC 174, 206) a hotchpotch of enactments of limited scope passed into law to meet specific situations or to strengthen the powers of specified courts.

The Criminal Law

6-10   One spouse is not entitled by reason of the marriage to inflict violence on the other against his or her will. In appropriate cases, therefore, a husband can be prosecuted for offences ranging from murder to common assault. However, a man cannot usually be convicted of raping his wife.

Criminal law not adequate remedy

6-11   For a number of reasons the criminal law does not provide an adequate response to the problems of marital violence. First, the primary objective ①of the criminal law is the punishment of the offender, not the protection of the victim. Fining (or even imprisoning) a brutal husband will not necessarily improve things for the wife. Secondly, there may be ②formidable problems in pressing a charge, given the traditional reluctance of the police and other agencies to become involved in domestic disputes. Thirdly, (as Atkins and Hoggett, *Women and the Law* (1984), p. 135 point ③out) a woman may have ambivalent feelings about the fact that she has "shopped" her husband; and these emotions may lead her to withdraw the co-operation with the prosecution which is in practice essential if a conviction is to be obtained. This remains true notwithstanding the fact that a wife can now be compelled to give evidence against her spouse: Police and Criminal Evidence Act 1984, s.80.

Civil remedies

A wife will therefore usually need to seek the assistance of the civil law   6-12
to provide her with reasonably effective protection against violence:

(a) She may seek an injunction against her husband in the High Court or in the county court under the Domestic Violence and Matrimonial Proceedings Act 1976. She may also seek an order under the Matrimonial Homes Act 1983.
(b) If divorce or judicial separation proceedings are pending, she may seek an injunction in those proceedings.
(c) She may seek a personal protection or exclusion order from the Magistrates' Court under the Domestic Proceedings and Magistrates' Courts Act 1978.

(a) Injunctions under the Domestic Violence and Matrimonial Proceedings Act 1976 ("the 1976 Act") or under the Matrimonial Homes Act 1983 ("the 1983 Act")

The advantages of obtaining an injunction are, first, that there is a   6-13
speedy procedure available; and secondly that there are effective methods of compelling obedience to the terms of the order—breach of an injunction constitutes a contempt of court, and may be punished by fine or imprisonment; whilst in some cases the court has power to attach a "power of arrest" to the injunction: see para. 6–21 below.
The main features of this legislation are as follows:

(i) *No need to seek any other relief*
The 1976 Act empowers the county court to grant injunctions in   6-14
specified terms whether or not any other relief is sought in the proceedings. It is no longer the law that injunctions can only be granted if divorce or other proceedings are imminent.

(ii) *No conditions for grant of injunction*
The 1976 Act does not specify any conditions which have to be satisfied   6-15
before an injunction can be granted. The decision whether to make an order is in the court's discretion: see para. 6–17 below.

(iii) *Orders that can be made*
The court has power to grant an injunction containing one or more of   6-16
the following provisions:

Non-molestation order. The injunction may contain a provision restraining the other party to the marriage from molesting the applicant, or a child living with the applicant: 1976 Act, s.1(1)(a), (b). The courts have not been anxious to give a definition of "molest." The word would certainly extend to physical attacks: but any "pestering" suffices:

> In *Horner* v. *Horner* [1982] Fam 90, for example, it appears that the husband hung scurrilous posters about the wife on the railings of the school at which she taught.

6-17 *Ouster orders.* The 1976 Act provides (s.1(1)(*c*)) that an injunction may contain a provision excluding the other party from the matrimonial home or a part of the matrimonial home or from a specified area in which the matrimonial home is included. This power enables the court to make an ouster order—with the drastic consequence that the husband may be put out on the street with nowhere to go. But the statutory power may also be used for more limited purposes—for example, the order may simply exclude a spouse from part of the matrimonial home (*e.g.* the kitchen or a bedroom)—and the court may also order a spouse not to go to the street, town or other district in which the matrimonial home is situated.

The effect of the decision of the House of Lords in *Richards* v. *Richards* [1984] 1 AC 174 is that an application by a spouse for an ouster injunction will normally be made under the Matrimonial Homes Act 1983: and the question of whether the court will grant such a drastic order will in any case be governed by principles laid down in the 1983 Act. For that reason, this subject is dealt with further at para. 9–06 below.

6-18 *Re-entry orders.* The 1976 Act (s.1(1)(*d*)) also empowers the court to insert a provision requiring the applicant to be permitted to enter and remain in the matrimonial home or a part of the matrimonial home—an applicant who has been driven from the matrimonial home is thus to be allowed to return in safety. Again, applications for such orders—which are often sought in conjunction with an ouster order—will usually now be made under the Matrimonial Homes Act 1983, and are governed by the principles laid down by that Act: para. 9–06 below.

(b) Injunctions in pending matrimonial proceedings

6-19 The Supreme Court Act 1981, consolidating earlier legislation and effectively supplanting what used to be called the "inherent" jurisdiction, empowers the High Court to grant an interlocutory or final injunction "in all cases in which it appears to the court to be just and convenient to do so"; and similar powers are conferred on the county court by section 38 of the County Courts Act 1984. The Divorce courts may exercise the power thereby conferred to grant injunctions ancillary to divorce, nullity or judicial separation proceedings, and in practice they frequently make non-molestation and other orders in this way. However, in *Richards* v. *Richards* [1984] 1 AC 174 the House of Lords held that applications for *ouster* injunctions in proceedings between spouses must be made by originating summons under the Matrimonial Homes Act 1983. If a petitioner for divorce wants an ouster order he must therefore issue separate proceedings seeking an order under the 1983 Act; but those proceedings will now normally be heard by the court which is dealing

with the divorce. The important point is that the principles upon which
the court will act in deciding the ouster application are laid down in the
1983 Act: see para. 9–06 below.

Enforcement of injunctions

Breach of an order is a contempt of court which may in the last resort be   **6–20**
punished by committal to prison.

It is true that in most cases stern warnings or an adjournment to allow
tempers to cool will be the best way of minimising the damage to the
family unit (see Ormrod L.J. in *Ansah* v. *Ansah* [1977] Fam 138, 144) but if
necessary the offender can be dealt with severely. For example:

> In *Re H (A Minor) (Injunction: Breach)* [1986] 1 FLR 558 the defendant continued
> to try to see his daughter and her mother in defiance of an injunction. He
> smashed his way into the house, waylaid the mother in the small hours of the
> morning, and assaulted her by putting his hands round her neck and squeezing
> her throat. He was sent to prison for three months; and the Court of Appeal
> made it clear that the sentence would have been longer but for the fact that this
> was the first reported breach.

However breach of an injunction does not constitute a criminal offence,
and until the enactment of the 1976 Act the police had no power to arrest
the husband even if they were aware that he was acting in breach of an
injunction. This caused difficulties for battered wives; and the 1976 Act
therefore empowered the court to attach a power of arrest to certain
injunctions in terms specified in the Act.

Powers of Arrest

The court may attach a power of arrest to any injunction—whether it   **6–21**
was granted under the 1976 Act, the 1983 Act, or otherwise—which
restrains the other party to the marriage from using violence against the
applicant (or against a child living with her) or which excludes the other
party from the matrimonial home or from a specified area in which the
matrimonial home is included: 1976 Act, s.2(1). But a power of arrest can
only be inserted if it is proved that the party enjoined has caused actual
bodily harm to the applicant (or child), and if the court considers that he is
likely to cause actual bodily harm again. Even then, the court has a
discretion whether or not to attach a power of arrest to an injunction, and
it has been said (see Ormrod L.J. in *Lewis* v. *Lewis* [1978] 1 All ER 729) that
the power should only be used in exceptional situations "where men and
women persistently disobey injunctions and make nuisances of themselves to the other party and to others concerned."

A power of arrest will be registered at a police station for the applicant's
address; and it empowers a constable to arrest, without warrant, a person
whom he has reasonable cause for suspecting of being in breach of a
provision of the injunction: 1976 Act, s.2(3). A person arrested under such
a power must be brought before a judge (who may exercise his powers to
punish for disobedience to the injunction) within 24 hours from the time
of arrest.

(c) Orders in the Magistrates' Court

6-22   The domestic jurisdiction of magistrates' courts originated in the need recognised by Parliament in 1878 to protect "women of the poorer classes" from physical assaults by their husbands. The legislation is now much more ambitious in scope. Complex, detailed, but in many respects restricted, provisions are now contained in the Domestic Proceedings and Magistrates' Courts Act 1978 ("the 1978 Act"). Under sections 16–18 of that Act either party to a marriage may apply to a magistrates' court for orders usually described as personal protection orders and exclusion orders. The main features of each are set out below.

(i) *Personal protection orders*

6-23   *What the applicant must prove.* To obtain a personal protection order, the applicant must prove two separate facts:

> (i)   that the respondent had used or threatened to use, violence against the person of the applicant (or a child of the family: see para. 16–03 for the definition), and;
>
> (ii) that it is necessary for the protection of the applicant (or a child of the family) that an order be made: 1978 Act, s.16(2).

6-24   *Restrictively drafted.* This provision is narrowly drafted in three important respects. First there must have been "violence" either used or threatened. There is no power to act on proof of molestation short of threatened violence even if that behaviour has caused or is likely to cause psychological damage to the wife or child. Secondly, the violence (or threat) must be directed against the person of the applicant or a child of the family. A wife will be unable to obtain an order merely because her husband has used or threatened violence against some other member of the family circle (such as the wife's mother) or even if he has done so against a child who falls outside the definition of "child of the family." Finally the court must be satisfied that the granting of the order is "necessary" for the protection of the applicant or child, a condition which Parliament deliberately removed from the Domestic Violence and Matrimonial Proceedings Bill because it was considered to be potentially too restrictive.

6-25   *Terms of the order.* If these conditions are satisfied the court can order that the respondent should not use, or threaten to use, violence against the person of the applicant (or against the person of a child of the family), or to incite or assist others to do so. But the magistrates have no power to grant an order against molestation, in the sense of pestering: contrast the powers of the county court: para. 6–16 above.

(ii) *Exclusion orders*

6-26   *What the applicant must prove.* The court has power to grant this "drastic remedy" only if it is satisfied of two separate facts: 1978 Act, s.16(3):

(i) *Violence by respondent.* It is not sufficient that the respondent has simply threatened to use violence. Even if there is the clearest possible evidence that a wife or child is in danger of serious physical injury a magistrates' court will be unable to grant an exclusion order unless the applicant can prove that the respondent has either:

(a) "used violence against the person of the applicant or a child of the family;" or
(b) "threatened to use violence against the person of the applicant or a child of the family and has used violence against some other person;" or
(c) threatened to use violence against the person of the applicant or a child of the family" in contravention of a personal protection order.

(ii) *Danger of physical injury.* The applicant must also satisfy the court **6–27** that the applicant or a child of the family is in danger of being physically injured by the respondent (or would be in such danger if the applicant or child were to enter the matrimonial home). It is not sufficient to prove that there is a risk of damage to mental health.

Terms of the order. An exclusion order is the counterpart of an ouster **6–28** order (para. 6–17 above). The court may (i) require the respondent to leave the matrimonial home; and/or (ii) prohibit the respondent from entering the matrimonial home. The court may also order the respondent to permit the applicant to enter and remain in the matrimonial home. Orders may be for a specified term and subject to exceptions (*e.g.* that the husband be permitted to enter one room) or conditions. But the magistrates have no power to order one spouse to keep away from the neighbourhood in which the home is situated: contrast the powers of the superior courts, para. 6–17 above.

Emergency procedures
There are two provisions designed to ensure that action can be taken **6–29** quickly. First, if the court considers that it is essential that the application—whether for a personal protection or exclusion order—should be heard without delay it may do so in spite of the fact that some of the usual rules about the composition of the court (for example, that it include both a man and a woman) cannot be observed. Secondly, the court (which for this purpose may consist of a single justice) may make an expedited order, lasting for up to 28 days, notwithstanding that the usual procedural safeguards for notice to the respondent have not been complied with. But this expedited procedure is only available in respect of personal protection orders; and the court can only act if it is satisfied that there is "imminent danger of physical injury to the applicant" or a child; 1978 Act, s.16(6). These restrictions make the procedure much less flexible than in the superior courts, where orders—even, in exceptional circumstances ouster orders—can be made *ex parte* (*i.e.* without notice to the respondent), and administrative arrangements have been made to ensure that a judge is always available to hear applications.

Enforcement of orders

6-30   The 1978 Act provides two special procedures designed to facilitate enforcement of orders.

(i) *Arrest and punishment for breach.* If an order has been disobeyed, the court, on the application of a spouse, can issue a warrant of arrest: 1978 Act, s.18(4). The court may then fine the respondent (up to £50 for every day on which the respondent is in default, but with a maximum of £1,000) or commit him to prison for a period not exceeding two months.

(ii) *Insertion of a power of arrest.* The court may attach a power of arrest if the respondent has "physically injured" the applicant or a child of the family and considers that he is likely to do so again: 1978 Act, s.18(1). The effect of such an order is comparable to that of an order made under the Domestic Violence and Matrimonial Proceedings Act 1976: see para. 6-21 above.

PART II—PROPERTY AND FINANCIAL ASPECTS OF FAMILY LAW

Introduction

In *Hyman* v. *Hyman* [1929] AC 601, 625, Lord Atkin said that agreements whereby a couple agreed to regulate their financial affairs on separation were to be dealt with "on precisely the same principles as any respectable commercial agreement, of whose nature indeed they sometimes partake." This may be thought an excessively cynical view; but few would deny that property and money issues can be vitally important, particularly perhaps when a relationship breaks down. The first five chapters (Chapters 7 to 11) in this Part therefore consider the financial position of the family created by marriage. Chapter 7 deals with the relevance of property law. Chapter 8 examines property regimes—does the fact that a couple get married affect their property rights, and if so how? Chapter 9 deals with a separate, albeit related, issue—does the fact that a couple are married give them any particular rights to occupy the home which they have established? Chapters 10 and 11 look at various procedures under which financial matters can be resolved when a marriage breaks down. The final chapter in this part (Chapter 12) deals with the financial position of the family outside marriage.

Chapter 7

MATRIMONIAL PROPERTY

DOES PROPERTY LAW MATTER?

Divorce Court's adjustive powers more important?

In practice the powers of the courts to make financial provision and   **7-01**
property adjustment orders in divorce proceedings (which are dealt with
in Chapter 11) have greatly reduced the importance of matrimonial
property law in the traditional sense. A couple whose marriage is still
functioning will rarely be interested in the answer to the question: "who
owns this particular item of property which we use?"—or perhaps it
would be more accurate to say that they will rarely wish to pursue their
interest to the point of engaging in expensive and uncertain litigation in
order to find the answer. If their marriage has broken down they will find
that the court has extensive powers to make orders for financial support
and to divide up family assets on a discretionary basis, so that it will only
rarely be relevant to ask: "to whom does this belong?" Instead the divorce
court will decide: "to whom should this be given?"

Property law irrelevant?

Does this mean that the very complex rules about beneficial ownership   **7-02**
can safely be ignored? The answer is that, for at least two reasons, they
cannot. First of all, there are still those who believe that the law governing
the ownership of property is not in all respects fair; and it is desirable to be
able to evaluate these arguments. Secondly, notwithstanding the great
shift towards reliance on the discretionary powers of the divorce court to
deal with property issues, there remain a number of circumstances in
which the question of beneficial ownership—the "cold legal question"—
can be relevant in practice.

Relevance of cold legal question

The circumstances in which the question of beneficial ownership may   **7-03**
be relevant can be summarised as follows:

(a) *Third Party affected*

The dispute may not be between two spouses; but between a spouse   **7-04**
and a third party—for example, a creditor of the husband; see for example
the case of *Williams & Glyn's Bank Ltd.* v. *Boland* [1981] A.C. 487
considered at para. 8–26 below. The creditor may be able to enforce his
legal rights of recovery against the property of the husband; but he will
not generally be entitled to attack property which is beneficially owned by
the wife.

This will be particularly important if one spouse is adjudicated
bankrupt. In that case all his property vests by operation of law in his

trustee in bankruptcy whose duty is to realize the assets for the benefit of the bankrupt's creditors. The wife's property, in contrast, does not vest in the trustee; and she is in principle entitled to keep it.

(b) *No marriage*

7-05   Not all disputes between a couple who have been living together can be resolved by the divorce court exercising what are called its "ancillary" powers. The divorce court can only exercise those powers if there is a decree—whether of divorce, nullity or judicial separation; and it is self-evident that if a couple have never bothered to get married they cannot get a divorce. The cynical may—falsely—argue that the only real consequence of marriage today is that it gives the parties the right to divorce one another, with the very extensive financial consequences which may be involved in a divorce settlement. If there is no marriage the divorce court can have no adjustive powers to use. The question of whether the "unmarried housewife" is to be entitled to any share in the home in which she may have brought up a family thus has to be resolved by reference to the principles of beneficial ownership. As will be seen in Chapter 12 the main contemporary relevance of the law about the ownership of what may be called "family assets" is now in such cases. But paradoxically, the relevant legal principles were developed in disputes between married couples at a time before the divorce court had its wide adjustive powers.

(c) *No divorce*

7-06   There are still people who have conscientious scruples about recourse to divorce: see *e.g. Shinh* v. *Shinh* [1977] 1 All ER 97. If a couple choose not to bring matrimonial proceedings the court will have to resolve any questions about the beneficial entitlement to their property without using the adjustive powers which would be available in divorce. A married couple may of course use judicial separation as a way of invoking adjustive powers without dissolving the marriage; but it also has to be remembered that the majority of marriages are terminated by death, and not by divorce. It is true that if a man dies leaving all his property by will to charity, say, or to his mistress, his wife now has a right to apply to the court under the Inheritance (Provision for Family and Dependants) Act 1975 for reasonable provision to be made for her out of his estate: see para. 8–30 below; but the court in deciding such applications may have to balance the wife's claim against those of others. A wife may therefore find it more advantageous to claim that she actually owned the matrimonial home (for example) so that it does not pass under her husband's will at all.

(d) *Disputes about use of property rather than its ownership*

7-07   Such disputes—for example, as to whether a jointly owned house should be sold—are still sometimes dealt with by reference to property law rather than the adjustive jurisdiction of the divorce court. This is particularly the case when a third party is involved—for example, if the husband's share in the property has become liable to enforcement action in respect of his debts.

Chapter 8

MATRIMONIAL PROPERTY REGIMES

A property owning society?

8-01   In spite of economic policies in the first three-quarters of this century which were intended to promote greater equality in the distribution of wealth it is still true that 5 per cent. of the population own 55 per cent. of the wealth. The reader may therefore think that questions of whether marriage has any effect on property are of interest only to a comparatively small section of the community. This is not true; and the main reason why it is not true is connected with the great extension of home ownership financed by building society and bank credit.

The mortgage phenomenon

8-02   The result of this trend is that families often acquire—sometimes without really being conscious of it—what may be a very substantial capital asset. For example:

> In *Mortimer* v. *Mortimer-Griffin* [1986] 2 FLR 315 the couple bought their home in 1970 for £6,360. They put up £1,350 in cash and borrowed the rest on mortgage. By the time of the hearing the house was worth £70,000 after allowing for the outstanding mortgage.

Again:

> In *Wachtel* v. *Wachtel* [1973] Fam 70 the family home had been bought in 1956 in the husband's name for £5,000, all of which was in fact borrowed on mortgage. Over the years the debt was reduced by regular instalment payments to £2,000. Over the same period, the value of the house rose to £22,000 or more, so that some £17,000 (perhaps some £60,000 in 1987 values) had come into existence as a windfall gain.

Does the wife in cases such as *Wachtel* have any right to share in the gain, or could the husband say: "I bought the house, I was responsible for paying off the mortgage loan, so it all belongs to me?"

Family assets—the history

8-03   Today, as we have already said, questions like this would in practice usually be resolved by the divorce court exercising its wide discretionary powers over the whole of a couple's capital and income. The court will normally exercise those powers so as to give the wife a share in the home on the basis that she has "earned" such a share by her contributions to the welfare of the family, including her contribution to looking after the home and caring for the family (see MCA 1973, s.25(1)(f), para. 11–44 below) But it was only in 1971 that the court was given these extensive powers (Matrimonial Proceedings and Property Act 1970, the relevant provisions

72

of which were subsequently consolidated in MCA 1973). Before that date therefore such issues had to be resolved in the context of property law. The question which had to be decided was: did the fact that a couple were married have any effect on their property rights? In particular did the wife acquire any rights to what were conveniently called "family assets" —"those things which are acquired by one or other or both of the parties, with the intention that there should be continuing provision for them and their children during their joint lives, and used for the benefit of the family as a whole." (*Wachtel* v. *Wachtel* [1973] Fam 72, 90.)

Injustice to wives

It seemed to many people only fair that a wife in the sort of case   **8-04**
mentioned above should be regarded as having earned a share in the family assets. After all, her services in the home were comparable in economic value to those of her husband, who had only been freed to go out and earn in the waged sector of society by her efforts. Lord Simon of Glaisdale put this point in a picturesque and much quoted dictum:

> "The wife spends her youth and early middle age in bearing and rearing children and in tending the home; the husband is thus freed for his economic activities. Unless the wife plays her part, the husband cannot play his. The cock bird can feather his nest precisely because he is not required to spend most of his time sitting on it." (With all my worldly goods . . . (1964).)

Husband and wife one?

At one time marriage did have a most profound effect at common law   **8-05**
on property entitlement: husband and wife became legally one—but (as Lord Denning has put it: see *Williams & Glyn's Bank Ltd.* v. *Boland* [1979] Ch 312, 332) the husband was that one. Much of the wife's property therefore vested in the husband; but the wife acquired a right to be supported by the husband, and she also had certain rights after his death. In the 19th century there was a powerful campaign against the injustice to married women of the common law rule; and in a series of enactments culminating in the Married Women's Property Act 1882 Parliament adopted the system of "separate property." In effect, marriage no longer had any immediate effect on entitlement to property. The result was intended to be beneficial to married women, and it certainly did have some advantages—for example, a married woman's earnings were her own to do with as she wished, whereas at common law her earnings belonged to her husband. However, in relation to claiming a share in the family assets the position was not so satisfactory.

Disadvantages of separate property regime

As a result of the acceptance of the principle of separate property there   **8-06**
was no longer "one law of property applicable where a dispute as to property is between spouses or former spouses and another law of property where the dispute is between others" (Viscount Dilhorne in

Gissing v. *Gissing* [1971] AC 886, 899). A wife who wanted to make out a claim to (say) a share in the family home would thus have to base it on some recognised principle of property law, and in effect she could only do so if someone who had never been married to the husband could equally have done so. (In 1969 the House of Lords had unequivocally ruled that the provisions of section 17 of the Married Women's Property Act 1882 empowering a judge to "make such order . . . as he thinks fit" in disputes about title to or possession of property did not, as Lord Denning and others had claimed, give the court, a "free hand to do what is just" in all the circumstances: *Pettitt* v. *Pettitt* [1970] AC 777.)

Not easy to make out claim to family assets

8–07   A brief examination of the relevant principles of property law under the regime of separate property must therefore be made. It will become clear that there were (and are) formidable difficulties facing a wife who seeks to make a claim to family assets.

The student should also note that the parties in some of the cases which are referred to in paras. 8–08 to 8–27 were not in fact married, but had simply lived together in a common household. It follows from the principle adopted by the House of Lords (see para. 8–06 above) that such cases may be equally relevant to a discussion of the property rights of husband and wife. The situation is analysed specifically from the perspective of the unmarried in Chapter 12 below.

RELEVANT RULES OF LAND LAW—WHO IS BENEFICIALLY ENTITLED?

8–08   Most of the disputes about family assets have centred on the family home; and the following rules of land law and equity are particularly relevant:

(1) Deed needed for transfer of legal estate

8–09   Section 52 of the Law of Property Act 1925 stipulates that a deed is necessary to convey or create any legal estate in land. If the conveyance of the matrimonial home was taken in the husband's name it follows that (in the absence of any subsequent conveyance to her) the wife can make no claim to be entitled to the legal estate.

(2) Writing necessary for other interests in land

8–10   Section 53 of the Law of Property Act 1925 stipulates that no interest in land can be created or disposed of except by a signed written document. Hence in *Gissing* v. *Gissing* [1971] AC 886, HL the matrimonial home had been conveyed into the husband's sole name. When the marriage broke up he told her: "Don't worry about the house—it's yours. I will pay the mortgage payments and all other outgoings." However, the wife had no claim on the basis of that statement: there was no deed which could displace the legal estate, and no written document which could give her any other interest.

(3) But interest may be claimed under implied resulting or constructive trust

Section 53(2) of the Law of Property Act 1925 provides that the above **8–11** rules do not affect the "creation or operation of resulting, implied or constructive trusts." A spouse may therefore be able to establish a claim under these equitable doctrines, which are based on the underlying principle that it would in the circumstances be unconscionable to allow the legal owner to continue to assert the absolute ownership which appears on the title documents to be his: see Lord Templeman in *Winkworth* v. *Edward Baron Development Company Ltd.* [1987] 1 All ER 114.

However, the student should be warned that there is still considerable uncertainty in this area. As Mustill L.J. put it in *Grant* v. *Edwards* [1986] 1 All ER 426, 435, CA, the time has not yet "arrived when it is possible to state the law in a way which will deal with all the practical problems which may arise in this difficult field, consistently with everything said in the cases." The following summary of principles should accordingly be treated with reserve:

(a) *Payment of purchase price—resulting trust*

If one partner provides all or part of the purchase price of a matrimonial **8–12** home conveyed into the name of the other, he or she will, in the absence of admissible evidence that some other result was intended, be entitled in equity to a share in the property proportionate to the amount of his or her contribution: if the wife pays £10,000 and her husband pays £30,000 of a total purchase price of £40,000 she will in principle be entitled in equity to a one-quarter interest in the property by way of resulting trust: see generally *Cowcher* v. *Cowcher* [1972] 1 WLR 425. (If the husband pays part of the price of a property conveyed into the name of his wife the usual presumption of resulting trust illustrated above may sometimes be rebutted by the so-called presumption of advancement, *i.e.* that he intends to make a gift to her: see *Silver* v. *Silver* [1958] 1 WLR 259, 261.)

(b) *Common intention acted on to claimant's detriment—implied trust*

If there is admissible evidence that, at the date of the acquisition, the **8–13** parties intended the home to be jointly owned, the court will imply a trust of the proceeds of sale to that effect, provided that the claimant has acted to her detriment in a way which is referable to the acquisition. There are two stages in this analysis:

(i) *Is there evidence of intention?* In answering this question, the courts **8–14** are prepared to scrutinise all the circumstances, and draw inferences which a reasonable person would draw from the parties' conduct at the time of the acquisition or subsequently: *Re Densham* [1975] 1 WLR 1519. In particular, if the wife has made a direct contribution to the acquisition costs the court will usually infer an intention that the matrimonial home be jointly owned. The making of a cash contribution to the initial deposit on a house being bought on a mortgage is the best example of such a contribution; but regular and substantial direct contributions to the mortgage instalments will also suffice: see Lord Diplock in *Gissing* v. *Gissing* (above) at p. 908. Occasional payments, on the other hand, may not suffice: see Buckley L.J. in *Kowalczuk* v. *Kowalczuk* [1973] 1 WLR 930, 935.

8-15   *Indirect contributions.* The basic principle seems to be that contributions are relevant as furnishing evidence of intention; and the question will usually be whether the contributions which have been made can be shown to have been referable to the acquisition of the property. There is little difficulty in establishing such a link in the case of direct contributions of the type discussed above. On the other hand:

> In *Winkworth* v. *Edward Baron Development Company Ltd.*, [1987] 1 All ER 114, H and W were the sole shareholders and directors in a company which, at a cost of £70,000, bought a house for their occupation. Some time later, H and W sold their former home, and the net proceeds were paid into the company's overdrawn account. W (who knew nothing about business and left the management of the company in H's hands) would not in fact have agreed to a mortgage on the couple's home; but the company nonetheless borrowed £70,000 from Mr Winkworth, and executed a legal charge in his favour over the house for that amount. W's signature (which appeared on the charge—apparently as a director—and on a letter acknowledging that neither she nor her husband had any beneficial interest in the property) had been forged. The House of Lords unanimously dismissed what Lord Templeman described as the "bold and astonishing" proposition that W had, by the payment of the sale proceeds of the former home into the company's account, acquired an equitable interest in the house. That payment was not referable to the acquisition of the house which had already been bought and paid for in full; but had simply been paid into the company's account and became part of its assets managed by H and W as sole and equal shareholders. Mr Winkworth was entitled to possession.

In practice, the question which has proved most troublesome is whether the court will be prepared to draw the necessary inference of intention from the making of so-called "indirect" contributions. Suppose for example that the wife goes out to work, and uses her wages to pay for food and other housekeeping expenses? Since the question is essentially one of intention there seems no reason why the court should not draw an appropriate inference in such a case; but on one view the court will not usually do so unless there has been a contribution in money (or at least in money's worth—for example, helping with building work). In this view, merely helping with the housekeeping expenses (Mustill L.J. in *Grant* v. *Edwards* [1986] 2 All ER 426, 436) or "keeping house, giving birth to and looking after and helping to bring up the children" would not be a sufficient basis for a claim: see *Burns* v. *Burns* [1984] Ch 317, CA, discussed at para. 12–09 below. (However, those were cases involving an unmarried couple, and the courts have in practice shown themselves less ready in such cases to draw inferences of a commitment to sharing: see *Bernard* v. *Josephs* [1982] Ch 391; para. 12–06 below.)

Establishing intention by other means. Many of the cases have been **8-16** concerned with the inferences about the parties' common intention which the courts will draw from the fact that the claimant has contributed in some way to the acquisition of the property. But the Court of Appeal has recently made it clear that the making of contributions (for example, by incurring expenditure) is not a necessary condition; and that other evidence of common intention can be accepted:

> In *Grant* v. *Edwards* [1986] 2 All ER 426, CA, the claimant was told that her name was not going to go on the title because if it did there might be problems in her then pending divorce proceedings. The court accepted that this fact coupled with evidence that the parties treated the house as belonging to them both and that they had a principle of sharing everything constituted sufficient proof that she was intended to have an interest in the house.

(ii) *Detrimental reliance by claimant.* The Court of Appeal has recently **8-17** asserted that it is not sufficient for the court to infer an intention that both parties should have a beneficial interest in the property. Because of the principle that equity will not assist a volunteer, it must also be shown that the claimant has acted to his detriment in reliance on that intention. It is for this reason that the making of contributions is in practice so important: such contributions will both constitute evidence from which the parties' common intention can be inferred, and also establish that the claimant has acted to her detriment in reliance on that agreement. If there has been no such contribution it may be difficult to show the necessary detrimental reliance:

> In *Midland Bank plc* v. *Dobson and Dobson* [1986] 1 FLR 171, CA, the court accepted that husband and wife had a common intention to share the beneficial interest in the matrimonial home; but the wife nonetheless failed in her claim to a beneficial interest because there was no evidence that she had acted to her detriment on the basis of that intention. She had made no direct contribution to the acquisition costs or mortgage instalments, and her contributions in buying domestic equipment and in decorating the house were unrelated to the intention that the ownership of the house be shared.

(c) Other techniques—equitable estoppel and the constructive trust

So far, the agreement of the parties—express or inferred—has been a **8-18** crucial factor; but it is not always necessary to find such an agreement in order to uphold a claim to a share in property. In particular, the doctrine of equitable estoppel may be relevant: if one partner has incurred expenditure or done other acts to his or her detriment (for example, carrying out improvements) in the reasonable belief that she already owned or would be given a proprietary interest in the property, equity will give effect to that belief:

> In *Pascoe* v. *Turner* [1979] 1 WLR 431, CA, the plaintiff, on the breakdown of their relationship, told the defendant, that the house "is yours and everything in it." So far, there seems nothing to distinguish the case from *Gissing* (para. 8–10 above); but the crucial distinction between the two cases appears to be that in *Pascoe* v. *Turner* the defendant, in reliance on this assurance, then used a large

proportion of her small capital in paying for repairs, improvements, and maintenance. It was held that the plaintiff's encouragement and acquiescence gave rise to an estoppel which could only be satisfied by ordering him to do what the defendant had been led to expect, namely that he would transfer the property to her.

Equitable estoppel is a doctrine of potentially great importance (see Browne-Wilkinson V.C. in *Grant* v. *Edwards* [1986] 2 All ER 426, 439) since it goes some way towards allowing the court to give effect to the parties' assumptions if to do otherwise would be unfair or unjust; but the doctrine does not provide a general remedy for injustice. For example:

In *Coombes* v. *Smith* [1986] 1 WLR 808 M assured F that he would always provide for her; but it was held that she was not entitled to an interest by way of estoppel since she had not been under any misapprehension about her legal rights.

Estoppel as a defence. Even if one party is unable to establish a proprietary interest under the doctrine of equitable estoppel, there may nonetheless be circumstances in which he can resist an action for possession on the basis that there has been a representation that he would be allowed to stay in the property for a period, and that the representation was intended to be acted upon and was in fact acted on: see *Maharaj* v. *Jai Chand* [1986] 3 WLR 440, PC.

8-19   *The remedial constructive trust doctrine.* On one view it is unnecessary to have too much concern for the niceties of estoppel or the implied or resulting trust, since (it is claimed) equity can in any case impose a constructive trust, irrespective of the parties' intentions, whenever it is necessary to do so to satisfy the demands of justice and good conscience. In this view in resolving disputes between husband and wife the court must simply look at all the circumstances—including such matters as the wife's contributions to the family budget: *Hazell* v. *Hazell* [1972] 1 WLR 301, CA—as they exist at the time that their marriage breaks down, and impose a constructive trust on their property in such shares as justice and equity requires: see Lord Denning M.R. in *Williams & Glyn's Bank Ltd.* v. *Boland* [1979] Ch. 312, 329, CA.

8-20   *Wide doctrine not accepted in England.* If the courts were to adopt this view of the constructive trust as a broad and flexible equitable tool to be imposed whenever justice and good conscience require (see *Hussey* v. *Palmer* [1972] 1 WLR 1286, CA) it would certainly avoid much of the artificiality and injustice involved in the judicial quest for the fugitive or phantom common intention (as Dixon J. put it in the Canadian Supreme Court decision, *Pettkus* v. *Barker* [1980] 117 DLR (3d) 257, 280). But it seems clear that such a broad doctrine, although accepted in some common law juridictions, is not yet part of English law as laid down by the House of Lords in *Pettitt* v. *Pettitt* and *Gissing* v. *Gissing* (above). For the time being, therefore, the constructive trust has only a limited part to play in accordance with recognised equitable precedents.

(4) Quantification of beneficial interest

Once the existence of a beneficial interest has been successfully asserted **8-21** under the trust principles set out above, it will still be necessary to determine its size. In principle, the question to be asked is: what did the parties intend?; and in answering that question the courts can take any evidence into account, including (it would appear) the making of indirect contributions, for example by way of contributions to household expenses: see *Grant* v. *Edwards* [1986] 2 All ER 426 (particularly Browne-Wilkinson V.C. at p. 439). If the court finds an interest by way of estoppel, the question becomes "what is the most appropriate way to give effect to the equity?"

Legal estate conveyed to both parties

Even if the legal estate has been conveyed into the joint names of **8-22** husband and wife there may nonetheless be a dispute about the nature and extent of their interests—is the wife entitled to a quarter share as tenant in common, for example, or are the couple joint tenants equally entitled to the proceeds of sale? Judges have urged solicitors to deal with these questions directly in the conveyance in order to avoid disputes; and it is settled law that an express declaration of beneficial entitlement in the conveyance can only be rebutted by proof of fraud or mistake: *Goodman* v. *Gallant* [1986] 2 WLR 236, CA. But all too often this advice is not followed; and the courts will then have to examine the evidence to see whether it indicates an intention by the parties that the beneficial ownership should be other than equal: *Bernard* v. *Josephs* [1982] Ch 391, 402–403.

OTHER LAND LAW QUESTIONS

Will the court order a sale?

Even if the wife (say) does make out a claim under these rules, it may **8-23** also be necessary to decide what is to happen if, for example, she wants to keep the property whilst her husband wants it sold. Such a dispute may be resolved by an application to the court under section 30 of the Law of Property Act 1925. In exercising its discretion under that section the Court will take account of the underlying purpose for which the property was acquired: if the parties' relationship has come to an end the court will often regard the purpose as having also come to an end, and order a sale: *Jones* v. *Challenger* [1961] 1 QB 176. But if there are still young children their interests will also be relevant, and the court will be less ready to order a sale (*Chhokar* v. *Chhokar* [1984] FLR 313) even though the children are not strictly speaking beneficiaries under the trust: *Burke* v. *Burke* [1974] 1 WLR 1063.

Sales in bankruptcy cases

If the husband's interest has vested in his trustee in bankruptcy the **8-24** trustee will usually apply to the bankruptcy court for an order for sale under section 30. That court is by statute (Insolvency Act 1986, s.336(4)) required to have regard to the interests of the bankrupt's creditors, to the conduct of the spouse or former spouse "so far as contributing to the bankruptcy," to the needs and financial resources of the spouse or former spouse, to the needs of any children and to all the circumstances of the case (other than the needs of the bankrupt); but after one year from the bankruptcy the court is required (unless the circumstances of the case are "exceptional") to assume that the interests of the bankrupt's creditors outweigh all other considerations: Insolvency Act 1986, s.336(5).

Severance of joint tenancy

8-25   It is of the nature of a joint tenancy that it can be severed—*i.e.* converted into a tenancy in common. This may be particularly important where a marriage is breaking down. For example, one spouse may want to ensure that his half interest in the matrimonial home should on his death pass under his will or intestacy (perhaps to his children by a previous marriage) rather than to the other spouse. There are a number of ways in which severance can be achieved, of which the simplest is by giving written notice to the other under the provisions of section 36 of the Law of Property Act 1925. (Simply asking for an order in matrimonial proceedings is not by itself sufficient: *Harris* v. *Goddard* [1983] 1 WLR 1203.) It is also important to note that it is impossible to sever a joint tenancy by will.

Does the wife's interest bind third parties?

8-26   In principle property rights bind third parties: a husband who purports to sell the matrimonial home cannot give a purchaser a greater interest than he owns. But in most cases, the wife's interest will be only equitable, and purchasers are not necessarily bound by such interests. The position is: (a) *If the title is not registered* under the Land Registration Act 1925, a spouse's equitable interest under a trust for sale will bind the purchaser of a legal estate in land only if the purchaser has actual or constructive notice thereof. The question is usually whether the purchaser has made such inspections as ought reasonably to have been made (LPA 1925, s.199); and a purchaser will thus normally be treated as having notice of the rights of a wife who is in occupation at the time of the transaction:

> In *Kingsnorth Finance Co. Ltd.* v. *Tizard* [1986] 1 WLR 783 a purchaser was held to be bound by the wife's interest notwithstanding the fact that his surveyor had inspected the property and seen no evidence of occupation by her or any other female. This was because the inspection had taken place by prior appointment on a Sunday afternoon, and the husband had been able to conceal any evidence of his wife's existence.

(b) *If the title to the property is registered* under the Land Registration Acts a wife's beneficial interest will bind a purchaser if the wife was "in actual occupation" at the time of registration unless the purchaser made enquiry of her which failed to reveal her rights: see *Williams and Glyn's Bank Ltd.* v. *Boland* [1981] AC 487, HL:

> Michael Boland obtained a loan from the bank, to whom he charged the family

home as security. The business got into financial difficulties; and the bank brought proceedings for possession. They failed. Mrs Boland had (it was conceded) a beneficial interest in the property, notwithstanding the fact that Michael Boland was registered as sole proprietor. She had been "in actual occupation" at the time when the loan was made; and the Bank had made no enquiries of any kind of her about her rights. Hence the Bank took subject to her interest which constituted an overriding interest. It was said that the words "actual occupation" were ordinary words of plain English, connoting physical presence; but there may well be cases in which it is not easy to say whether or not a claimant is in actual occupation or not.

The decision in *Boland* gave rise to many difficulties in conveyancing practice (which are analysed by the Law Commission in its *Report* on the implications of the decision: Law Com. No 115, 1982); but it is important to remember that the first question must always be whether the claimant can establish a beneficial interest under the principles set out above. In *Boland* it was conceded that the wife had such an interest; but:

In *Winkworth* v. *Edward Baron Development Company Ltd.,* [1987] 1 All ER 114, para. 8–15 above) the mortgagee contested the wife's claim that by allowing the proceeds of sale of the matrimonial home to be paid into the legal owner's bank account she had thereby acquired a beneficial interest in the house which it had previously acquired; and, as already stated, Lord Templeman rejected the claim which he described as "bold and astonishing." Lord Templeman (whose first instance decision in favour of the mortgagee in *Boland* was overturned by the Court of Appeal and House of Lords) stated that some responsibility for the six-figure litigation costs incurred in what the Law Lords obviously regarded as an unmeritorious claim was shared by the decision of the House in *Boland*.

Waiver of interest by wife

In practice lenders and others normally get wives to execute a   **8–27** document authorising the husband to enter into a transaction involving the house—for example, mortgaging it to raise money for improvements or other purposes—and giving that transaction priority to her beneficial interest. Even if there has been no express waiver it has been held that the court may infer such an authorisation: *Bristol and West Building Society* v. *Henning* [1985] 1 WLR 778, CA. If the courts are ready to do this, the protection apparently given to the interests of wives by the *Boland* and *Tizard* decisions may prove to be illusory.

PROPERTY RIGHTS ON DEATH

Widows favourably treated

Most marriages are still ended by death rather than divorce; and   **8–28** marriage does have a significant effect on the devolution of property on death. If a married person dies intestate then his spouse will be entitled to his personal chattels and to a "statutory legacy" amounting, if he leaves issue, to £40,000. (If he leaves any of certain specified close relatives, but no issue, the sum is raised to £85,000.) In addition the surviving spouse will be entitled to an interest in any balance of the estate—a life interest in one-half if there is issue, or half absolutely if there are close relatives but no issue. (If there are no close relatives the surviving spouse takes the whole estate.)

Freedom of testation

8-29　　Most people die intestate; but if there is a valid will its terms will over-ride the intestacy rules—English law, unlike many foreign systems, does not stipulate that a spouse has a right to a certain proportion of the deceased partner's estate.

Court may over-ride will or intestacy provisions

8-30　　If a widow or widower feels that the provision to which he is entitled under the will or intestacy is not reasonable he or she may apply to the court under the Inheritance (Provision for Family and Dependants) Act 1975. The court will consider whether or not reasonable financial provision has been made. If not, it will ask whether provision should be ordered and if so in what form—for example, by way of periodical income payments, or payment of a lump sum, etc. In deciding these questions the court is directed to consider all matters which it considers relevant, and its attention is specifically drawn to a number of matters. These include the duration of the marriage, the contribution made by the applicant to the welfare of the family of the deceased (including any contribution made by looking after the home or caring for the family), and it is also required to have regard to the provision which the applicant might reasonably have expected to receive if the marriage had been ended in divorce. The "divorce expectation" is "obviously a very important consideration" (Oliver L.J. in *Re Besterman* [1984] Ch 458, 469, CA); and reference must be made to Chapter 11 where the court's powers on divorce are considered. Some idea of how important the 1975 Act can be may be derived from the facts of *Re Besterman* itself:

> The deceased, after 18 years of marriage, left his wife his personal chattels and an annual income of £3,500 out of a total estate of £1,500,000. The court made an order that she should receive one-quarter of the estate on the basis that since the estate was large the wife should have sufficient money to ensure that she should not fall into need.

Of course most estates are far smaller, but the court will equally be concerned to meet the applicant's reasonable needs: see for example *Stead v. Stead* [1985] FLR 16 where the court made a complicated order primarily designed to ensure that the applicant would be properly housed.

THE MOVE FOR FURTHER REFORM

Community of Property

8-31　　In the late 1960s there was considerable pressure for the introduction into English law of a system of community of property in order to

minimise the unfairness of the separate property regime. Indeed in 1969
the House of Commons gave a second reading, against government
advice to a private member's bill designed to introduce a community
regime. In 1971 the Law Commission published a detailed Working Paper
(No. 42) on family property; and in 1973 the Commission published its
First Report on Family Property: A New Approach.

Between publication of the Working Paper and the First Report the
Court of Appeal in *Wachtel* v. *Wachtel* [1973] Fam 72, had emphasised the
great potential of the wide discretionary powers conferred on the divorce
court in 1970 to bring about an equitable sharing of family assets; and the
Commission's First Report concluded that, in the light of this decision, it
would be unnecessary to superimpose a general community structure
upon those powers. However, the Commission was conscious of the fact
that these rights depended on the exercise of a judicial discretion; and
recommended that the law should be reformed by the introduction of a
principle of co-ownership under which the matrimonial home—in
practice usually the only significant capital asset—would, in the absence
of contrary agreement, be owned jointly by husband and wife. The
conferment of such a right would (the Commission evidently thought)
suffice to remedy what it had in 1971 described as the fundamental cause
of dissatisfaction with the law:

> "In effect what women are saying, and saying with considerable male
> support, is: 'We are no longer content with a system whereby a wife's
> rights in family assets depend on the whim of her husband or on the
> discretion of a judge. We demand definite property rights, not
> possible discretionary benefits.'" (Law Com. Working Paper No. 42,
> para. 0.22)

Law Commission's proposed scheme not implemented

The details of the scheme necessary to give effect to this policy, as set   8-32
out in the draft legislation annexed to the Law Commission's *Third Report
on Family Property* (1978, Law Com. No. 86) proved to be exceedingly
complex. There were also a number of arguments of principle against the
scheme (many of which are tellingly summarised in the Report of the
Scottish Law Commission on *Matrimonial Property* (1984) para. 3.10)
Why, for instance, single out the matrimonial home for special treatment?
Why give a windfall advantage to one party to a, perhaps very short,
marriage whose spouse happened to have inherited a very valuable
house? Why impose a system of co-ownership on one particular asset at a
time when in practice the great majority of married couples decide for
themselves that co-ownership is the régime they wish to choose?

But above all, by the time the draft legislation was produced, the
mischief which it was concerned to remedy seemed no longer to be so
pressing. Case law after *Wachtel* made it clear that, if a marriage broke
down, the divorce court would ensure that wives got adequate recognition
for their contributions to the matrimonial home; and no-one any longer
suggested that the co-ownership scheme could replace the court's

discretionary powers on divorce. In these circumstances, the Government decided that the co-ownership proposals were unlikely to produce advantages commensurate with their manifest disadvantages in terms of complexity and consequent cost. There seem to be no prospects for legislative implementation of the Law Commission's scheme.

Other statutory reforms

8–33 The detailed examination of family property law undertaken by the Law Commission did lead to the enactment of the Inheritance (Provision for Family and Dependants) Act 1975. This important enactment, as explained above, enables the court to order financial provision for a surviving spouse and other specified dependants.

Minor reforms

8–34 In comparison, other statutory provisions dealing with the beneficial ownership of matrimonial property are unimportant, and can be summarised in chronological order as follows:

8–35 (i) *The Married Women's Property Act 1964* was intended to reverse the common law rule under which the husband was entitled to any savings made by his wife out of a housekeeping allowance. The (unsatisfactorily drafted) Act provides that such savings shall in the absence of contrary agreement be treated as belonging to husband and wife in equal shares. The Law Commission has now provisionally proposed further reform: see Working Paper No. 90, *Transfer of Money Between Spouses* (1985). In practice the Act seems rarely to be invoked.

8–36 (ii) *The Matrimonial Proceedings and Property Act 1970, section 37*, seeks to clarify the law relating to the effect of one spouse's contributions to the improvement of property. Provided that the contribution is substantial and in money or money's worth, the contributing spouse is, in the absence of contrary agreement, to be treated as acquiring a share (or an enlarged share) in the property. If the parties do not do so it is for the court to quantify the share according to what it considers to be just. It should be emphasised that the section is not concerned with the effect of contributions to the acquisition or to the maintenance of property.

Chapter 9

OCCUPATION OF THE MATRIMONIAL HOME

INTRODUCTION

The fact that a wife cannot establish a beneficial interest in the **9–01** matrimonial home under the rules set out in Chapter 8 does not mean that she has no right to live there. Even at common law a married woman had a right to be provided with a roof over her head, although she would forfeit this right if, for example, she committed adultery. The Matrimonial Homes Act 1967 (now consolidated in the Matrimonial Homes Act 1983: "MHA 1983" hereafter) effectively supplanted the common law, and MHA 1983 now codifies the law governing the occupation of the matrimonial home.

THE RIGHTS CONFERRED ON SPOUSES BY THE MATRIMONIAL HOMES ACT 1983

Rights of Occupation
In its original form, the Matrimonial Homes Act was primarily **9–02** concerned with the situation in which one spouse was entitled to occupy the home "by virtue of a beneficial estate or interest or contract" or by statute, and the other spouse was not so entitled. The latter—the non-owning spouse who was at common law potentially so vulnerable—is given "rights of occupation" by the Act (s.1(1)):

    (a) if in occupation, a right not to be evicted or excluded from the dwelling house or any part thereof by the other spouse except with the leave of the court . . . ;
    (b) if not in occupation, a right with the leave of the court . . . to enter into and occupy the dwelling house."

Duration of Rights of Occupation
Broadly speaking, rights of occupation last only for as long as the **9–03** marriage. But the court is given power, "in the event of a matrimonial dispute or estrangement" to over-ride this general principle. If an application is made during the subsistence of the marriage the court may in effect extend the rights of occupation either for a specified period (which could be as long as the wife's life) or "until further order": MHA 1983, s.1(4), s.2(4).

Application to the court
So long as one spouse has rights of occupation, either spouse can apply **9–04** to the court for orders governing the occupation of the home: MHA 1983, s.1(2). Thus, a wife may seek an order excluding her husband from the home (or from part of it, for example her bedroom), and she can do so

even though she accepts that as a matter of property law he is the sole beneficial owner. Correspondingly a husband-owner could apply for an order bringing the wife's rights to an end, for example so that he could sell the house with vacant possession.

Joint owners

9-05   As has already been pointed out, the Act was originally concerned with protecting the non-owner; but the procedure was found to be so useful that it is now provided that, even where the spouses are jointly entitled, they may apply under the Act for an order relating to the occupation of the home: MHA 1983, s.9; s.1(11).

THE PRINCIPLES APPLIED

The order must be "just and reasonable"

9-06   The Act provides (MHA 1983, s.1(3)) that in determining applications the court "may make such order as it thinks just and reasonable having regard to the conduct of the spouses in relation to each other and otherwise, to their respective needs and financial resources, to the needs of any children and to all the circumstances of the case." In this context the interests of the children are not "paramount," in the sense that they over-ride all other factors as they do in cases in which custody and access are directly in issue. The essential requirement is that the order be "just and reasonable"

> In *Richards* v. *Richards* [1984] 1 AC 174 the wife applied to turn her husband out of the matrimonial home because she could not bear to be in the same household with him. Although the judge found that she had no reasonable ground for refusing to live in the same house, he granted her application in the interests of the three children (who were in the wife's care). The House of Lords held he had been wrong to do so; the order (as the judge had appreciated) was not "just and reasonable."

> In *Summers* v. *Summers* [1986] 1 FLR 343 husband and wife had repeatedly had violent quarrels. The husband would lose his temper, call the wife names, and smash the furniture. On one occasion the wife threw lager over the husband. As a result, the children were frightened and affected by the atmosphere which the judge found to have become "quite impossible." At first instance, the judge ordered the husband to leave, apparently partly "to allow the dust to settle for a time which might perhaps then lead to a fresh reconciliation". It was held that he had been wrong to do so. In particular, the judge had failed to take into account the "draconian nature" of an ouster order expelling the husband and the effect which such an order would have on the husband.

Children's needs important, although not paramount

9-07   Although the court must not treat the children's interests as "paramount" in the sense explained above (and see further Chapter 14) they are nonetheless extremely important. In particular, it will often be desirable for the court first of all to decide which parent is to have the care of the children so that it can properly assess their "needs" in accordance with the provisions of the Act: see *Essex CC* v. *T, The Times*, March 15, 1986.

Ancillary powers

MHA 1983, s.1(3) gives the court wide and flexible powers. It can exclude part of the house from a spouse's rights of occupation—so that a dentist could apply for an order that his wife be not permitted to come into the surgery and waiting room notwithstanding the fact that these were part of the home. It may also deal with repair, maintenance and other obligations, and can order one spouse to make periodical payments to the other in respect of the occupation.   9–08

Act concerned with occupation of home—other remedies available against violence, molestation, etc.

It is important to remember that the MHA 1983 does not exhaust the legal remedies available to deal with domestic violence. The courts also have fairly extensive powers to make orders intended to protect wives and others against violence and molestation. These procedures are summarised at para. 6–12 above.   9–09

EFFECT OF SPOUSES' RIGHTS UNDER ACT ON PURCHASERS, MORTGAGEES ETC.

Rights bind third parties if registered

In *National Provincial Bank Ltd.* v. *Ainsworth* [1965] AC 1165, the House of Lords had held that the wife's common law right to be provided with housing by her husband was an essentially personal right, intrinsically incapable of binding third parties—even if the third party knew of her claims. The MHA 1983 therefore introduced a procedure whereby rights of occupation may be made to bind third parties. But if such rights are to bind a purchaser of the land or any interest therein they must be protected by registration as a Class F land charge.   9–10

If a purchaser finds a charge registered against the property he will in practice refuse to complete unless and until it is removed—even though in legal theory the charge will only protect the rights under the MHA 1983 and not other rights (such as a beneficial interest in the property or the sale proceeds):

> In *Barnett* v. *Hassett* [1982] 1 WLR 1385 the parties' marriage had broken down, and the husband and children had left the matrimonial home. He had no wish to return to it, but registered a Class F charge in order to prevent the wife completing her planned sale of the house until a dispute about money had been settled. The Court held that the Act was intended to protect the right to occupy the home, and did not extend to protect other claims. Hence, registration had not been a proper use of the Act; and the charge was set aside.

Effect of spouse's insolvency on occupation rights

What is the position if the husband is adjudicated bankrupt—can the   9–11 wife assert her rights of occupation against the husband's creditors? It was originally specifically provided that her rights were void against the trustee; but under the Insolvency Act 1986 the position has been changed in an attempt to strike a fairer balance between the interests of the husband's family and his creditors. The rights of occupation do now bind the trustee; and it will be for him to apply to the bankruptcy court for an order terminating the wife's rights. The court will apply the same criteria to such an application as to an application for the sale of jointly owned property (see para. 8–24 above); and in effect the family will get a year's grace: Insolvency Act 1986, s.337.

Chapter 10

FINANCIAL REMEDIES—I

INTRODUCTION

At common law a husband had a duty to maintain his wife; but the extent **10–01** of this right was limited, and the methods of enforcing it were inadequate. Gradually more effective ways of enabling dependants to obtain support have been developed; and today the common law duty is rarely of direct practical significance. Chapters 10 and 11 seek not only to summarise those legal remedies; but more generally to provide material to answer the question: "what is a wife to do if her husband refuses to provide what she regards as adequate support for herself and the children?"

The financial procedures which are primarily relevant in situations of marital breakdown fall into four main groups:

(i) The Supplementary Benefit system;
(ii) Proceedings in the High Court or County Court based on failure to provide reasonable maintenance;
(iii) Proceedings in the magistrates' court based on such failure, or on other grounds specified in the Domestic Proceedings and Magistrates' Courts Act 1978; and—perhaps most important of all—
(iv) "Ancillary" claims for financial provision and property adjustment, divorce, nullity, or judicial separation proceedings. Because of the importance of this procedure it has a chapter (Chapter 11) to itself.

THE SUPPLEMENTARY BENEFIT SYSTEM

Main features

The Supplementary Benefits Act 1976 provides (s.1) that "every person **10–02** in Great Britain of or over the age of 16 whose resources are insufficient to meet his requirements shall be entitled to benefit. . . . " However, the terms "requirements" and "resources" have to be interpreted in accordance with elaborate statutory rules—it is no use an individual claiming that he has become used to living in the Ritz Hotel and that his requirements should be assessed accordingly. Moreover, the supplementary benefit system also stipulates that the resources and requirements of what is (in effect) the supplementary benefit household shall be aggregated. In particular, aggregation applies to dependent children, to a married couple who are members of the same household, and to an unmarried couple living together as husband and wife (a concept which gives rise to great difficulty in practice). But a married couple are only affected by the aggregation principle if they are members of the same "household" (an expression discussed at para. 4–33 above) so that if a marriage breaks down the wife who is left behind will be able to claim benefit in her own right.

How "requirements" are calculated

10-03　　　Regulations stipulate a standard scale of normal requirements; which as at July 28, 1986 was as follows:

Couple	£48.40
Single householder	29.80
Dependent children—	
aged 18 or more	23.85
aged 16 or 17	18.40
aged 11 to 15	15.30
under 11	10.20

(In certain circumstances a higher long term scale applies).

Additional and Housing Requirements

10-04　　　In addition to these "normal" requirements, certain "additional requirements" are allowed—for example an extra £2.20 is allowed for heating costs if a member of the household is less than 5 years old. Finally, "housing requirements" are brought into the calculation of the claimant's total requirements. In practice rent and rates are now dealt with through Housing Benefit schemes administered by local authorities; but the interest element of mortgage instalments due in respect of the claimant's home will usually be allowed as a supplementary benefit "requirement" (since January 26, 1987 owner-occupiers under 60 are, for the first sixteen weeks, only entitled to have half the mortgage interest paid. The Supplementary Benefit (Housing Requirements and Resources) Amendment Regulations 1987. However, this change in the regulations —which has been severely criticised: see the Report of the Social Security Advisory Committee (1986, Cm. 35)—will not affect the long term position of the one-parent family with which this Chapter is concerned.)

Calculation of "resources"

10-05　　　Having calculated a claimant's requirements in this way the next step is to calculate his "resources." The regulations distinguish between "capital resources" and "income resources." So far as "income resources" are concerned the general principle is that the whole of the earnings and other income of members of the family is calculated on a weekly basis and taken into account. Periodical payments made to a member of the family by a "liable relative" (for example, a separated spouse: see para. 10-11 below) are taken into account in full as income, as are all payments of child benefit, family income supplement, and so on.

Certain resources disregarded

By way of exception to the general rule, certain resources are left out of account—in particular, the earnings (but not any other income) of a dependant (but not of a spouse or cohabitant) are disregarded, so that entitlement to benefit is not affected by, for example, a child's earnings from a part-time job. In the case of a single parent, the first £4 of earnings and half of any earnings between £4 and £20 are disregarded. **10–06**

Striking the balance

The aggregate of the claimant's resources is set against his "requirements". If resources exceed requirements no benefit is payable; if requirements exceed resources the difference is payable by way of a weekly allowance. **10–07**

Capital

This assumes that the claimant has no capital resources. If he does have any capital it must be taken into account in accordance with the regulations. If the total of a claimant's capital resources (other than those disregarded: see para. 10–09) exceeds a specified amount (currently £3,000) he is not entitled to a supplementary allowance. This all or nothing rule has the advantage of simplicity; it is not clear that it has any other. **10–08**

Capital disregarded

The potential hardship of the rule set out in para. 10–08 is in some cases mitigated because of the existence of important "disregards." Of these, the most important—certainly in the context of family breakdown—is the disregard of the value of the accommodation "normally occupied by the claimant and any other members of the same household as their home." The result is that it will often be far better for a wife to accept a transfer of the matrimonial home rather than to seek an order for periodical payments from her husband. This is because periodical payments would simply increase her "resources" and thus, pound for pound, reduce her entitlement to benefit, whereas her ownership of the family home will not affect it at all. Moreover, mortgage interest payable by her will increase her "requirements" and thus the sum total of her benefit: see para. 10–04 above. **10–09**

An example

Suppose that H, a welder earning £120 weekly, leaves W and their three children aged 8, 12, and 16 in the matrimonial home. W earns £15 weekly as a home-worker assembling bell-pushes; the 16 year-old child earns £10 working on Saturdays in a store. The matrimonial home, which is jointly owned, is worth £30,000, but it is subject to a mortgage of £25,000 at 12 per cent. The family have no other assets. W can claim benefit as follows: **10–10**

W's requirements:

For herself	£29.80
For children	£43.90
Housing Requirements	£57.69
Total	£131.39

Deduct resources:

Child Benefit	£21.30	
W's income	£6.50	
		£27.80
		£103.59

N.B. In practice this calculation will be inaccurate. For example, if W has been on benefit for a year she will normally become entitled to the so-called "long-term" rate of benefit; some allowance will be made for repair and insurance costs, and there will often be other "requirements"—for example, in connection with heating costs—which can be claimed.

Recovery from liable person

10–11   Ignoring these complications, we can assume that W will receive £103.59 weekly from the DHSS by way of benefit. However, that is not the end of the story. Benefit will be paid to a woman who has been left unsupported, but under the liable person procedure the DHSS may attempt to recover from the so-called "liable person" the sums it has disbursed. We need to know: who is a liable person for this purpose? What tests are applied in deciding whether he is in breach of his obligation to maintain? What procedures are used to enforce the liable relative's obligation?

(a) *Who is a liable person?*

10–12   Section 17(1) of the Supplementary Benefits Act 1976 provides that for the purpose of the Act (a) a man shall be liable to maintain his wife and his children, and (b) a woman shall be liable to maintain her husband and her children.

(b) *When is a liable person in breach of his obligation to maintain?*

10–13   This question is governed by administrative practices which do not have the force of law. If the whereabouts of a liable person can be ascertained, he will be contacted by a specially trained official, the so-called "liable relative officer" (L.R.O.) The L.R.O. will ask the liable person to fulfil his obligation; and an offer by him to do so will be accepted if it equals or exceeds the amount of benefit in payment or if the Department accepts that it is as much as he can reasonably afford. The authorities apply a formula to decide this issue, which starts from the basis that a man should be left with the amount he would get on benefit, plus one quarter of his net earnings.

(c) *Procedures for enforcing the obligation to maintain*

If the DHSS is unsuccessful in getting an acceptable offer from the   **10-14** husband it may seek to coerce him; and this may be done directly or indirectly:

(i) *DHSS application to magistrates' court* for an order that husband pay   **10-15** "such sum, weekly or otherwise, as the court may consider appropriate." In deciding whether to make an order the court is directed to "have regard to all the circumstances and in particular to the resources of the liable relative."

(ii) *Wife takes proceedings.* The wife may of course herself take   **10-16** proceedings—as we shall see—for financial relief against her husband; and it was for long the policy of the Supplementary Benefit Authorities to "encourage and assist" a woman to take such proceedings herself. However, since 1975 the policy has been one of "explanation" rather than "encouragement." Claimants are given a leaflet, which explains that it is entirely up to the claimant to decide whether to apply for a maintenance order. Since maintenance orders are usually for smaller sums than benefit there will be no immediate advantage for most women in bringing proceedings which would not improve their financial position. However, it should be remembered that a court order obtained by the wife will not be automatically affected if she ceases to be eligible for benefit—for example because her means increase—and that it is always possible that she will receive a periodical payments award in excess of her supplementary benefit entitlement.

(iii) *Criminal prosecution.* It is a criminal offence persistently to refuse or   **10-17** neglect to maintain any person whom under the Act one is obliged to maintain: Supplementary Benefits Act 1976, s.25. The DHSS may, therefore, start a prosecution against the offending husband, but such prosecutions are rare in cases of genuine separation.

(iv) *The diversion procedure.* If a woman obtains a maintenance order   **10-18** under one of the procedures discussed below, the payments made thereunder count as income, and reduce a woman's entitlement to supplementary benefit. As the Finer Report put it in 1974, this often led to a woman finding herself "on a see-saw" between the court collecting office and the supplementary benefit office. Now the court clerks are required to pay over maintenance by post. This benefits all women payees, whether or not they are in regular receipt of supplementary benefit. Secondly, a practice has developed whereby, if a woman qualifies for supplementary benefit, and has a maintenance order within the scale rate, the DHSS will, in return for her authorising the court to pay over any maintenance receipts to the DHSS, pay her the full supplementary benefit scale rate. The result is that the wife receives regularly her full entitlement regardless of whether the order is paid regularly, intermittently, or never. It seems that nearly 80 per cent. of maintenance orders in favour of women on supplementary benefit are diverted in this way.

Passport effect of supplementary benefit

10-19   It may be worth claiming even a very small weekly supplementary benefit payment. This will, as the law now stands, qualify the recipient for single payments to meet certain special needs (such as clothing, and removal expenses) and will confer automatic entitlement to a wide range of welfare benefits—such as free school meals, free prescriptions, exemption from dental charges, and free legal advice under the green form scheme.

Reform of the supplementary benefit system

10-20   The Social Security Act 1986 envisages sweeping changes in the supplementary benefit system—starting by renaming it "income support." However, the new system is not expected to come into operation until April 1988, and it is not possible to give an account of it until the Regulations authorised by the Act have been published. In practice, the main principles of the supplementary benefit system in its application to marital breakdown will remain substantially unchanged: see, for example, the "liable relative" procedure, Social Security Act 1986, ss.24-6. But many important details—for example, the system of lump sum payments for exceptional needs referred to in para. 10–19, the long term rate and the additional "requirements" for heating etc. referred to at para. 10-04 above, are to disappear.

COURT ORDERS FOR FINANCIAL SUPPORT—FAILURE TO MAINTAIN

Applications in superior courts

10-21   MCA 1973, s.27 (as amended) provides that either party to a marriage may apply to the High Court or to a Divorce County Court for an order on the ground that the other party has failed to provide reasonable maintenance for the applicant, or that he has failed to provide or to make a proper contribution towards reasonable maintenance for any child of the family. In deciding whether there has been such a failure, and if so what order to make, the court is to "have regard to all the circumstances of the case" including the matters which are specifically referred to under the divorce legislation (considered in detail at para. 11–23 below.) Where the application is in respect of a child of the family (see para. 16–03 below) who is under 18 the court must (as in divorce proceedings) give "first consideration" to the welfare of that child while a minor. If the case is made out the court can make orders for periodical payments (secured or unsecured) and a lump sum.

Housekeeping orders?

10-22   There is no statutory provision preventing the court from making an order while the parties are living together; and an order may continue whilst they live together.

Not often used

In practice there are few applications to the superior courts under this   **10-23**
provision—121 in 1985. However there are far more applications to the
magistrates' court which also has power to make orders on this ground.

APPLICATIONS TO THE MAGISTRATES' COURT

Historical evolution

Since 1878 magistrates' courts have had power to make financial orders   **10-24**
in domestic cases; and their powers are now codified in the Domestic
Proceedings and Magistrates' Courts Act 1978 ("the 1978 Act" hereafter)—a reforming Act intended to bring the family jurisdiction of the
magistrates' courts into line with the law administered in the divorce
court, and to remove any justification there might have been for the
allegation eloquently voiced in the Finer Report (Vol. 2, App. 5, para. 6)
that the magistrates' domestic jurisdiction was a "secondary system" of
family law "designed for what were considered to be the special and
cruder requirements of the poor."

Resgned to high mags. Dom. jursdic.
i line with Div. crs.

Powers to make financial orders

The court has power to make financial orders if the applicant can   **10-25**
establish one of the grounds set out in section 1 of the 1978 Act. Broadly
speaking those grounds involve an element of wrongdoing on the part of
the respondent. However, the court is also given power to make certain
financial orders in cases where the parties are living apart by agreement;
and it is given an express power to make orders for payments which have
been agreed by the parties.

Grounds for complaint

There are four grounds:

(a) *Failure to provide reasonable maintenance for spouse*: 1978 Act, s.1(a)
This ground is in substance identical to the ground for an application to   **10-26**
the superior courts: para. 10–27 above. The Act gives no guidance as to
what has to be established to make out this ground; but if it is made out
the court is directed in deciding how to exercise its powers to have regard
to certain specified matters such as the income, earning capacity and other
financial resources of the parties as well as their conduct if it would be
inequitable to disregard it: 1978 Act, s.3(2).

(b) *Failure to provide, or to make proper contribution towards, reasonable
maintenance for any child of the family*: 1978 Act, s.1(b)
The term "child of the family" is explained at para. 16–03 below. There   **10-27**
are special guidelines which may apply in cases where the child in
question is, for example, a step-child and not the respondent's own child.

(c) *Respondent has behaved in such a way that the applicant cannot reasonably be expected to live with the respondent*: 1978 Act, s.1(c)

10-28   This ground is identical in substance to the "fact" evidencing breakdown of marriage for the purposes of the divorce law: see para. 4–15 above.

(d) *Desertion* 1978 Act, s.1(c)

10-29   Desertion has the same meaning as in the law of divorce (see para. 4–29 above). However, a deserted spouse can apply immediately for a magistrates' order; it is not necessary to prove a two year period.

Time limits
10-30   Proceedings under the 1978 Act are subject to the general rule applicable in magistrates' courts (Magistrates' Courts Act 1980, s.127) that an application must be made within six months of the date when the cause of complaint arose.

Orders that can be made
10-31   If the applicant satisfies the court of a ground of complaint the court may make any of the following orders:

(a) *Periodical payments*
    There is no formal restriction on the amount of the payments which may be ordered; but the magistrates, unlike the divorce court, have no power to order secured periodical payments.

(b) *A lump sum (not exceeding £500)*
    This power was apparently intended to be used to cover payment of expenses such as outstanding hire purchase debts, gas or electricity bills or removal expenses, and to reimburse the wife for maintenance expenses incurred before the date of the order: see Law Com. No. 77, para. 2.34.

    Periodical and lump sum orders may also be made in respect of children of the family.

Guidelines for exercise of discretion
10-32   The 1978 Act (s.3) requires the court to have regard to all the circumstances (including in particular certain specified matters) first consideration being given to the welfare while a minor of any child of the family. These guidelines are now similar to those applicable in divorce— for example, in requiring the court to give priority to the welfare of children, to take account of any increase in earning capacity which it would be reasonable to expect a party to the marriage to take steps to acquire, and to take conduct into account only if it would be inequitable to disregard it: see para. 11–23 below. But the powers of the magistrates are limited, particularly in relation to property; and it may not always be possible for a magistrates' court to do what the divorce court would consider appropriate, for example in relation to the enjoyment of the

matrimonial home. In practice, in many (perhaps most) of the cases coming before magistrates, the conclusive factor will be the inability of the husband to provide for all his dependants.

The voluntary separation ground   **10–33**

Section 7 of the 1978 Act contains a novel provision intended to provide greater security where husband and wife have separated by consent. The intention was to give a degree of security and certainty to the wife, rather than making her wait "for the month when the cheque does not arrive" (when she would be able to start neglect to maintain proceedings: see para. 10–26 above). Accordingly the court may (subject to a number of complex restrictions) make a periodical payments order if: (i) the parties have been living apart for a continuous period exceeding three months; and (ii) neither party has deserted the other; and (iii) one party has during the period of three months preceding the application been making periodical payments for the benefit of the other. In practice, however, this provision is hardly ever used.

Consent orders   **10–34**

Section 6 of the 1978 Act empowers the court to make a consent order for financial provision for a spouse or a child of the family provided: (i) there is adequate proof of the agreement and (ii) the court has no reason to think that it would be contrary to the interests of justice to do so. The intention was (in the Law Commission's words: see Law Com. No. 77, para. 4.4) to provide a means "by which, where a marriage has temporarily broken down, the parties to the marriage can obtain the assistance of the courts in regulating the financial arrangements between themselves without having to parade before the court their marital difficulties." Such a power is particularly useful because if a court order is made—even by consent—the parties' tax liabilities may be reduced; a simple agreement between them will not be effective to "split" income: *Harvey v. Sivyer* [1986] Ch 119, para. 11–60 below. It is perhaps for this reason that many orders are made under this provision.

Duration of orders   **10–35**

The court may make an order for a limited period—for example, 12 months from the date of the order. But even if the order is not in terms limited it will be subject to the following rules:

(a) *Remarriage*

Periodical payment orders in favour of a spouse automatically determine if that spouse remarries.

(b) *Cohabitation*

Although an order can be obtained even if the parties to the marriage are living with each other, a periodical payments order will cease to be enforceable if they continue to live with each other, or subsequently resume living with each other, for a continuous period of six months. The result is that a wife can go to court and obtain an enforceable "housekeeping order" albeit only for a limited period.

Effect of divorce

10–36   Magistrates' orders do not automatically determine on divorce; and although the divorce court has a statutory power to direct that a magistrates' periodical payments order should cease to have effect, in practice magistrates' orders often continue in force.

Variation

10–37   The court has power to vary or revoke a periodical payment order but it has no power to vary a lump sum order. In exercising its variation jurisdiction, the court gives effect to any agreement between the parties "so far as it appears just to do so". The court is directed to have regard to "all the circumstances of the case, first consideration being given to the welfare while a minor of any child of the family who has not attained the age of 18," and the circumstances of the case "shall include any change in any of the matters to which the court was required to have regard when making the order": 1978 Act, s.20(11). In practice, variation is often sought by husbands who have got into arrears.

Registration of divorce court orders

10–38   A maintenance order made by the divorce court may be registered for enforcement in the magistrates' court—thereby possibly giving the wife rather more effective methods of enforcement than are available in the superior courts. One important consequence of registration is that the magistrates may thereafter vary the order as if it had originally been made by them. Research has shown that 65 per cent. of all orders being enforced in magistrates' courts were cases in which the spouses had in fact been divorced; and it has been pointed out that the paradoxical result is that the major role of the magistrates' matrimonial jurisdiction has thus changed from the intended purpose of making and enforcing mainte- nance orders for the benefit of the separated wife to that of an enforcement agency for the divorced wife: C. Gibson (1982) 12 Fam Law 138.

Chapter 11

FINANCIAL REMEDIES II—ORDERS IN DIVORCE NULLITY AND JUDICIAL SEPARATION PROCEEDINGS

INTRODUCTION—EVOLUTION OF THE LAW

Money often most important issue in divorce

In 1984, no fewer than 90,342 orders for what is described as "ancillary relief" were made by the courts. In theory, these applications for financial orders are ancillary (or subordinate) to the main suit for divorce, etc. The reality is that in many cases now it is these financial matters which lie at the heart of the issue between the parties. If either party to a marriage wants a divorce sooner or later he will, unless the case is wholly exceptional, be able to obtain one; and there is thus rarely any point in persisting in resisting the grant of a decree. But financial issues loom correspondingly large, and can give rise to long and bitter disputes. **11–01**

Pressure to safeguard blameless wives

Under the pre–1969 divorce law the courts' powers to deal with financial matters on divorce were limited, and the legislation was virtually silent as to the principles to be applied by the court in exercising such powers as it had. There was much opposition to the 1969 reforms, particularly on the ground that blameless wives would be repudiated by their husbands and left in severe economic difficulties. In response, the Lord Chancellor gave an undertaking that the reformed divorce legislation would not be brought into force until legislation had been brought in to deal comprehensively with the financial consequences of divorce. Mr Leo Abse (one of the prime movers of the divorce reforms) has said that the result was the price which had to be paid to get the divorce reforms on the statute book: Hansard (HC), Vol. 54, col. 416. **11–02**

Reforming the reformed law

The Matrimonial Proceedings and Property Act 1970 (the provisions of which were subsequently consolidated in the Matrimonial Causes Act 1973) gave the courts extensive powers to redistribute virtually all the parties' economically valuable assets and to order maintenance to be paid periodically—perhaps throughout the other spouse's life. In the event, it was not long before its provisions were themselves the object of criticism. This criticism did not focus on the extent of the court's powers; but rather on the criteria which the court was directed to apply in exercising those powers—particularly the so-called minimal loss statutory hypothesis which required the court, having considered all the circumstances, "so to exercise (its) powers as to place the parties, so far as it is practicable and, having regard to their conduct, just to do so, in the financial position in which they would have been if the marriage had not broken down . . ." **11–03**

(MCA 1973, s.25). Critics said that this was inconsistent with the philosophy of the modern divorce law, which tried to give recognition to the fact that a marriage had irretrievably broken down. In particular, it was said sometimes to be unjust to order a husband to support his former wife for the rest of her life—particularly if the result was to impoverish him and the family created by his remarriage.

The 1984 reforms

11-04   The Matrimonial and Family Proceedings Act 1984 ("the 1984 Act" hereafter) was enacted in a controversial attempt to remove any justification for complaints of injustice. By amendment to the 1973 Act, it sought to bring about a change of emphasis rather than a radical restructuring of the law. The changes it introduced were intended to be of an evolutionary rather than a revolutionary nature: see Law Com. No. 112, para. 23. *Subsequent references to MCA 1973 are to that Act as amended.*

ORDERS THAT THE COURT CAN MAKE

M.C.A., 1973

Extent of powers

11-05   The orders which the court can make (which have remained virtually unaffected by the 1984 Act) are extremely wide. Courts can, by using a combination of the available powers, usually achieve whatever result is regarded as fair, just, and reasonable—however flexible and sophisticated may be the orders sometimes required to this end. The process has been graphically described by Lord Denning in *Hanlon* v. *The Law Society* [1981] AC 124, 146. The court (he said):

> "takes the rights and obligations of the parties all together and puts the pieces into a mixed bag. Such pieces are the right to occupy the matrimonial home or have a share in it, the obligation to maintain the wife and children, and so forth. The court then takes out the pieces and hands them to the two parties—some to one party and some to the other—so that each can provide for the future with the pieces allotted to him or to her. The court hands them out without paying any too nice a regard to their legal or equitable rights but simply according to what is the fairest provision for the future, for mother and father and the children."

MCA 1973 distinguishes (section 21) between "financial provision orders" and "property adjustment orders." It also has power to order a sale of property:

1. Financial provision orders

(a) *Maintenance pending suit*

11-06   MCA 1973, s.22 empowers the court to order either party to make periodical payments for the other's maintenance for any period (beginning not earlier than the date of the presentation of the petition and ending with the date of the determination of the suit) as it thinks reasonable. Such orders are intended to provide for the petitioner's immediate needs; but in practice there may often be a considerable delay in getting an order. If the husband does not pay maintenance voluntarily a wife without an independent source of income will often have to rely on supplementary benefit.

(b) *Periodical payments—secured or unsecured: MCA 1973, s.23(1)(a)(b) and (e)*

Orders for regular income payments—for example, £10 weekly; £150   **11–07**
monthly; £5,000 annually—are the traditional way of providing mainte-
nance. The most common form of order is for unsecured payments. If the husband fails to make the payments the wife will have to take enforcement proceedings against the husband—perhaps by means of a charging order (under which his property may be sold in satisfaction of the debt), or more usually by registering the order in a magistrates' court (see para. 10–38 above), and seeking to attach the husband's wages (so that his employer will have to deduct the specified sums and pay them over direct to the court). But in practice it is often difficult to enforce maintenance orders—perhaps because the husband has no employer, and he has no property which can be found.

If the order is *secured*, the husband is required to set aside a fund of capital (usually stocks and shares) which will be vested in trustees. The fund remains the property of the husband; but if he defaults in making the stipulated payments recourse can be had to the fund to make good the default. A secured order has two significant advantages over an order for unsecured periodical payments. First, the order can be effectively enforced even if the husband disappears, parts with all his other assets, or ceases to earn. Secondly, a secured order may continue throughout the lifetime of the wife. The husband may die, but the fund remains. In contrast, there is no power to order unsecured payments to continue beyond the parties' joint lives.

Secured or unsecured periodical payment orders may be made for either party, and also in respect of children of the family (defined at para. 16–03 below). These orders may in appropriate cases require payment to be made direct to the child. Payment direct to the child can have significant tax advantages: see para. 11–60 below.

Duration of periodical payment orders—joint lives or specified term?   **11–08**
Periodical payments orders may be for such term as the court directs, and the traditional form of order was to make payments during the parties' joint lives. However, under the provisions designed to emphasise self-sufficiency introduced by the 1984 Act (see para. 11–63 below) the court may now perhaps be more inclined to make orders for a specified term—*e.g.* three years—to give the wife time to find a new job or to arrange for the care of the children so that she is able to go out to work.

Death and remarriage have an automatic effect on periodical payment   **11–09**
orders. The death of either party terminates an unsecured periodical

101

payments order; and the death of the payee must terminate a secured order.

The payee's remarriage automatically terminates both a secured and unsecured order: MCA 1973, s.28(1); but it is submitted that the enactment of this rule was unfortunate. A divorced woman may lose substantially if she marries a man poorer than her first husband; and the loss may cause hardship if the mother has the care of a child. It is true that periodical payments in respect of the child's maintenance will not be affected by the mother's remarriage; but the child may suffer unfortunate consequences if the mother's own standard of living suddenly drops. Moreover, a woman may be tempted to cohabit rather than remarry: cohabitation does not automatically affect her maintenance order, and although the court may reduce or extinguish the order if her partner is able to provide for her financially the existence of such a relationship does not (in contrast to remarriage) debar her from subsequently seeking support from her former husband if circumstances change.

(c) *Lump sum orders: MCA 1973, s.23(1)(c), (f)*

11-10 The powers considered so far are concerned with income payments; and it is not altogether clear why the draftsman should have grouped the court's power to make an order for payment of capital in the form of a lump sum under this head rather than that of property adjustment. The sums involved may be very large—£600,000 in the case of *Preston* v. *Preston* [1982] Fam 17. However the power is sometimes used in relation to those of modest means. For example, in *Cumbers* v. *Cumbers* [1974] 1 WLR 1331 the court wanted the wife to have one-third of the proceeds (after paying off the mortgage) from the sale of the former matrimonial home (*i.e.* £500). Unfortunately, the husband had already spent the whole of the proceeds on buying another house, and had no other capital. The court exercised its power to order payment by instalments; and also ordered that payment of such instalments be secured—in this case on his new house. Again, the court is specifically empowered to order a payment to cover liabilities or expenses reasonably incurred in maintaining the spouse or a child of the family before the making of the application.

A lump sum order may be made in favour of a child of the family or to someone else for his benefit: see further para. 11–59.

2. Property adjustments orders

(a) *Transfer of property: MCA 1973, s.24(1)(a)*

11-11 This power enables the court to order that specified property (such as the matrimonial home, or investments) be transferred to the other spouse (or to or for the benefit of a child of the family).

(b) *Settlement of property: MCA 1973, s.24(1)(b)*

11-12 The court may direct that property to which a party to the marriage is entitled be settled for the benefit of the other spouse and/or the children of the family. This power is now often used to make fair arrangements in connection with the former matrimonial home, so that it can continue to be used as a home for dependent children whilst preserving both spouses' financial interest in it. For example, the court may make what is called a *Mesher* order (see [1980] 1 All ER 126), under which the home is held on trust for sale for husband and wife in equal shares, but no sale is to take place until the youngest child of the marriage has attained the age of 17. The techniques used are considered in more detail at para. 11–36 below.

(c) *Variation of nuptial settlements: MCA 1973, s.24(1)(c), (d)*

The court may make an order varying for the benefit of the parties **11–13** and/or the children of the family any "ante-nuptial or post-nuptial" settlement made on the parties to the marriage. This power can, of course, be used to make appropriate variations in those (comparatively rare) cases in which the parties have interests under a traditional marriage settlement; but the term "settlement" has been widely interpreted, and has been held to extend to a dwelling-house in which the parties both have a property interest. The decision whether to use this or some other property adjustment order will usually be a matter of conveyancing technique and convenience—if, for example, the matrimonial home is held by the spouses as beneficial tenants in common, and the court thinks that one spouse should be solely entitled, this can be achieved either by a transfer of property order requiring the husband to transfer his interest to the wife, or by an order varying the "nuptial settlement" by ordering that the property be held on trust for her absolutely.

3. Power to order sale

The court now has (MCA 1973, s.24A) an express power to order sale on **11–14** making any order for financial relief other than an order for unsecured periodical payments. In effect, the power is ancillary to the making of the other orders already considered.

CONCLUSION ON ORDERS THAT CAN BE MADE—COURT'S POWERS WIDE BUT NOT LIMITLESS

In *Jenkins* v. *Livesey* [1986] AC 424 the House of Lords emphasised that **11–15** the court could only act in accordance with the Act. Thus it has for example no power to order one party to pay insurance premiums on the former matrimonial home direct to the insurers; and in *Milne* v. *Milne* (1981) 2 FLR 286 the Court of Appeal held that since the statute did not permit the court to order payments to be made save to the other party to the marriage or for the children of the family it could not order the husband to execute and pay for a life insurance policy and assign the benefit to the wife. (If the policy had already been in existence the court could of course have made a transfer of property order.) In practice, therefore, provisions dealing with insurance, repairs, and payment of mortgage interest and other outgoings are often dealt with by the parties giving undertakings which are then annexed to the court's order in a schedule.

Other limitations

11-16   There are three other matters which may affect the court's ability effectively to redistribute the family's wealth:

(i)   The court has no powers over assets which, by their nature, are not "owned" by either spouse. This may perhaps seem self-evident, but it follows that the court can have no power to make orders dealing with expectations under many pension schemes; see further para. 11-50 below.

(ii) The court has no power to deal with the capital of a settlement which is not a nuptial or post-nuptial settlement. It a testator settles property on his bachelor son for life, the settlement would fall outside the definition of a nuptial settlement, and accordingly the court could not vary the settlement. (It could of course order the son to settle his life interest, but that could not affect the settled capital).

(iii) The exercise of the court's powers cannot prejudice the rights of third parties not before the court. Thus, if the matrimonial home is subject to a mortgage, a transfer of the home to the wife cannot affect either the mortgagor husband's contractual liability to pay the mortgage instalments, nor the rights of the mortgagee to take enforcement action if the mortgage covenants are broken. (In practice mortgage deeds usually contain prohibitions against the mortgagor transferring the property without the mortgagee's consent; hence the mortgagee should have notice of the application and be given an opportunity to be heard.)

HOW THE COURT EXERCISES ITS POWERS

No sex discrimination

11-17   The legislation does not discriminate between the sexes. Orders can be, and are, made in favour of either party to the marriage. As Scarman L.J. put it (*Calderbank* v. *Calderbank* [1976] Fam 93, 103): "husbands and wives come to the judgment seat . . . upon a basis of complete equality". Orders—sometimes substantial—have been made against wives: in *B* v. *B (Financial Provision)* (1982) 3 FLR 298, CA, a wife was ordered to pay £50,000 to her husband; and in *Wills* v. *Wills* [1984] FLR 672 (which was in fact a case under the Domestic Proceedings and Magistrates' Courts Act 1978) it was accepted that an order for periodical payments might be made against a wife in favour of her disabled husband who (with her concurrence) had become a student. But in practice economic realities normally dictate that financial orders will be made against the husband in favour of the wife.

Guidelines for exercise of discretion
(i) *Maintenance pending suit*

The legislation contains no detailed guidelines; it simply directs the   **11–18**
court to make such order as it "thinks reasonable." But there is no
difference of principle in relation to quantification between this and other
orders. The court may therefore take account of all the matters referred to
in the guidelines considered below which are known to it: *F* v. *F* (1982) 4
FLR 382; but in practice it obviously cannot make the final settlement of
financial matters which is appropriate on final decree, not least because it
cannot at this stage deal with the parties' capital—notably the matrimonial home.

Need the crucial factor

The court will usually consider the wife's needs and the husband's   **11–19**
ability to meet those needs having regard to his other needs and
obligations as the most important factor:

> In *Peacock* v. *Peacock* [1984] 1 WLR 532 the wife was living on supplementary
> benefit; the husband had take-home pay of some £82, out of which he had to
> meet travelling expenses of £10; and he also paid insurance premiums of £7. His
> board and lodging in his parents' home currently cost him £20, but he was
> about to set up in a new home which might cost as much as £35 weekly. He was
> making a voluntary payment of £20 weekly to the DHSS under the procedure
> described at para. 10–13 above, but he did not get any tax relief (see para. 11–31
> below) on that amount. The court ordered him to pay maintenance pending suit
> of £15 i.e. £10.50 after tax relief—on the basis that this was a proper figure for
> the three or four months before the financial position could be finalised. No
> doubt the DHSS, although not formally bound by this award, would accept that
> the amount ordered was a reasonable contribution by him under the liable
> relative procedure discussed at para. 10–11 above.

(ii) *All other orders*   M.C.A. 2.25

The scheme of the legislation is, in outline, as follows: **11–20**

(a) It is the duty of the court in deciding whether to exercise its powers
and, if so, in what manner to have regard to all the circumstances of
the case, first consideration being given to the welfare while a
minor of any child of the family who has not attained the age of 18:
MCA 1973, s.25(1).
(b) As regards the exercise of the powers to make financial provision
orders, property adjustment orders, or orders for the sale of
property in relation to a party to the marriage it is provided that the
court shall "in particular have regard to" certain specified matters:
MCA 1973, s.25(2).
(c) The Act also directs the court "in particular" to have regard to
certain specified matters as regards the exercise of its powers to
make such orders in relation to a child of the family: MCA 1973,
s.25(3), (4).
(d) Finally, the Act contains a number of provisions designed to direct
the court's attention to the principle of self-sufficiency, and to

facilitate the making of a "clean break" between the parties to the marriage in appropriate cases: MCA 1973, s.25A.

No governing principle
11-21   The Matrimonial and Family Proceedings Act 1984 removed the statutory directive whereby the court was obliged to seek to place the parties in the financial position in which they would have been had the marriage not broken down; and does not substitute any comparable directive. This fact makes it all the more necessary to remember that the factors involved in matrimonial cases are almost infinitely various; and the value of precedents is accordingly much restricted. *The Times* headlined its report of the case of *Sharpe* v. *Sharpe*, *The Times*, February 17, 1981 "Forget the Cases"; and although that is an injunction which law students should view with some caution it nevertheless embodies an element of truth. The court's task is simply to apply the words of the statute to the facts of the cases.

1. All the circumstances

All the circumstances to be considered
11-22   MCA 1973, s.25(1) directs the court to consider "all the circumstances", and "in particular" to have regard to an elaborate list of specific matters. But the court must not simply confine its attention to those specified matters; it must also (as Scarman L.J. put it in *Trippas* v. *Trippas* [1973] 1 WLR 134, 144) investigate all other circumstances "past, present, and, in so far as one can make a reliable estimate, future" which arise on the facts of any particular case. Examples can be taken from decided cases of such matters:

(i)   Wife had remarried at date of financial hearing: *H* v. *H* [1975] Fam 9; *Jenkins* v. *Livesey* [1986] AC 424. The court will need to consider how far the financial implications of her new status should affect the distribution of capital assets from the first marriage.

(ii) Wife had made substantial contributions to the husband's business *before* the marriage: *Kokosinski* v. *Kokosinski* [1980] Fam 72 (*cf.* MCA 1973, s.25(2)(*f*), para. 11-44 below, applicable to such contributions during the marriage).

(iii) Husband had made his money after the breakdown with the assistance of another woman: *Lombardi* v. *Lombardi* [1973] 1 WLR 1276.

(iv) Husband had brought up the children of the marriage: *Lombardi* v. *Lombardi* (above).

(v)   Husband's behaviour disabled the wife from resuming her professional career: *Jones (MA)* v. *Jones (W)* [1976] Fam 8.

(vi) Husband had put the family assets at risk by entering into unwise business transactions: *Martin* v. *Martin* [1976] Fam 335.

The specified matters

Most of the matters to which the court is now directed "in particular" to   **11–23**
have regard in relation to a party to the marriage are substantially
unchanged from those originally contained in the Matrimonial Proceedings and Property Act 1970. A vast body of case law has developed.
Although most of this remains relevant, it is impossible to consider it in
detail. Instead points of particular significance which have arisen in
practice in relation to each of the statutory provisions are highlighted.

**"the income, earning capacity, property and other financial resources
which each of the parties to the marriage has or is likely to have in the
forseeable future, including in the case of earning capacity any
increase in that capacity which it would in the opinion of the court be
reasonable to expect a party to the marriage to take steps to acquire"
(MCA 1973, s.25(2)(a)**

This provision directs the court's attention to the parties' assets, in the   **11–24**
broadest possible terms. Nothing is excluded: a flat bought by the wife
with personal injury damages awarded to her was accordingly taken into
account in working out her financial position: *Daubney* v. *Daubney* [1976]
Fam 267; and the court can take account of the likelihood that a party will
benefit under the will of a relative who is terminally ill: *Morgan* v. *Morgan*
[1977] Fam 122; contrast *Michael* v. *Michael* [1986] 2 FLR 389 where there
was no evidence that the testatrix's death was imminent.

The duty to disclose

It is the parties' duty to reveal all relevant information (*Jenkins* v.   **11–25**
Livesey [1986] AC 424), and standard forms are available to deal with
straightforward cases. In practice detailed probing is often called for. An
applicant may require the production of documents and information; and
it is sometimes suggested that this process may exacerbate the bitterness
between the parties: see Booth Committee Consultation Document,
para. 8.10, and Report para. 4.158.

Common problems include the following:

(a) *Earning capacity*

The court is concerned with what each spouse could reasonably have.   **11–26**
For example:

> In *Hardy* v. *Hardy* (1981) 2 FLR 321 the husband worked in his father's racing
> stables for much less than he could have earned on the open market. The court
> saw no reason why he should enjoy this privilege at the expense of his wife and
> children.

But there must be *evidence* that there is better paid work available:
contrast *Williams (LA)* v. *Williams (EM)* [1974] Fam 55 where the trial court
wrongly failed to take account of the telling fact that the supplementary
benefit authorities had accepted that the husband could not find work.

11-27   *Earning potential.* The requirement of evidence is particularly significant in the light of the addition made by the 1984 Act of a reference to "any increase in earning capacity which it would be reasonable to expect" a spouse to take steps to acquire. This (it is submitted) requires proof of two separate matters: firstly, that a spouse could in fact increase his or her prospects of earning; secondly, that it would be reasonable for him or her to be expected to do so. For example, if a wife had experience as a secretary before marriage there might be evidence that by retraining in the use of modern office equipment (such as word processors) she could again find well remunerated secretarial work. But that hurdle is difficult to surmount. As Sir Roger Ormrod said in *Camm* v. *Camm* (1982) 4 FLR 577, 586:

> "...experience in this court indicates that it is much easier to talk about married women who have not been working for a good number of years getting back into full time employment than it is to get the employment. It is to be remembered that 15 years or more of looking after children and not earning is a serious economic handicap..."

Even if there is evidence that the wife could increase her earning capacity the court must still be satisfied that it is reasonable to expect her to do so:

> In *Leadbeater* v. *Leadbeater* [1985] FLR 789 the wife, aged 47, had been a secretary, but at the date of the hearing earned only £1,680 p.a. as a part-time receptionist. The judge thought she could, by working longer hours, reasonably earn somewhat more; but that it would not be reasonable to expect her at her age to familiarise herself with modern office technology.

In contrast:

> In *Mitchell* v. *Mitchell* [1984] FLR 672 the court—even under the old law—thought that it would be reasonable to expect a woman who had been a full-time secretary for a period during the marriage once again to take up such comparatively highly paid work when her children had left school in preference to a part-time job as a canteen assistant.

(b) *New partner's earnings and earning capacity*
11-28   The court has no power to order that a third party—such as the husband's second wife or cohabitee—should provide for the applicant or for the children of their family; and it must not make an order which can only be satisfied by dipping into a third party's resources: *Re L (Minors) (Financial Provision)* (1979) 1 FLR 39; see also *Berry* v. *Berry* [1986] 1 FLR 618. But the fact that such a person has means available may be relevant, because the husband can thereby more readily make appropriate provision: *Macey* v. *Macey* (1981) 3 FLR 7. As the Law Commission put it (Law Com. No. 112, para. 41) the husband is not allowed in such cases to say that he needs all or most of his income in order to provide for the needs of his new family. In effect the means of the cohabitee are taken into account at what is often the decisive stage of calculating the net effect of the proposed order: see para. 11–80 below.

(c) *Availability of supplementary benefit*
Two questions arise: **11-29**

(i) *Should an order ever be made against a spouse who is on supplementary
benefit?* Benefit rates are pitched at subsistence levels which give recipients
nothing to spare beyond what is needed for their own support. Hence,
although the court will always consider the merits: *Stockford* v. *Stockford*
(1982) 3 FLR 58 (and there may indeed be exceptional circumstances—for
example where a young man is living with his parents: *Billington* v.
Billington [1974] Fam 24, 29—in which an order for periodical payments
will be made) the probability is that no such order will be made: *Fletcher*
v. *Fletcher* [1985] Fam 92. The court may of course make a nominal order
(*e.g.* 5p a year) which can be varied if circumstances change: see
para. 11–89 below. It may also make orders dealing with capital
assets—in practice usually the matrimonial home.

(ii) *Should the court order a spouse to make payments which will simply*   **11-30**
reduce the recipient's benefits? Obviously the court would not allow a
wealthy husband to say: "my former wife is receiving benefit which keeps
her alive; why should you expect me to support her?" But the situation is
far more difficult where both parties are near subsistence level. Should the
court effectively reduce the already low standard of living enjoyed by the
husband by compelling him to make payments to the wife when these
will merely reduce her supplementary benefit payments? The courts
apply two coherent principles. First, a husband is not to be allowed to
throw onto the state the cost of supporting his dependants. Secondly, he
is to be allowed to keep for himself and his new family at least a
subsistence level of income. In practice, therefore, the courts will work out
what the husband would get if he were entitled to benefit for himself and
his new family; and they will add onto that figure his outgoings for
housing and his travelling and other working expenses. The court will
also possibly add some additional "inducement" allowance, and a sum to
take account of any special circumstances—such as the husband's need to
establish a new home: *Stockford* v. *Stockford* (above); *Freeman* v. *Swatridge*
[1984] FLR 762; *Peacock* v. *Peacock* [1984] 1 WLR 532. Only the balance
over that sum will be regarded as available to support his ex-wife and
their children. The result is to produce rough equality, at more or less
supplementary benefit levels. The courts have not accepted suggestions
that in deciding what is subsistence level they should apply the "formula"
used by the DHSS (see para. 10–13 above) in calculating whether a liable
relative's offer of support is reasonable: Ormrod L.J. in *Shallow* v. *Shallow*
[1979] Fam 1, 6; but recent cases show a readiness to allow a significant
inducement to the husband:

In *Allen* v. *Allen* [1986] 2 FLR 265, CA the Court held that a husband had acted
reasonably in buying a modest house for his own occupation with the aid of a
mortgage, and that the full costs of the mortgage should be taken into account
in assessing what he could afford to pay. The order which had been made at
first instance would have left the husband only very little above the long-term

rate of supplementary benefit (see para. 10–03 above); and on appeal it was reduced so that he would be left with a surplus of £5.71 weekly over the long term rate. The fact that the wife was on benefit meant that the order would not affect her financial position; but if she ever ceased to be on benefit it would be necessary to reconsider in variation proceedings the consequences of the order on her financial position: see para. 11–89 below.

(d) *How far is taxation relevant?*

11-31   The court initially works on the parties' gross incomes, without making any deduction for tax. This is because the tax system incorporates its own machinery for making allowances for maintenance payments: periodical payments made by a taxpayer under court order in favour of his wife or children cease to be his income for tax purposes. Normally, the payer deducts tax at the basic rate on making the payment—so that a man ordered to pay £100 monthly to his wife will actually pay her £710, *i.e.* £1,000 less tax of £290 at the basic rate of 29 per cent. The wife is then treated as having received an income of £1,000 from which basic rate tax has been deducted. If she is not in fact liable to pay that much tax she can make a claim for repayment of the tax.

Making repayment claims is a nuisance. If the sums payable are within the definition of "small maintenance payments" the husband pays the whole sum ordered without deducting tax, and his overall tax liability will be adjusted subsequently. The wife will then not need to bother with a repayment claim, but of course if her income is high enough to involve liability to tax she will have to pay it.

If the husband is liable to higher rate tax, he deducts the sum paid (£1,000 in the example) from his total income on which tax is assessed and obtains relief in that way. Conversely, if the wife's income, including the maintenance, is such as to make her liable to higher rate tax she will have to pay it.

11-32   *Spendable income relevant in final assessment.* Although, for these reasons, the court works initially on the gross sums, it will at the end of the day want to know the net effect of what has been done and the parties must put calculations before the court:

> In *Allen* v. *Allen* (above) the fact that an order for £15 weekly against the husband would, taking tax relief into account, only take £10.50 out of his pocket was a significant factor in making the calculation of the appropriate order.

"the financial needs, obligations and responsibilities which each of the parties to the marriage has or is likely to have in the foreseeable future" (MCA 1973, s.23(2)(b))

"Needs"

11-33   When assessing financial orders it is in practice usually the "reasonable needs" of the parties and the children of the family, and the "net effect" which the order will have on them in the light of their reasonable expenses and tax and benefit position: see *Stockford* v. *Stockford* (1981) 3 FLR 58; *Furniss* v. *Furniss* (1981) 3 FLR 46. At the most basic, this involves provision of an income at least sufficient for subsistence; and a roof over the families' heads. In terms of the low income groups, we have already seen how the courts now pay close attention to supplementary benefit standards: para. 11–30 above. The Appendix to this book contains a "net effect" calculator, used in some courts to facilitate these comparisons.

Needs of the affluent

If the parties are more affluent, the question is inevitably more   **11-34** subjective:

> In *Leadbeater* v. *Leadbeater* [1985] FLR 789, for example, the court decided that a wife, who had during a fairly short (4 year) marriage enjoyed a lavish life-style, "needed" a two-bedroom house (rather than the three bedrooms she had claimed); and that this would cost £10,000 to furnish—rather than the £20,000 which she had claimed, or the £6,000 which the husband had offered on the basis of prices taken from a Habitat catalogue. She also needed a Ford Fiesta car (costing some £1,450 to run annually), £2,500 for housing outgoings, and £4,000 for household and private expenses.

What do the wealthy need?

Need is a relative term; and the wife of a wealthy man has been held to   **11-35** be entitled to a high and even luxurious standard of living:

> In *Bullock* v. *Bullock* [1986] 1 FLR 372, CA the husband was a director and shareholder in a family business. The wife had no capital. She had tried, unsuccessfully, to find work and had no income. The court ordered that the husband pay her £100,000 (to be satisfied in part by a transfer of his interest in the matrimonial home). A reasonable requirement of the wife, or one of her needs (said Sir J. Arnold P.) was "to have money on which to live."

> In *Preston* v. *Preston* [1982] Fam 17, the husband had capital assets of £2.3m, and an annual income of £40,000 (which was only subject to a low rate of income tax in Jersey). The court held that "needs" was equivalent to "reasonable requirements," and that in this sense the wife's needs included a house costing up to £300,000, and also having the reasonable financial security conferred by the availability of a significant sum of free capital. A £600,000 lump sum order was upheld.

Housing

The courts have given a lot of attention to the best way of satisfying the   **11-36** need of the parties for a secure home. There may of course be cases in which it seems best to transfer the house outright to the wife: see for example *Hanlon* v. *Hanlon* [1978] 1 WLR 592 where the husband had rent-free housing available to him by reason of his employment as a police officer. Such a transfer can be particularly advantageous if the wife is on supplementary benefit. Any periodical payments paid by the husband would simply reduce the wife's entitlement to benefit, but if the house is transferred to her that will not affect her entitlement to benefit, and the DHSS will pay the interest on any outstanding mortgage: see *S* v. *S (Note)* [1976] Fam 1.

Mesher orders

11-37   For many years the commonest type of order made where the wife had custody of the children was the so-called *Mesher* order: (1973) [1980] 1 All ER 126. In its simple form such an order would direct a transfer of the matrimonial home into the joint names of husband and wife on trust for sale for themselves in (say) equal shares, provided that the property be not sold until the youngest child had attained the age of 17 or stopped full-time education. (In practice it would be desirable to make provision for a number of other eventualities—for example, the wife wishing to move house before the trust for sale had become exercisable—but all appropriate terms could be included in the court's order under its power to direct a settlement of property: see generally Hayes and Battersby (1985) 15 Fam Law 213; 16 Fam Law 142 and Cleary (1987) 17 Fam Law 43.)

The decline of the Mesher order

11-38   More recently, the tide has moved somewhat against Mesher orders —partly because in some cases it was not clear how the wife was to be housed when the time for sale came, partly because (contrary to the "clean break" philosophy: para. 11–63 below) such an order preserved a financial link between the parties, and might effectively tie her to the former matrimonial home because she lacked the means to buy another more suitable home. The modern practice is either to make an outright transfer see *Mortimer* v. *Mortimer-Griffin*, para. 11–68, or if that is not thought appropriate to make a so called *Martin* order (see *Martin (BH)* v. *Martin (D)* [1978] Fam 12) giving the wife the right to occupy the house until her death or remarriage (or, sometimes, her becoming dependent on another man or living with him as his wife: *Chadwick* v. *Chadwick* [1985] FLR 606). In appropriate cases the wife will be required to pay an occupation rent once the children are 18: *Harman* v. *Glencross* [1986] 1 All ER 545, 556, CA.

Obligations and responsibilities

11-39   How far can a man claim that his income is not as high as it seems because, for example, he has large travelling expenses, or that he has to service a large mortgage on the house in which he is living with his second wife? The general answer—as is so often the case—is that it depends on what is reasonable:

> In *Slater* v. *Slater* (1982) 3 FLR 364, CA, the court thought the husband had been extravagant in deciding to live in a country house with consequent heavy transport and property maintenance expenses; and he was not allowed to deduct those expenses in working out his available income. But if the husband has reasonably decided to buy a new house with a heavy mortgage, leaving his divorced wife and family in the former matrimonial home, the court will not make an order against him which would make it impossible for him to service the mortgage: *Stockford* v. *Stockford* (1981) 3 FLR 58.

Claims of the reconstituted family

11-40   The courts now accept that a man will in practice want to maintain his newly formed family: although the first wife has a claim, it is accepted that the second marriage will result in a reduction in his capacity to support the first wife: *Barnes* v. *Barnes* [1972] 1 WLR 1381. However, since 1984 (see para. 11–54 below) the legislation has required the court to give "first consideration" to the welfare of the children of the family; and this may suggest that some preference should be given to the children of the first marriage as against the claims of other dependants: see para. 11–56.

"the standard of living enjoyed by the family before the breakdown of the marriage" (MCA 1973, s.25(2)(*c*))

A wife is not entitled to expect to enjoy the standard of living she **11-41** enjoyed during the marriage merely because she has been a wife, but "adequate recognition" should be given to it in deciding what is reasonable as between the parties:

> In *Leadbeater* v. *Leadbeater* [1985] FLR 789 the wife had been married for four years to a man worth £250,000, and had in consequence enjoyed a "much enhanced" life-style. The high standard of living was taken into account; but so was the modest life-style she had enjoyed before the marriage. Taking all the factors into account (see para. 11–81 below for the facts) a comparatively modest £37,500 lump sum was ordered.

> In *Attar* v. *Attar* [1985] FLR 649 the wife (who had previously been an air-hostess with an Arab air-line earning some £15,000 per annum net) was married for only six months to a man worth more than £2m. The court ordered a lump sum payment of £30,000 to enable her to adjust over a period of two years (based on an assessment of what she had lived on before the marriage) to the ending of the marriage.

"the age of each party to the marriage and the duration of the marriage" (MCA 1973, s.25(2)(*b*))

It will often not be necessary to consider the parties' ages as a matter **11-42** distinct from the court's assessment of their needs and resources—if a wife is young and healthy her needs will not be so great because she will be able to work; if she is elderly and inform her needs will be that much greater. In contrast there is now likely to be much more concern with the duration of the marriage, since Parliament has decisively repudiated the notion that a wife is entitled solely by virtue of the status of marriage to be maintained on a scale appropriate to her husband's standard of life:

> In *Brett* v. *Brett* [1969] 1 WLR 487, under the pre-1969 law, the wife—a childless 23 year old solicitor, whose marriage had lasted for less than six months—was awarded (in 1987 values) yearly periodical payments of some £13,000 and a lump sum of some £125,000.

> In contrast, in *Attar* v. *Attar* (referred to above) the court thought a single capital payment of £30,000 was sufficient to enable the wife of an exceedingly wealthy man to retrain over a two year period after a six month marriage; and in *Leadbeater* v. *Leadbeater* [1985] FLR 789 the court first of all calculated the wife's reasonable needs along the lines already explained, and held that they could be satisfied by a payment of £50,000. Since the marriage had only lasted four years

that was reduced by 25 per cent. to £37,500, to be paid by way of once-for-all settlement of all her claims.

"any physical or mental disability of either of the parties to the marriage": (MCA 1973, s.25(2)(d))

11-43   This provision seems to add little to the matters which will be considered under other heads. It does not appear to have been considered in decided cases.

"the contributions made by each of the parties to the welfare of the family, including any contribution made by looking after the home or caring for the family" (MCA 1973, s.25(2)(f))

11-44   The law governing property regimes was felt by many not to give adequate recognition to the contributions which wives make towards the acquisition of so-called "family assets"—"those things which are acquired . . . with the intention that there should be continuing provision for (the parties) and their children during their joint lives, and used for the benefit of the family as a whole," as Lord Denning put it in *Wachtel* v. *Wachtel* [1973] Fam 72: see para. 8–04 above. That case made it quite clear that such contributions would be taken fully into account by the Divorce Court and that where a young couple with little or no starting capital acquired a home with the help of mortgage finance it would usually be regarded as their joint investment.

The court will of course equally have regard to a wife's contribution to a business:

> In *O'D* v. *O'D* [1976] Fam 83 the wife had worked as receptionist, chambermaid, cook, waitress and clerk while building up a hotel business. The court awarded her a lump sum of £70,000 (and periodical payments) in partial recognition of this fact, although her needs could have been satisfied by a payment of £30,000.

The court will take account of contributions to be made "in the foreseeable future"—for example, by a wife who is clearly going to have the care of the children during their infancy.

"the conduct of each of the parties, if that conduct is such that it would in the opinion of the court be inequitable to disregard it" (MCA 1973, s.25(2)(g))

Importance of conduct under matrimonial offence doctrine

11-45   So long as divorce was based on the matrimonial offence doctrine the parties' conduct was of crucial importance: an "innocent" wife was entitled to full compensation for the loss of her status and the right to support which a wife had at common law, but a "guilty" wife would not in principle be entitled to maintenance at all. Over the years the harshness of this rule were mitigated; and in the end it became accepted that a wife's misconduct would only be allowed to affect her right to maintenance if it could be described as really serious, disruptive, intolerable, and unforgivable: *Ackerman* v. *Ackerman* [1972] Fam 1 (Sir George Baker, P.).

Policy of the Divorce Reform Act

Although the 1969 was intended to allow the empty legal shell of a   **11-46**
broken marriage to be destroyed with the minimum bitterness distress
and humiliation, the legislation dealing with the financial consequences of
divorce specifically required the court to have regard to the parties'
conduct in determining how far it was just to place them in the financial
position they would have been in had it not been for the breakdown. Did
this mean—as was suggested in some of the early cases—that the courts
would have to carry out an investigation into responsibility for the
breakdown of the marriage? Did it mean that the judge had to hear the
parties' "mutual recriminations and ... go into their petty squabbles for
days on end, as he used to do in the old days"?

In *Wachtel* v. *Wachtel* [1973] Fam 72 the Court of Appeal refused to
allow the policy of the divorce law to be subverted in this way. In the vast
majority of cases (said Lord Denning) both parties would have contributed to the breakdown. In such cases the court should not reduce its
order for financial provision merely because of what was formerly
regarded as guilt or blame. Nevertheless, there would remain a "residue
of cases" where the conduct of one of the parties had been (in the words
of Ormrod J. at first instance) "both obvious and gross," so much so that
to order one party to support another whose conduct fell into this
category would be "repugnant to anyone's sense of justice." It was only in
such cases that the financial order should be reduced.

Conduct only relevant in exceptional cases

As a result of the acceptance of this decision, considerations of conduct   **11-47**
were held rarely to be admissible; and it was the intention of the
draftsman of the Matrimonial and Family Proceedings Act 1984 to codify
the practice of the Court of Appeal developed on the basis of *Wachtel*,
whilst avoiding the use of the expression "obvious and gross" which had
become in danger of being used as it were a statutory formula describing
the sort of conduct which exceptionally might be taken into account.
Conduct was to be relevant only in those (exceptional) circumstances in
which it would be "inequitable" to disregard it. For example:

In *Jones* v. *Jones* [1976] Fam 8 the husband attacked the wife inflicting serious
and lasting injury; and it was held that it would be wrong to ignore this conduct.

In *Bailey* v. *Tolliday* (1982) 4 FLR 542 the wife had an adulterous relationship
with her husband's father; and that fact was held relevant in assessing the
financial provision which should be made for her.

On the other hand, in *Leadbeater* v. *Leadbeater* [1985] FLR 789 the wife (who had
an alcohol problem) had committed adultery with several men whilst on
holiday; the husband had insisted on a 15 year old girl moving into the family
home, refused to turn her out, and indeed subsequently had a child by her. The
court, applying the wording of the statute as amended in 1984, held that it

would not be "inequitable" to disregard the wife's conduct; it was a classic case in which (to use Lord Denning's words in *Wachtel*) "both parties are to blame."

"Conduct" not limited to matrimonial misconduct

The Court will take account of any conduct which it would be inequitable to disregard—for example dissipating the family property. As Cairns L.J. put it in *Martin v. Martin* [1976] Fam 335, 342, "a spouse cannot be allowed to fritter away the assets by extravagant living or reckless speculation and then to claim as great a share of what was left as he would have been entitled to if he had behaved reasonably."

May be positive factor

11-48   In appropriate cases the court will regard conduct as a circumstance which should be taken into account as a positive factor in influencing the provision. For example:

> In *Kokosinski v. Kokosinski* [1980] Fam 72 the wife had (said the judge) "given the best years of her life to the husband. She had been faithful, loving and hard-working. She had helped the husband to build what was in every sense a family business. She had managed the husband's home and been a mother to and helped bring up a son of whom they were both justly proud." However, all this had occurred before the parties were able to marry; so that it could not be taken into account under MCA 1973, s.25(2)(*f*) (para. 11–44 above). But it would be inequitable not to take those matters into account as "conduct"; and the wife was held to have earned for herself some part of the value of the family business.

"in the case of proceedings for divorce or nullity of marriage, the value to each of the parties to the marriage of any benefit (for example, a pension) which by reason of the dissolution or annulment of the marriage, that party will lose the chance of acquiring

11-49   Marriage is a status, which automatically confers certain rights and privileges. For example, a widow (the woman to whom a man was married at the date of his death) has substantial rights to succeed to his property if he dies intestate: para. 8–28 above. A widow also has pension rights under the National Insurance scheme; and if her husband belonged to an employer's pension scheme she would almost invariably have rights—often substantial—under that scheme. If a spouse is divorced all those expectations and contingent rights will be lost. The present provision is intended to direct the court's attention to the need to take such matters into account.

The problem of pensions

11-50   In practice it has been the loss of the right to a pension which has caused most difficulty, largely because the court will not usually be able to make orders directly affecting the pension entitlement. (This is because the beneficiaries' rights are usually merely discretionary; and the assignment or commutation of benefits will often be prohibited—either by the terms of the scheme or, in the case of some public sector pensions (see, *e.g.*

Walker v. *Walker* [1983] Fam 68; *Roberts* v. *Roberts* [1986] 2 All ER 483) by statute.

Sometimes possible to take pension benefits into account

The court will sometimes adjourn the wife's application until the **11–51** husband receives the retirement lump sum; but adjournment will only be contemplated for a comparatively short period, such as two or three years: see *Morris* v. *Morris* (1977) 7 Fam Law 224, CA, and contrast *Roberts* v. *Roberts* (above) where the payment was not due until 2003. Moreover, the court may sometimes be able by an immediate order to compensate the wife for the loss:

> In *Milne* v. *Milne* (1981) 2 FLR 286 the husband was ordered to pay a deferred lump sum equal to one half the amount ultimately received on retirement or death.

> In *Richardson* v. *Richardson* (1978) 9 Fam Law 86 the husband would be entitled on retiring some three years after the divorce to a civil service pension and a lump sum of £9,000; if the wife had survived she would have been entitled to a widow's pension. There was other capital available; and the court ordered the husband to pay the wife an enhanced lump sum to take account of her loss of these expectations.

Husband may undertake to give provision

The husband may be prepared to undertake to do what the court could **11–52** not order him to do—for example to pay premiums on a life policy taken out for her benefit: see *Milne* v. *Milne* (above). His readiness to do so may be increased by the fact that if his petition is based on the five years living apart "fact" (see para. 4–58 above) loss of a pension entitlement may constitute grave financial hardship such as would entitle the court to refuse to grant a decree: *cf. Parker* v. *Parker* [1972] Fam 116 (where the court was satisfied that the wife's loss of a police widow's pension could be offset by alternative insurance arrangements secured on the husband's house.)

Position unsatisfactory

In spite of these methods of taking pension rights into account, it has long **11–53** been accepted that the situation is not satisfactory; and in 1985 the Lord Chancellor's Department published a Consultation Paper, Occupational Pension Rights on Divorce containing provisional proposals under which application could be made to the court for pension provision after divorce.

2. First consideration to the welfare of children

The policy

In 1984 148,501 children under the age of 16 were involved in their **11–54** parents' divorce. Notwithstanding the fact that in custody matters the court is specifically directed to regard the welfare of the children as the first and paramount consideration (Guardianship of Minors Act 1971, s.1; see para. 14–01 below) and that the divorce court has special duties to satisfy itself about the arrangements made for the welfare of such children (para. 16–07 below) the Law Commission said in 1981 that the impression was widespread that making financial provision for children was "regarded as a matter of secondary importance to the making of provision for the former spouse": Law Com. No. 112 para. 24. The Commission thought the law should "emphasise as a priority" the need to make the financial provision necessary to safeguard the maintenance and welfare of the children, and the 1984 Act introduced the requirement that it should be the duty of the court in deciding whether to exercise its powers in financial matters and if so, in what manner, to "have regard to all the circumstances of the case, first consideration being given to the welfare while a minor of any child of the family who has not attained the age of eighteen."

Although this provision is important, there are three significant limitations on its scope:

(a) *First, but not paramount*

11–55   In deciding custody issues the court regards the welfare of the child as the "first and paramount" consideration even if that means overriding the claims of the child's parents or others affected: see para. 13–10 below. In considering financial matters, in contrast, the court is not required to go so far. It need only give "first" consideration to the welfare of the child in question. The court must thus consider all the circumstances, always bearing the children's welfare in mind; and it must then try to make a financial settlement which is just as between husband and wife: *Suter* v. *Suter and Jones, The Times,* January 9, 1987; see also *R* v. *Avon CC, ex parte K and Others* [1986] 1 FLR 443, a decision on the identically formulated provision of child care legislation: para. 18–16. The court is not required to allow the welfare of the child to prevail over the needs and interests of other persons affected by the divorce (who may, as we shall see, include other children).

(b) *Applies only to children of the family*

11–56   The expression "child of the family" is widely defined in the legislation and extends to any child who has been treated by both of the parties to the marriage as a child of their family: see para. 16–03 below. But although this definition is wide, it does not extend to all those children who may, actually or prospectively, be affected by the orders made in the matrimonial proceedings in question. For example, the child born to a husband and his cohabitee after the marriage breakdown is unlikely to be within the definition. The legislation thus seems now to embody the principle that the court is to put the interests of the children of a first marriage before the interests of other children affected. However, this does not mean that the interests of those other children are to be ignored—merely that they yield priority to the children of the family.

(c) *Applies only during infancy of children*

11–57   The court is only required to give first consideration to the welfare "while a minor" of any child of the family who has not attained the age of eighteen. This has two particular consequences. First, the court is not obliged to give such consideration to the welfare of any child of the family who has at the date of the hearing already attained the age of eighteen, even if he is undergoing advanced education or training, or if he is (for example) disabled. Secondly, even in the case of children of the family who are, at the date of the hearing, under eighteen, the court is only obliged by this provision to give first consideration to their welfare whilst they remain minors. The court is not required to take account of the fact that children in practice often stay in their homes until a later age whether because they are undergoing education or training or because they are disabled or unemployed, or simply because they prefer to do so particularly during the early stages of their career. Once again, this does not mean the court will ignore such considerations, but they do not have priority.

The child's needs

Before the court can decide what the child's welfare requires, it must **11–58** ask what he needs—in relation to housing, food, education and so on. There was some evidence that in the past the court underestimated the real costs of providing for children, and that having made an order for the spouse the court would simply make an order at a conventional level—apparently in 1982 £12.50 weekly: *Titheradge* v. *Titheradge* (1982) 4 FLR 552—for the child. Under the new law there should be greater emphasis on the children; and, in an attempt to provide realistic data, the courts are now provided with:

(a) *The supplementary benefit scale rates for the "requirements" of children*
The scale in force at November 1986 was as follows:

Age of Child	Weekly Allowance
under 11	£10.20
11–15	£15.30
16–17	£18.40

These figures of course relate to a subsistence level of support.

(b) *The recommended scale published by the National Foster Care Association*
This is accepted by many local authorities as the basis for calculating fostering allowances. The scale in force (in April 1986: see (1986) 16 Fam Law 202) was—

Age of Child	Weekly Allowance
0–4	£28.07
5–7	£32.76
8–10	£35.91
11–12	£38.99
13–15	£42.14
16–18	£56.21

Methods of giving effect to welfare directive

11-59 The court can promote the financial interests of children in two ways:

(a) *In exercising powers to make financial orders in favour of a parent*

For example, the court will usually try to ensure that the child has stable housing; and make an order settling the home on terms that it be not sold during the child's dependency: see para. 11–38 above. The child is not as such a beneficiary under that settlement, but his welfare is promoted by making it. Again, the court may think that the welfare of the children means that—notwithstanding the provisions encouraging self-sufficiency considered at para. 11–63 below—the wife should have periodical payments to enable her to stay out of the full-time labour market, at least so long as the children are still at school.

(b) *In making provision for children*

The court has, and may exercise, powers to make financial provision and property adjustment orders for the child himself: MCA 1973, s.23(1)(d), (e), (f) and s.24(a) to (c). The legislation contains guidelines (MCA 1973, s.25(3)) about the exercise of these powers; but it suffices to say that the courts view the family as a whole, and are disinclined to order provision of a capital endowment for children once they have ceased to be dependent: see *Harnett* v. *Harnett* [1973] Fam 156, 161 (Bagnall J.) and *Lilford (Lord)* v. *Glyn* [1979] 1 WLR 78.

There can be significant tax advantages in ordering periodical payments in favour of the child direct. This requires a brief explanation.

Tax advantages of orders for children

11-60 A court order for payment to the child direct will be effective to transfer the income ordered to be paid from the payer to the child for income tax purposes: *Harvey* v. *Sivyer* [1986] Ch 119. Since a child—however young—is entitled to a single person's personal allowance (£2,335 annually in 1986/7) an order against his father to pay £2,000 per annum will not involve the child in any tax liability, and the father (who may have been paying as much as £1,200 per annum by way of income tax at the top rate on this slice of his income) will cease to be liable to any income tax on the amount involved. The effective result in this example is that £2,000 can be made available for the child at a net cost to the father of only £800.

Since the payment is less than £2,496 per annum the father would simply pay it over as stated under a procedure designed to deal with what are called "small maintenance payments." But if the amount ordered exceeded that limit, the father would deduct 29 per cent. (tax at the basic rate) and a claim would have to be made on behalf of the child to the revenue to recover that amount. Although the order is in favour of the child it will usually be paid to the mother as his guardian. There is a procedure (which, however, is likely to be reviewed by the House of Lords: see *Sherdley* v. *Sherdley* [1986] 1 WLR 732, CA) whereby orders to pay the child's school fees can be treated as orders in the child's favour for the purpose of tax relief: see *Practice Direction (School Fees)* [1983] 1 WLR 800.

Where the spouse is not the child's parent

A spouse may be liable to have financial orders made against him in respect of a child of the family (such as a step-child) who is not biologically his own child. Special criteria—such as the basis on which he assumed responsibility and the maintenance liability of others to the child—apply in such cases: MCA 1973, s.25(4). For example:

> In *Leadbeater* v. *Leadbeater* [1985] FLR 789 the Court refused to order a husband to make any payment in respect of his step-daughter. The primary responsibility in the circumstances was on her own natural father.

11–61

Duration of child support

The legislation contains (MCA 1973, s.29) complex provisions about the maximum duration of orders in favour of children. In essence, the cut-off comes not later than 18; but support may be ordered beyond then if the child is in continuing education or training or if there are "special circumstances which justify" the making of a different order. Moreover, in *Downing* v. *Downing (Downing Intervening)* [1976] Fam 228 it was held that a child who has attained the age of 18 may himself intervene in divorce proceedings (notwithstanding the fact that the decree may have been pronounced many years ago) and claim financial provision if, for example, he wishes to pursue further education or can satisfy the court that there are special circumstances which justify the making of an order.

11–62

3. Provisions designed to encourage self-sufficiency—the "clean break"

The Law Commission recommended (Law Com. No. 112, para. 27) that the legislative guidelines governing the court's financial powers be revised to give greater emphasis to the importance of the parties doing everything possible to become self-sufficient. The Act now contains four provisions designed to achieve this objective; and the modern practice is to favour the so-called "clean break" wherever possible (Balcombe L.J. in *Harman* v. *Glencross* [1986] 1 All ER 545, 557).

11–63

(1) Court to consider potential increase in earning capacity

The matters to which the court's attention is particularly directed now include a reference to any increase in earning capacity which it would in the opinion of the court be reasonable to expect a party to the marriage to take steps to acquire: (see para. 11–27 above).

11–64

(2) Duty to consider termination of obligations

If the court decides to exercise its financial powers in favour of a party to the marriage, it must consider "whether it would be appropriate so to exercise those powers that the financial obligations of each party towards

11–65

the other will be terminated as soon after the grant of the decree as the court considers just and reasonable": MCA 1925, s.25A(1).

The "clean break" principle

11-66   This provision requires the court to consider the principle of the "clean break," which has been stated by the House of Lords to be one of the principles of the modern divorce law. The objective is to encourage the parties "to put the past behind them and to begin a new life which is not overshadowed by the relationship which has broken down," (see Lord Scarman in *Minton* v. *Minton* [1979] AC 593, 608) and thus to bring to an end the bitterness and hostility which (as the Booth Committee remarked: see para. 2.21) "may attach to long-standing maintenance orders." However, there is some danger of the expression "clean break" being indiscriminately used to express different and sometimes contradictory ideas (Ormrod L.J. in *Pearce* v. *Pearce* (1979) 1 FLR 261, 266); and it is particularly important to pay close attention to the details of the legislative structure.

First, the duty arises whenever the court decides to exercise its property adjustment or financial provision powers in favour of a party to the marriage. (It has no application to orders for children). Secondly, the question is whether it would be "appropriate" to exercise those powers in a certain way—most often perhaps by ordering a capital settlement in preference to continuing periodical payments. Thirdly, the financial obligations are only to be terminated when it would be "just and reasonable" to do so.

Wealthy parties

11-67   If there is substantial capital available it will often be possible to secure a "just and reasonable" settlement, providing for the parties' reasonable requirements (see para. 11–34 above):

> In *Preston* v. *Preston* [1982] Fam 17 the husband was ordered to pay the wife £600,000 in settlement of all his obligations.

> In *Attar* v. *Attar* (No 2) [1985] FLR 653 the husband, who had assets worth more than two million pounds, was ordered to pay the wife a comparatively modest lump sum (£30,000) after a marriage which only lasted some six months.

Matrimonial home adequate provision

11-68   In many cases, where the husband's income is only sufficient to support his new family and make some contribution to his children's maintenance, the court may decide simply to transfer the matrimonial home to the wife and dismiss any claim by her for periodical payments. (Periodical payments would still normally be ordered for the children). This technique may well be particularly appropriate if the wife has earnings or earning capacity, and it would also be an efficient way of maximising the wife's claims to welfare benefits (see para. 10–09 above):

> In *Livesey (formerly Jenkins)* v. *Jenkins* [1984] AC 424 the parties, who had two children aged 15 and 13, were divorced after a 24 year marriage. The parties

agreed to a consent order whereby the husband was ordered to make periodical payments of £7.50 weekly to each child, and to transfer his interest in the former matrimonial home to the wife (who was to be solely responsible for the mortgage and other outgoings). The wife's application for periodical payments was dismissed.

In *Mortimer* v. *Mortimer-Griffin* [1986] 2 FLR 315, CA the marriage had lasted for ten years. The husband had become unemployed, and was living on supplementary benefit which covered the mortgage interest on the house he had bought: see para. 10.04 above. The wife had retrained as a teacher and was earning £10,000 per annum. She lived with their 14 year old daughter in the former matrimonial home, worth £70,000. At first instance a *Mesher* order (see para. 11–37 above) was made giving the husband 40% of the value of the house when sold. The Court of Appeal substituted an order that the husband should receive an immediate lump sum of £2,500 (the most he could get without having to pay off the costs incurred by the legal aid fund) and that the house be transferred to the wife outright. In making this order the court took into account the financial burdens which the wife had shouldered since the breakdown of the marriage; but was primarily influenced by the fact that under a *Mesher* order the wife would have faced difficulty in rehousing herself when the time came for a sale; and that the husband was unlikely to benefit significantly by receiving a larger lump sum.

Other cases

The question of what is just and reasonable is obviously to some extent **11-69** subjective; and although May L.J. has rightly said (see *Morris* v. *Morris* [1985] FLR 1176, 1179) that the "clean break" thinking clearly now has Parliament's approval" as a general principle, it is equally true (in the words of the Solicitor-General's Memorandum to the House of Commons Special Standing Committee considering the 1984 Bill) that the legislation "does not lay down that a clean break is to be the norm, or anything like it." (Official Report, March 20, 1984, col. 10). Perhaps the most striking case in which the clean break has been applied is:

Seaton v. *Seaton* (1986) 16 Fam Law 267, CA where the 42 year old husband had suffered a heart attack and a stroke, as a result of which he could barely speak, and had only limited powers of concentration. After the breakdown of his 14 year marriage to a 36 year old teacher (who earned some £8,000 per annum) he was cared for by his elderly parents, who contributed financially to his upkeep. He had no income apart from a state disability pension, and the prognosis was that he would in due course have to go into a state-provided home, where his needs would be provided for. The Court of Appeal upheld a decision that there should be an immediate clean break, largely on the basis that he had no significant needs, and that no periodical payments by the wife could have any material effect in enhancing his life.

Does not override duty to consider children's welfare

The court's duties under the present provision must be taken in **11-70** conjunction with its duty to give first consideration to the welfare of the children.

In *S* v. *S* [1986] 3 All ER 566 the husband was extremely wealthy; and the question was whether the court should exercise its variation jurisdiction [see para. 11-89 below] to substitute a once-for-all capital payment to the wife for a periodical payments order under which she would receive £70,000 per annum. (Periodical payments of £10,000 per annum would continue for the 15 year-old daughter). It was held that the substitution could only be made if it accorded with the statutory requirements relating to welfare; and Waite J. said that the most important factor in reaching a decision to end the wife's periodical payments was that to do so would remove the sole remaining source of serious dispute between the girl's parents.

At one time it was thought that the court might be reluctant to impose a clean break where there were children particularly if there could be any risk that the wife's financial position might subsequently deteriorate to the children's disadvantage: see *Moore* v. *Moore* (1980) 11 Fam Law 109; but more recently the courts do not seem to have hesitated to make a "clean break" order even when there are children (see e.g. *Mortimer-Griffin*, above) provided that the settlement can be shown to be consistent with the children's welfare:

> In *Suter* v. *Suter and Jones, The Times,* January 9, 1987 the Court of Appeal held that it is wrong in law to say that there could be no "clean break" until the children were grown up. The children's welfare is a matter of first importance which should be borne in mind throughout the consideration of the circumstances which culminates in the court seeking a result which is fair and just as between the husband and wife; but the welfare of the children is not paramount, overriding all other considerations (see para. 11-55 above), and the court always has a duty to consider the clean break—whether immediately or at some future time—as a solution. On the facts of the case it would be premature to terminate H's obligations to W; but a nominal order (see para. 11-77 below) was substituted for periodical payments of £100 monthly.

It should be emphasised that what is in issue is whether or not the court will terminate one spouse's obligation to the other spouse—taking into account the impact that such a termination may have on the child. There is no power to terminate a parent's potential obligation to provide for a child of the family: see para. 11-59 above.

Termination may be at future date

11-71   In a proper case the court will have to consider whether it should order financial provision for only a limited period; and the possibility of making an order for a specified term is the subject of a special provision, considered below.

(3) Duty to consider a specified term order
11-72   If the court has decided to make a periodical payments order in favour of a party to the marriage. MCA 1973, s.25A(2) then requires it "in particular" to:

> "consider whether it would be appropriate to require those payments to be made or secured only for such term as would in the opinion of the court be sufficient to enable the party in whose favour the order is

made to adjust without undue hardship to the termination of his or her financial dependence on the other party."

Court must consider maintenance for specified term, such as six months or three years
The court may be particularly inclined to do so in those cases in which it considers that one spouse (usually the wife) has a potential for increasing her earning capacity—for example, by taking a retraining course: see the discussion of MCA 1973, s.25(2)(*a*) at para. 11–27 above. But two points should be noted: **11–73**

(i) *Specified term may be extended.* The court will have power to extend   **11–74** the term specified in such an order at any time during its currency, unless it has exercised the power conferred by MCA 1973, s.28(1A) to direct that no such application be entertained. For example, a wife may be given a periodical payments order for a year to enable her to retrain; but she might still find it impossible to find work. In such circumstances she could apply for an extension of the term. However, the onus in such a case would obviously be on her to make out a case for a variation of this sort:

> In *Sandford* v. *Sandford* [1986] 1 FLR 412, CA, the judge had made an order for periodical payments of £33 weekly to the wife until 31 December 1987. The Court of Appeal said that it was wrong to think the order was finite and incapable of extension, and that the wife could apply for a variation of the period if she could show that she would suffer undue hardship unless this was done.

(ii) *No undue hardship.* In deciding whether to make a specified term   **11–75** order the court must direct its mind to the question of whether the specified term is likely to be sufficient to enable the party concerned to adjust "without undue hardship" to the termination of the financial dependency. It seems likely that the courts will be well aware of how difficult it can be for a wife to become self-sufficient in practice (see *e.g.* *Mercer* v. *Mercer* (1986) 17 Fam Law; and see also *Camm* v. *Camm* (1982) 4 FLR 577, para. 11–27 above); and in any event a court may well conclude on the facts of a particular case that it would be inappropriate to expect the wife to do so:

> In *Leadbeater* v. *Leadbeater* [1985] FLR 789 the court did not think that it was reasonable to expect a 47 year-old wife who had been a secretary some years ago to familiarise herself with modern office technology (but contrast *Mitchell* v. *Mitchell* [1984] FLR 387 where the court—albeit not for the purposes of applying this provision—considered that a wife currently working as a canteen assistant could resume work as a qualified secretary once her children had left school.)

> In *Morris* v. *Morris* [1985] FLR 1176, CA, (a case on the rather different variation provisions: see para. 11–89 below) the trial judge had ordered that periodical payments in favour of a woman who had been married for 23 years should cease when the husband retired in five years time, or earlier if he lost the accommodation provided by his employer. The judge had not considered the hardship which this order might have caused the wife; and the order was set aside.

(4) Power to impose clean break without spouse's agreement

11-76   In *Dipper* v. *Dipper* [1981] Fam 31 the Court of Appeal held (to the surprise of many) that the divorce court had no power under the provisions of the Matrimonial Causes Act 1973 as originally enacted to dismiss a spouse's claim for periodical payments without his or her agreement. It could, of course, make a nominal order (for example, that the husband pay the wife 50 pence per annum); but so long as such an order was in existence it was always open to the wife to come back to the court and seek a variation: see *Jessel* v. *Jessel* [1979] 1 WLR 1148. The husband thus remained contingently liable if the wife's financial position altered for the worse—perhaps because of illness in old age. The court was therefore debarred from imposing a clean break—although it might indicate to the parties the orders which it had in mind on the alternative contingencies of the wife consenting to the dismissal of her claim, or insisting on at least a nominal order: see *Leadbeater* v. *Leadbeater* [1985] FLR 789, 797H (Balcombe J.). The 1984 legislation now specifically empowers the court to dismiss an application for periodical payments and to direct that the applicant be debarred from making any further application in relation to that marriage for such payments if it considers that no continuing obligation to make such payments should be imposed: MCA 1973, s.25A(3).

Summary of clean break options

11-77   The various options in practice open to the court under these provisions include:

(i) Immediate clean break. the court may consider that it would be appropriate to terminate the parties' financial obligations immediately. In that case it may make a property adjustment order; but it will dismiss any claim for periodical payments, and it will direct that neither party be entitled to make any further application for such an order. It will also order that neither party be entitled to apply for provision under the Inheritance (Provision for Family and Dependants) Act 1975.

(ii) Periodical payment order—nominal, or specified term? If the court considers that it would not be appropriate to terminate the financial obligations of the parties to one another it will wish to make a periodical payments order (although this may only be for a nominal amount, with the consequences mentioned at (iv) below.) The court must then consider whether it would be appropriate to order the periodical payments for only a specified term.

(iii) Deferred clean break. If the court decides that it would be appropriate to make a specified term order it must decide whether to direct that the applicant be debarred from applying for any extension of the term. Such an order may be called a "deferred clean break." In the absence of such a direction the applicant will be entitled to apply to have the term extended.

(iv) Nominal order. If the court makes a nominal order for periodical payments it will (in the absence of any such direction) be possible for the

applicant to apply to have the order varied at any time. In one sense the existence of a nominal order is the antithesis of the clean break philosophy, since it leaves the husband always open to the possibility that he will be required to make substantial periodical payments at some date, perhaps long in the future.

How are the Courts' Powers Exercised in Practice?

Introduction

It is difficult to find reliable up-to-date information about the operation **11–78** of the law in practice. The statistics are inadequate, and there has been no recent research which throws any real light on these issues. The published Judicial Statistics do however suggest that fairly extensive use is made of the self-sufficiency provisions. For example, in 1985 3,341 applications for ancillary relief were dismissed under the power conferred by MCA 1973, s. 25A; and 15,893 orders were made for a specified term. The courts' powers in determining the amount of orders are wide, and the statutory guidance certainly gives the court the flexibility which is, on one view, needed in order to achieve justice and fairness between the parties. But it is equally desirable that the law should be predictable and certain in its operation—not least so that advisers can assess the likely bracket of an award and negotiate a consensual settlement in the light of that prediction.

Different approaches

In *Wachtel* v. *Wachtel* [1973] Fam 72 the Court of Appeal approved the **11–79** then traditional *one-third* approach to the assessment of financial relief for the parties to a marriage—the parties' incomes are added together and divided by three, and the order calculated so as to bring the wife's income up to that proportion. (A similar approach might also be applied to capital). Subsequently the death of the one-third approach has frequently been announced, but it refuses to disappear. The courts still refer to it as a useful check on the figure which emerges from working through the matters specifically referred to in the legislation: see *Preston* v. *Preston* [1982] Fam 17, 25 (Ormrod L.J.); and:

> *Bullock* v. *Bullock* [1986] 1 FLR 372, CA, the court ordered the husband to pay the wife £100,000 which was one-third of the asset value of his shareholding in a family company. The court asserted that what it described as the "one-third convention" was still a proper approach.

However the courts have tended to attach greater weight to trying to satisfy the *reasonable needs* of the parties, and have also emphasised the desirability of working out the *net effect* of the proposed orders—taking everything into account (including tax and welfare benefits) what will the financial position of each of the two households be: *Stockford* v. *Stockford* (1981) 3 FLR 58; and *S* v. *S* [1977] 1 All ER 56)?

The practical approach

11-80   It seems that in practice an approach along the following lines is often used:

(a) *Children's needs*

The first step is to consider the needs of the children, and how they can be safeguarded.

(b) *Provisional assessment*

The court then considers all the circumstances of the case including those matters to which attention is specifically directed. In the light of that assessment, it seeks to work out the reasonable needs of the parties; and it will form a provisional view on the orders which might be indicated. In particular, it will consider the applicability of the self-sufficiency principles discussed at paras. 11–63 to 11–77 above.

(c) *Testing net effect of provisional assessment*

The court then assesses the net effect which such an order would have on the parties. In some cases an adjustment will be called for because the proposed order would put one party below subsistence level: see para. 11–30 above. In other cases it will check the proposed order against the one-third guideline; and possibly adjust it if it is too far away from it. (In making these calculations, some courts use pro-forma "calculators" of the kind set out in the Appendix to this book).

Application where substantial resources available

11-81   The decision in *Leadbeater* v. *Leadbeater* [1985] FLR 789—which has already been referred to as illustrating many specific points on the application of the legislation—is a good example of the court's approach along these lines in a case in which the parties had substantial means. The 45 year old husband's net assets amounted to £250,000; the 47 year old wife's to £80,000. During a marriage which had lasted effectively for only four years they had enjoyed a high standard of living:

(i) Welfare of the children. The only child of the family would shortly reach 18, and the order would thus not affect her during her minority.

(ii) The following factors were particularly relevant:

   (a) The wife needed a two bedroomed house for which £40,000 was needed; and she would need to furnish it at a cost of £10,000.

   (b) Her other needs could be assessed as a car (costing £1,450 yearly); private expenses aggregating some £8,000. The court rounded this up to £10,000.

   (c) The wife had a job bringing in £1,650 yearly. The court thought she could reasonably work longer hours, and earn thereby £2,500.

   (d) Duration of the marriage. Since the marriage had only lasted four years it would be just to reduce the sum which would otherwise have been ordered: see below.

   (e) Other factors. The court considered that it should give "adequate recognition" to the lifestyle the wife had enjoyed both before and after the marriage. But it refused to take either party's conduct into account, because each had been to blame.

(iii) Conclusion. This was a case where there were adequate funds for a "clean break." The wife's reasonable needs could best be satisfied by a lump sum payment of £50,000. That would be reduced by 25 per cent. because of the short duration of the marriage resulting in an order for £37,500.

Application where resources inadequate to support two families
In such cases the court will apply the principles discussed at   **11–82** para. 11–29 above. It may, of course, often make an order dealing with the former matrimonial home—often transferring it outright to the wife, particularly if the circumstances are such that no periodical award to meet her needs is appropriate.

CONSENT ORDERS—THE LIMITS OF PRIVATE ORDERING

A conflict of policy
It is the policy of the modern law to encourage the parties to resolve   **11–83** matters for themselves rather than seeking (to adopt the Law Commission's words) "an unattainable catharsis in a judicial forum." (Law Com. No. 103, para. 37). But the law also takes the view that the community as a whole has an interest in the financial arrangements made by a couple on divorce: a wife's rights are not to be settled by private agreement, and statute provides that any provision in a maintenance agreement restricting the parties' right to apply to the court is void: MCA 1973, s.34(1). The compromise between these two somewhat conflicting principles has been found in permitting the parties to seek an order by consent from the court, which will then be decisive—even if it provides for a "clean break" with no right to apply for any subsequent variation. This is because the order will derive its legal effect from the decision of the court rather than from the agreement of the parties which lead up to it: *de Lasala* v. *de Lasala* [1980] AC 546. The result can be summarised as follows:

(a) *Information to be provided*
Statute (MCA 1973, s.33A) provides that the court may make a consent   **11–84** order on the basis of specified information laid down by Rules of Court. The information required deals with such matters as the duration of the marriage, the age of the parties, the parties' capital resources, the arrangements proposed for the parties' accommodation; similar information about the children; whether either party has remarried or has any present plans to marry or cohabit; and "any other specially significant matters." (MCR 76A).

(b) *Court's duty to enquire*

11–85   The role of the court in considering an application for a consent order is not reduced to "putting a rubber stamp on the parties' agreement" (Booth Report, para. 2.20, echoing Balcombe J., *Tommey* v. *Tommey* [1983] Fam 15, 21.) On the contrary, it has a statutory duty to consider "all the circumstances" including those specified in MCA 1973, s.25 and discussed at paras. 11–23 to 11–49 above; and the parties have a duty to provide all relevant information and to ensure that it is correct, complete, and up-to-date: *Livesey (formerly Jenkins)* v. *Livesey* [1985] AC 424. For example, it would seem to be necessary to disclose whether the wife's expectation of life was less than normal (in which case it might not be appropriate for a large lump sum to be paid to her); or whether she plans to realise a business—since this might put her in possession of more liquid funds than would at first appear. It is not sufficient merely to provide the information stipulated in the rule referred to in para. 11–84 above—that is simply the minimum required to give the court jurisdiction.

(c) *Order may be set aside for non-disclosure*

11–86   If it subsequently transpires that the requisite full and frank disclosure has not been made, the court may set aside any order it has made:

> In *Livesey (formerly Jenkins)* v. *Livesey* [1985] AC 424 the wife agreed with the husband that she would accept a transfer of the husband's interest in the matrimonial home in settlement of all financial claims. On the day before application was made for a consent order embodying these terms she became engaged to be married; and three weeks after the order was made she remarried. The House of Lords held that she had been under a duty to disclose her engagement since it could have affected the order made; and the order was set aside.

The House of Lords was however careful to emphasise that consent orders are not lightly to be overthrown; it is not "every failure of frank and full disclosure which would justify a court in setting aside" such an order. For example:

> In *Edgar* v. *Edgar* [1980] 1 WLR 1410 the wife of a multi-millionaire received proper professional advice and chose to ignore it. She accepted some £100,000 from her husband and agreed not to seek any further provision. Three years later she applied for financial relief, and at first instance was awarded some £760,000. The Court of Appeal held that she was bound by the agreement, and she got nothing more.

(d) *Effect of unforeseen change of circumstances*

What is to happen if there is a change of circumstances after the making of the order which was unforseen by either party? For example:

> In *Barder* v. *Barder* [1986] 3 WLR 145, CA, on February 20, 1985 the court by consent made a "clean break" order under which H was to transfer the matrimonial home to W within 28 days. On March 25 W killed her children and committed suicide. All her property would go under her will to her mother.

H had not yet executed the documents necessary to transfer the house to W. Was he obliged to do so, or would the court set aside the order?

The cases currently draw a distinction between the situation, likely to be uncommon, in which the parties are still within the prescribed time for appealing against the order; and other cases where the court's leave is required to appeal. If the parties are within the stipulated time to lodge an appeal, and the basis on which the consent order has been made has been completely falsified, the court (so it has been said: see Lord Brandon in *Livesey* v. *Jenkins* [1985] AC 424) will substitute whatever order is necessary to achieve substantial justice. But once that time has passed, the court will only grant leave to appeal in "very special and exceptional cases" (Woolf L.J. in *Barder* (above), justifying the refusal to upset the order made in that case.)

It is obviously unsatisfactory to make so important a matter turn upon a procedural distinction of this kind, and in any event there was little common ground between the different members of the Court of Appeal in *Barder* (above). Leave has been given to appeal to the House of Lords in that case; and it is to be hoped that some coherent principle will emerge.

(e) *Private agreement ineffective*

It should once again be emphasised that it is only by court order that a   **11-87** final determination of the parties' financial obligations can be made. There is statutory power to vary the terms of any maintenance agreement (see MCA 1973, s.35); and there is power—subject to the provisions discussed at para. 11–74 above—to vary any periodical payments order made in matrimonial proceedings (MCA 1973, s.31).

Conclusion—role of court not clear

These rules betray a somewhat ambivalent attitude to the role of the   **11-88** court; and it is not surprising that there is some difference of approach from court to court. The underlying problem is that, as the Booth Committee remarked, it is not altogether clear what is the purpose of the court's enquiry: is it to ensure that neither party is acting under pressure or ignorance, or is it to ensure so far as possible that neither party "will be a liability upon the public purse"? (para. 2.20).

VARIATION OF ORDERS AND AGREEMENTS

The court has wide powers to vary periodical payment orders: MCA 1973,   **11-89** s.31. In particular, it may vary the term set by a specified term order unless it has exercised its power to direct that no application for this purpose should be permitted: MCA 1973, s.28(1A). Generally speaking property adjustment and lump sum orders cannot be varied.

In deciding whether to exercise the power to vary a periodical payments   **11-90** order, the court is directed (MCA 1973, s. 31(7)) to consider all the circumstances of the case. In particular, it is directed to give first consideration to the welfare of any minor children of the family (see para. 11–54 above); and to consider whether in all the circumstances, and having regard to any change in the relevant matters since the order was made, it would be appropriate to terminate the periodical payments after a period sufficient to enable the recipient to adjust to the termination without undue hardship.

11-91   The court may therefore vary any continuing maintenance provision. In particular, as we have already seen, it may vary an order for nominal payments to an order for substantial payments if a change in circumstances makes that appropriate. But the court has no power to make a lump sum or property adjustment order on an application to vary a periodical payments order; and it follows that the court has no power in such proceedings to impose the commonest form of "clean break" on a husband (*i.e.* that he pay a sum of capital to his wife). However, it has been held that the court may terminate the periodical payments order on the husband undertaking to pay to the wife a specified sum of money (and presumably an order could equally be terminated if he were to undertake to settle capital for her benefit). The result seems to be that the court can in effect impose a "clean break" on an unwilling wife (provided that it is satisfied about the interests of the children and the wife's capacity to adjust to the break without undue hardship); but that it cannot impose such a solution on a husband who is unwilling to provide the capital sum the court considers appropriate:

> In *S* v. *S* [1986] 3 All ER 566 the ex-wife of an immensely wealthy pop-star spent what she needed regardless of her means; she professed an ignorance of, and (as the judge found) took as little interest as possible in the details of household budgeting. The husband tried to help by arranging for accountants to control and monitor her expenditure; but she found that control irksome. She felt that as the divorced spouse of so rich a man she ought to be wholly relieved of financial anxiety; and she became increasingly resentful at what she considered to be the husband's meanness. She applied for the periodical payments order for £23,000 per annum made on the divorce to be increased; the husband sought to be freed of any further liability on his paying to her £120,000 which would give her a total capital of some £420,000. Waite J. held that he had jurisdiction to do what the husband asked; but that the proper figure for him to pay was £400,000. If he did not do this, the periodical payments should be increased to £70,000 per annum.

11-92   Husband and wife may, of course, make a maintenace agreement which is not subject to the court's approval. Such an agreement cannot restrict the parties' right to apply to the court for financial relief; and for that reason such out-of-court agreements are today uncommon. The court has power to vary the terms of such an agreement; but the legislation requires it first to be satisfied that by reason of a change in the circumstances the agreement has become unjust or inequitable. This is a more difficult test to satisfy than that applied to the variation of court orders: see *Simister* v. *Simister* [1987] 1 All ER 233.

Chapter 12

MONEY AND THE FAMILY OUTSIDE MARRIAGE

INTRODUCTION

Marriage creates a status from which certain legal consequences automati-   **12–01**
cally follow. But today a large number of people, who for one reason or
another have not bothered to "go through with the paperwork," live
together in relationships which perhaps appear to be marriages to
outsiders. The traditional response might be simply to say (see Sir George
Baker P. in *Campbell* v. *Campbell* [1976] Fam 347), that "rights duties and
obligations begin on the marriage and not before"; but it has come to be
recognised that such an approach would be unrealistic. In particular, the
courts have been faced with the problem of deciding what is to happen to
property acquired by a couple who intended a long-term relationship; and
statutes have been passed to deal with particular problems—for example,
to provide remedies in respect of domestic violence which can affect the
unmarried housewife as easily as the married. This Chapter therefore
deals with:

(i)   the property rights of unmarried couples;
(ii) rights to occupy the family home;
(iii) rights on the death of one of the partners;
(iv) social security entitlements;
(v)   miscellaneous rights.

PROPERTY RIGHTS

The general principle of English law was succinctly stated by Purchas J.,   **12–02**
in *Dennis* v. *MacDonald* [1981] 1 WLR 810, 814: the law gives no rights to
a mistress by reason of her relationship with her lover, but neither does
she lose any rights she would have had at law or in equity. But before
discussing the application of the relevant principles of common law and
equity to the family outside marriage, there is a statutory provision which
may be relevant.

Has there been a broken engagement?
Where there has been an agreement to marry—which means a clear   **12–03**
agreement, not merely a vague recognition of the possibility of a marriage
at some unspecified time in the future: *Bernard* v. *Josephs* [1982] Ch 391,
406—and this agreement has been terminated, the Law Reform (Miscellaneous Provisions) Act 1970, governs the situation. Specifically, section
2(1) of that Act applies "any rule of law relating to the rights of husbands
and wives" to the resolution of disputes relating to property in which

either party had an interest during the engagement. These rules have been analysed in Chapter 8; and in fact there is now little difference between the law affecting the married and the unmarried—what counts is the nature of the relationship: see below. Applying the rules of common law and equity governing husband and wife to the unmarried will therefore normally make no difference; but there is one statutory provision which may be relevant. This is section 37 of the Matrimonial Proceedings and Property Act 1970 which (see para. 8–36 above) deals with the effect of one spouse making contributions to improvements to property. As a result of the assimilation by the Law Reform (Miscellaneous Provisions) Act 1970 of the position of the formerly engaged and the married, an unmarried person may be able successfully to claim an interest in property under section 37 which he would not otherwise have been able to do.

The rules of law and equity

12-04   The fundamental principle is that English law has no special property regime governing matrimonial property. Paradoxically, this fact has made it easier for the courts to develop principles to govern the property rights of the family outside marriage. Lord Upjohn, in *Pettit* v. *Pettit* [1970] AC 777, 813 stated that property disputes between husband and wife had to be decided by ordinary principles "while making full allowance" in view of the relationship between the parties. The question therefore becomes "what allowances have to be made?"; and the answer must depend on the content of the parties' relationship rather than their legal status—the "paperwork" should make no difference. Two couples who have had a similar relationship should find that they have comparable property rights, irrespective of the fact that one is a married couple and the other is unmarried.

The application of this principle has been worked out primarily within the framework of the *implied resulting and constructive trust*: in English law a "housewife," whether married or unmarried, may successfully claim a share in the family home if she can establish the existence of such a trust in her favour. The relevant principles of law have been set out at paras. 8–11 to 8–20 above; and their application to the unmarried can be summarised comparatively briefly, albeit at the cost of some cross-referencing and repetition:

12-05   (i) Implied and resulting trusts usually depend on proof that there was a *common, if usually unexpressed,* intention that both the parties should have a beneficial interest in the property. The question is therefore whether there is material on which a finding of such an intention can be based.

12-06   (ii) *Significance of marriage in assessing intention.* Marriage by itself involves a commitment to a permanent relationship; but there is no such commitment implicit in other relationships. Everything depends on the facts; and the courts have said that it is necessary to look most carefully at the precise nature of the relationship between an unmarried couple in order to be able to draw appropriate inferences as to the parties' intentions: *Bernard* v. *Josephs* [1982] Ch 391. The practical result is that it is much more difficult to satisfy the court that an unmarried couple had an intention to own property jointly than it is in the case of a married couple: see (v) below.

(iii) *Contributions particularly significant evidence of intention to share.*   **12–07**
The required intention will often be found by inference from the parties' conduct. Contributions which they have made to the acquisition of the property will be particularly significant, because in the case of the unmarried the court cannot draw any particular inference from the fact that a couple have lived under the same roof. But contributions are merely one kind of evidence, and if other evidence is available it can determine the issue: see below.

(iv) The following are *examples of contributions* which have been held to   **12–08**
justify the court drawing the inference that a sharing of the beneficial interest was intended:

(a) payment of part of the purchase price;
(b) regular contributions to the monthly mortgage payments;
(c) paying off a part of the outstanding mortgage debt;
(d) making a "substantial financial contribution to the family expenses so as to enable the mortgage instalments to be paid" (Fox L.J. in *Burns* v. *Burns* [1984] Ch 317).
(e) the making of "real and substantial" contributions which can be regarded as equivalent to financial contributions—for example heavy and skilled building work: see, *e.g. Cooke* v. *Head* [1972] 1 WLR 518 where a woman had used a sledge-hammer and cement mixer in the course of improvement works; and also *Eves* v. *Eves* [1975] 1 WLR 1338.

(v) In the absence of evidence of such direct contributions in money or   **12–09**
money's worth to the acquisition of the house the courts have shown some reluctance to infer the necessary intention in favour of an "unmarried housewife." The following "contributions" have been held to be insufficient:

(a) Living together for 19 years, and giving up a job to look after the male partner and the couple's two children for 17 of those years: see *Burns* v. *Burns* [1984] Ch 317. (The woman had also taken her partner's name and obtained a passport in his name; she had put her earnings into the housekeeping, and bought fixtures and fittings for the house, a washing machine and tumble drier);
(b) Laying a patio and doing internal decoration work: *Burns* v. *Burns* (above);
(c) Being a man's mistress for 13 years and living with him for five years, supplying him with house management, love, companion-

ship, and secretarial assistance in his business. This was held to be insufficient even though, as the judge put it, the "services she was expected to supply were, to all intents and purposes, those of a wife": *Layton* v. *Martin and Others* [1986] 2 FLR 227.

12-10   (vi) But the *question is one of evidence of intention,* and evidence other than that of "contributions" may in a proper case enable the court to find that the parties did intend that both should have a beneficial interest: see, for example, *Grant* v. *Edwards* [1986] 2 All ER 426, CA, para. 8–16 above. Again if one of the partners has joined in a mortgage because mortgage finance could not otherwise be obtained the fact that such a liability has been assumed may itself justify the court in inferring that he or she was intended to have a share in the property notwith-standing the fact that no actual payments were made: *Marsh* v. *Von Sternberg* [1986] 1 FLR 526, where the claimant, who had joined in the mortgage but made only insignificant contribution to repayment of capital was held to have a beneficial interest; contrast *Young* v. *Young* [1985] FLR 375.

12-11   (vii) The court *may look at the conduct of the parties after the breakdown* if that clarifies the terms of the original understanding: *Bernard* v. *Josephs* at p. 398 (Lord Denning) and *cf.* p. 404 (Kerr L.J.).

12-12   (viii) *Detrimental reliance necessary.* Even if the claimant succeeds in showing that there was a common intention, she will still have to show that she acted on that intention to her detriment—for example, by making financial contributions to the acquisition costs: *Grant* v. *Edwards* above; and see para. 8–17 above.

The terms of the agreement between the parties will determine their entitlement; but the terms may also have consequences for the relation-ship between the parties and an outsider who has dealt with them. In *Bristol and West Building Society* v. *Henning* [1985] 1 WLR 778 it was conceded that a woman had a beneficial interest in the family home, but the court held that this did not bind the Building Society which had put up the funds. The inference to be drawn from the facts was that it had been intended that the man (who as far as the Society knew was the sole owner of the property) should have the woman's authority to mortgage the house to finance the purchase.

12-13   (ix) If two parties do have a beneficial interest in land, any interested person may apply to the court for an order for sale under section 30 of the Law of Property Act 1925, discussed at para. 8–23 above. If the relationship has come to an end a sale will normally be ordered (see *Bernard* v. *Josephs* [1982] Ch 391) unless, for example, a house is still needed for the upbringing of children, or it can be shown that it would be inequitable to order a sale. If the application is by a trustee in bankruptcy the interests of the creditors will normally prevail—the statutory rule contained in Insolvency Act 1986, s.336 (see para. 8–24 above) which may often in practice give a wife 12 months from the bankruptcy does not apply.

Other doctrines

Although the trust has been the most fruitful technique for developing   **12–14**
concepts of family property other doctrines may sometimes be relevant.
For example, the court may be able to find that there was an *enforceable*
contract between the parties; or one of them may be *estopped* from
denying that the other has a proprietary interest in the property:

Contract

It is possible for a couple to regulate their affairs by contract; and in   **12–15**
appropriate cases the court may be able to infer the existence of a legally
enforceable agreement between them.

Requirements of contract

In order to establish a contract it must be shown: **12–16**

(i)   That there was a genuine meeting of minds between the parties—
      i.e. an offer and an acceptance;
(ii) That the parties intended to create a legally enforceable relation-
      ship;
(iii) The terms of the agreement must be sufficiently precise;
(iv) If the agreement is not contained in a sealed document, there must
      be consideration; and,
(v)   The terms which it is sought to enforce must not be illegal or
      contrary to public policy.

For the most part there will be no particular difficulty in applying the   **12–17**
ordinary rules of contract to the domestic situation. Two decided cases
illustrating the working of the law can be contrasted:

In *Tanner* v. *Tanner* [1975] 1 WLR 1341 the male partner purchased a house for
occupation by the defendant and the twin daughters of their relationship. The
defendant moved into the house; but subsequently the parties' relationship
broke down; and the plaintiff claimed possession on the basis that the
defendant was only a bare licensee under a licence which he had revoked. The
Court of Appeal held that there was an implied contractual licence under the
terms of which the defendant was to be entitled to occupy the house so long as
the children were of school age, or some other circumstance arose which would
make it unreasonable for her to retain possession.

In *Layton* v. *Martin and Others* [1986] 2 FLR 227 a woman accepted a man's offer
that if she would live with him he would give her what emotional security he
could, plus financial security on his death. She nevertheless failed in an action
against his estate after his death notwithstanding the fact that she had lived
with the deceased for five years after that offer had been made, and that she had
been his mistress for 13 years in all. This was because the court refused to find
that there had been any intention to create a legally enforceable contract—a
decision which seems somewhat harsh on the facts (but see also *Horrocks* v.

Foray [1976] 1 WLR 230 and *Coombes* v. *Smith* [1986] 1 WLR 808, in both of which the claim was unsuccessful.)

Contrary to public policy?

12-18   Even if a woman does prove the existence of a contract, questions of public policy could arise: if a contract is "founded on an immoral consideration" it may not be enforced. However, the position has been well summed up as follows: " . . . there is a large body of old authority which directly invalidates contracts for prospective cohabitation and a growing number of very recent cases which impliedly ignore this threat . . . The latter group has met with the approval of commentators." (C. Barton, *Cohabitation Contracts* (1985), p. 38) In the United States the common law rule has been extensively considered and restrictively interpreted (see *Marvin* v. *Marvin* (1976) 557 P 2d 106); and in the result it is difficult to believe that in cases of a genuine emotional relationship, an agreement would be affected by any general rule of illegality. There are, it is true, a number of specific rules of law which would still apply to the terms of a contract—particularly the rule now embodied in statute whereby any agreement to surrender or transfer parental rights or duties will not be enforced: see Children Act 1975, s.85(2)—but those rules are unlikely to affect property rights.

Estoppel

12-19   If one party to a relationship incurred expenditure or did some other act to her detriment in the belief, encouraged by the other, that she already owned or would be given some proprietary interest in it, an equity will arise to have made good, so far as may fairly be done between the parties, the expectations which have been encouraged—even, in appropriate cases, by requiring the owner of the legal estate in the property to transfer it to his former partner. The application of this equitable doctrine in the context of a non-marital relationship can be illustrated by reference to the case of *Pascoe* v. *Turner* [1979] 1 WLR 431:

> The defendant had lived with his former housekeeper as man and wife for many years. He then formed another relationship, and told the defendant that the house and its contents were hers. In reliance on that statement the plaintiff made substantial improvements to the house and bought furnishings for it, using for these purposes a large proportion of her small capital. The statement that "the property was to be the defendant's" was held to be ineffective because the appropriate formalities had not been observed (see para. 8–08 above, and compare *Gissing* v. *Gissing* [1971] AC 886, para. 8–10 above). But the court held that there was an equitable estoppel by reason of the defendant's encouragement and acquiescence in the actions which the plaintiff had taken in reliance on it. That estoppel could only be satisfied by transferring the legal estate in the property to her. (See also *Greasley* v. *Cooke* [1980] 1 WLR 1306).

> In contrast in *Layton* v. *Martin* (para. 12–17 above) the plaintiff failed to establish an estoppel interest because the expectations aroused by the deceased's very general representations did not relate to any specific item of property; and in *Coombes* v. *Smith* [1986] 1 WLR 808 the claimant failed because she did not have any mistaken belief about her legal position.

RIGHTS OF OCCUPATION AND PROTECTION AGAINST VIOLENCE

There are two relevant procedures: first, the county court will often have   **12-20**
jurisdiction under the Domestic Violence and Matrimonial Proceedings
Act 1976; secondly, the High Court and county court may sometimes
have jurisdiction under section 37 of the Supreme Court Act 1981 (or
section 38 of the County Courts Act 1984).

1. The Domestic Violence and Matrimonial Proceedings Act 1976

The provisions of the Domestic Violence and Matrimonial Proceedings   **12-21**
Act 1976 ("the 1976 Act" hereafter) governing the jurisdiction of the
County Court to grant injunctions and to attach a power of arrest to
injunctions apply "to a man and a woman who are living with each other
in the same household as husband and wife as it applies to the parties to a
marriage" (s.1(2); and see also s.2(2)).

Who can apply?
In order to qualify, the applicant must establish that the couple had   **12-22**
been living together in this way at the date of the incidents about which
complaint is made:

> In *Adeoso* v. *Adeoso* [1980] 1 WLR 1535 the couple had in fact been living in
> separate rooms and communicating only by note for five months prior to the
> application; but the court held that it had jurisdiction notwithstanding the fact
> that by the date of the application there were clearly two separate households:
> see para. 4–33 above.

Of course, if there has been a long delay in starting the proceedings the
court may decide that it would be inappropriate to exercise a jurisdiction
which is intended to provide short-term relief:

> Thus in *O'Neill* v. *Williams* (1984) 5 FLR 1 W went away on holiday and
> returned to find that her partner had changed the locks. On his subsequent
> return he assaulted W; and in October 1982 W went back to live with her
> parents. The court refused to make any order on an application filed at the
> beginning of March 1983.

The court's powers
The court may grant an injunction containing one or more of the   **12-23**
following terms (see generally paras. 6–16–6–18 above):

(i) *Not to molest the applicant or a child living with the applicant.* The best
single synonym for "molest" it has been said (see *Vaughan* v. *Vaughan*
[1973] 1 WLR 1159, where the man called at the woman's place of work,
came to the family home early in the morning and late at night and made
"a perfect nuisance of himself to her the whole time") is "pester."

(ii) *Excluding the respondent from the family home or a part of the family
home or from a specified area in which the family home is included.* Such a
provision is called an "ouster" order.

(iii) *Requiring one party to permit the applicant to enter and remain in the family home or part of the family home.*

Power of arrest

12-24 The court may attach a power of arrest to ouster orders and to orders restraining one party from using violence, provided that it is proved that the respondent has caused actual bodily harm to the applicant or child and the court considers that he is likely to do so again: see further para. 6–21 above. A power of arrest authorises a constable to arrest without warrant a person whom he has reasonable grounds for suspecting of being in breach of the relevant provisions. The limitations on the power of arrest are important: there is no power to attach such a power to a non-molestation injunction.

Limitations on court's powers

12-24 These powers, taken together, give the court wide powers to protect the "unmarried housewife"; but there are nevertheless some possible gaps. For example, the court has no power to prevent the man from removing his furniture from the family home; and he may thereby render it virtually uninhabitable:

> In *Davis* v. *Johnson* [1979] AC 264 the applicant, after litigation which was taken all the way to the House of Lords, successfully obtained an ouster order; but when she returned to the family home she found it empty save for some plastic ornaments and plates.

Basis on which the court exercises its powers

12-25 There is a distinction between ouster orders and non-molestation orders. Everyone, whether married or unmarried, has a legal right to integrity and security of the person. Hence the court will make non-molestation orders whenever it feels that to do so is necessary to protect the applicant or her child. But in the case of ouster orders, different considerations might apply—does the applicant have to show that she has some legal or equitable right to remain in the family home, for example? In *Davis* v. *Johnson* [1979] AC 264 the House of Lords held that it was not necessary to establish any such right, with the jurisprudentially perhaps rather strange result that the court is given power to provide a remedy (*e.g.* an ouster order) when there has been no breach of any legally recognised right.

Ouster orders normally temporary

12-26 It is perhaps because the applicant normally lacks any clear right to dispossess her partner that the 1976 Act is to be used primarily to provide "first aid but not intensive" (or, one might add, extended) care: Lord Salmon in *Davis* v. *Johnson* at page 73. It is true that it has been said that the jurisdiction should be exercised in precisely the same way as it would in a case between husband and wife (*Spindlow* v. *Spindlow* [1979] Fam 32)—and of course a wife has both common law and statutory rights in the matrimonial home: see para. 9–02 above. But this statement seems to mean no more than that the court should ask whether the order proposed is in all the circumstances "just and reasonable": see *Lee* v. *Lee* (1983) 127 SJ 696, and para. 9–06 above).

Short-term orders

At least in the first instance, the court will not normally grant an ouster **12-27** order for more than three months: *Practice Note (Domestic Violence: Power of Arrest)* [1981] 1 WLR 27. However, "liberty to apply" will usually be given, and either party can then apply for a variation; and in an appropriate case the court may grant an ouster order until further order—*i.e.* indefinitely:

> In *Spencer* v. *Comacho* (1983) 4 FLR 662 a series of three month orders was made against a man who continued to behave violently to his former partner. After an incident when the police were called, the order was extended "until further order."

2. Injunctions under section 37, Supreme Court Act 1981, etc

The court has a wide power to grant injunctions under section 37 (and the **12-28** analogous County Court legislation); but it has been held that this power should only be exercised if three conditions are satisfied:

(a) The injunction must be incidental to other proceedings—such as an action for damages for trespass to the person; and

(b) There must be a sufficient link between the relief sought by way of injunction and the other proceedings to which the grant of an injunction was ancillary; and—in practice perhaps most important

(c) An injunction will only be granted in support of a recognised legal or equitable right. Thus in *Re W (a minor)* [1981] 3 All ER 401 the applicant was the sole tenant of the council flat which had been the family home. This proprietary interest has been held sufficient to support her application for an injunction ousting her partner from the flat: Dillon L.J. in *Ainsbury* v. *Millington* [1986] 1 All ER 73, 77. In contrast, in the latter case the couple were joint tenants; and since neither joint tenant has the right to occupy the property to the exclusion of the other the applicant lacked the necessary right which the court would enforce. However, it should be noted that an appeal to the House of Lords in this case is pending at the date of going to press.

RIGHTS ON DEATH OF A PARTNER

Introduction

If one party to a relationship dies, all his or her property vests in **12-29** personal representatives who are under a duty to distribute it in accordance with the provisions of the deceased's will or (insofar as there is no valid will) in accordance with the rules of intestacy.

Circumstances in which unmarried partner may claim

12–30   The deceased's unmarried partner may be eligible to take some or all of the family property under one or other of the following heads:—

12–31   (a) *If the survivor can prove that he is beneficially entitled to the property under the rules of property law:* see paras. 12–02 to 12–12 above. This principle should really be self-evident, since it is only the deceased's own property which passes on his death to his personal representatives. But there are two particularly important applications of the general principle which may be relevant:

(i) The survivor may be able to establish an interest in property the legal title to which was in the deceased under an implied resulting or constructive trust: see para. 12–04 and see (for an unsuccessful example of such a claim) *Layton* v. *Martin and Others* [1986] 2 FLR 227.

(ii) If the partners were beneficial joint tenants of property, the interest of the deceased will automatically accrue to the other on his death, irrespective of the terms of his will. Questions may arise as to whether the joint tenancy had been severed and converted into a tenancy in common: see para. 8–25 above.

12–32   (b) *The survivor may be entitled to succeed to the deceased partner's tenancy* If the tenancy in question is a private sector tenancy the survivor may qualify if he can satisfy the court that he was a member of the deceased tenant's family who was residing with the deceased at the time of, and for the period of six months immediately preceding, the tenant's death: Rent Act 1977, Sched. 1, para. 3. There is some difficult case law on the interpretation of the expression "member of the original tenant's family"; but it seems probable that the question is whether an ordinary man would say that the applicant was within that definition: *Dyson Holdings* v. *Fox* [1976] QB 503; *cf. Helby* v. *Rafferty* [1979] 1 WLR 13. The assumption of a common name, the duration of the relationship, and the bringing up of children are all relevant factors, although none of them is conclusive.

Public sector tenancies may be transferred to a "member of the tenant's family" who has resided with the tenant throughout the period of twelve months ending with the tenant's death: Housing Act 1985, s.87. It is provided (s.113(1)(a)) that a person is a member of another's family if "he and that person live together as husband and wife."

12–33   (c) *If the survivor can establish an interest binding the deceased under which she is entitled to stay in possession of the property:* see *Horrocks* v. *Foray* [1976] 1 WLR 230 where the defendant claimed that there was a contractual licence giving her the right to remain in the house bought for her occupation by the man whose mistress she had been for 17 years. (On the facts, however, she failed to establish the existence of such a licence.)

12–34   (d) *If the deceased made a valid will making provision for his partner she will of course be entitled to take under it.* (It may, of course, be that other members of his family will seek provision out of his estate under the provisions of the Inheritance (Provision for Family and Dependants) Act 1975: see para. 8–30 above.)

(e) *If the deceased died intestate his partner will not as such have any right*   **12–35**
of succession under the intestacy laws which only benefit certain specified
relatives: see para. 8–28 above. But if the deceased left no relatives qualified to inherit, so that the property would normally pass to the Crown as *bona vacantia*, the Crown may at its discretion make provision for the survivor as a "dependant" of the deceased: Administration of Estates Act 1925, s.46(1).

(f) *The survivor may be able successfully to make a claim for provision*   **12–36**
under the Inheritance (Provision for Family and Dependants) Act 1975. This merits separate treatment.

Claims under the Inheritance (Provision for Family and Dependants) Act 1975 (The 1975 Act)

This Act empowers the court to make financial orders in favour of a   **12–37**
deceased's surviving dependants if it is satisfied that reasonable financial provision has not been made for him.

When can an unmarried partner apply?

A person who "immediately before the death of the deceased was being   **12–38**
maintained, either wholly or partly, by the deceased" is eligible to apply as a "dependant" under the Act: 1975 Act s.1(1); and the Act provides that a person is for this purpose to be treated as being maintained if the deceased "otherwise than for full valuable consideration, was making a substantial contribution in money or money's worth towards the applicant's needs."

Financial dependence necessary

It follows from this that a claimant can only qualify under this head if   **12–39**
he has been financially dependent on the deceased; and the deceased must have assumed responsibility for the applicant's maintenance—although the court will readily infer that there had been such an assumption if the deceased has in fact maintained the applicant: *Jelley* v. *Iliffe* [1981] Fam 128. Hence, what is in issue in deciding whether a cohabitee is eligible to apply is not the emotional relationship between her and the deceased, but whether she had been financially dependent. A woman who—as in *Horrocks* v. *Foray* [1975] 1 WLR 1351—had been provided with a house and an allowance by the deceased would thus qualify; but the mere fact that a couple live together, sharing a bed and a common household is not sufficient. Indeed, if they each have jobs and contribute more or less equally to the household expenses the survivor can have no claim under the Act, since he will not have been dependent.

Time of dependence

The applicant must show that the maintenance relationship existed   **12–40**
"immediately before the death" of the deceased. It is true that the courts

have regard to the settled basis or general arrangement between the parties; and an applicant will not be disqualified merely because there was no factual sharing, for example during the last few weeks of a terminal illness: *Re Beaumont* [1980] Ch 444. But the plaintiff in *Layton* v. *Martin* [1986] 2 FLR 227 (see para. 12–17 above) would not have been eligible to apply under this Act because her relationship had come to an end two years before the death in spite of the fact that her lover had promised her financial security out of his estate (which exceeded £350,000 in value). Even more dramatically, an application failed in *Kourkgy* v. *Lusher* (1981) 4 FLR 65 where the deceased died on August 7 having abandoned his mistress of 10 years standing on July 29.

What applicant must prove

12-41   If the applicant qualifies as a dependant under this head, he must then satisfy the court that the will and/or intestacy fail to make "such financial provision as it would be reasonable in all the circumstances of the case for the applicant to receive for his maintenance": 1975 Act, s.1(2)(*b*). In deciding this question the court is required to have regard to a number of matters set out in the Act (1975 Act, s.3(1)) relating to all applicants (such as the resources and needs of those concerned), and also to one matter relating solely to those qualifying on the basis of having been maintained by the deceased, namely "the extent to which and the basis upon which the deceased assumed responsibility for the maintenance of the applicant, and to the length of time for which the deceased discharged that responsibility": 1975 Act, s.1(4).

What order will be made?

12-42   If the court decides that reasonable provision has not been made it must then decide whether to order provision, and if so in what form. The court's powers to make periodical payments, property orders etc. are exactly the same as in the case of relatives: see para. 8–30 above. Some examples of successful applications are:

In *Malone* v. *Harrison* [1979] 1 WLR 1353 a 38-year-old woman had been the deceased's mistress (but had not shared a home with him as his wife) for 12 years, during which time he had given her some £4,000 yearly. The court ordered a lump sum of £19,000 out of an estate of some £480,000—using the analogy of a claim under the Fatal Accidents Act (see para. 12–51 below) to quantify her financial dependency.

In *Harrington* v. *Gill* (1983) 4 FLR 265, a 72-year-old woman had given up her tenancy of a council flat to live with the deceased as his wife. When he died eight years later he left some £65,000. His only other relative was a married daughter who was well established in life. The court ordered a lump sum of £5,000, periodical payments of £5,000 for the applicant's life, and settled the house on her for her life.

SOCIAL SECURITY

12-43   The benefits provided by the social security system are conveniently

divided into two main groups—contributory benefits and non-contribu- **12–43**
tory benefits.

Contributory Benefits
In relation to contributory benefits—such as retirement pension and **12–44**
widow's benefit—the existence of marriage is often important: a widow is
entitled to benefit in right of her status; and a wife may in certain
circumstances be able to rely on her husband's contributions in order to
found a claim to a benefit. In these cases the existence of a valid legal
marriage is all important—the cohabitee has no comparable entitlement.
Indeed, broadly speaking, the only relevance of cohabitation in relation to
contributory benefits is that cohabitation may result in benefit ceasing to
be payable. It is for example provided that a widow's pension shall not be
payable for any period during which she and a man to whom she is not
married are living together as husband and wife: Social Security Act 1975,
s.26(3).

Non-contributory benefits
The most important non-contributory benefit for present purposes is **12–45**
supplementary benefit. The main features of the scheme have been
outlined in Chapter 10, but the application of the scheme to unmarried
couples requires some elucidation.

Marriage irrelevant
The general principle embodied in the Supplementary Benefits Act **12–46**
1976 is that every person of or over the age of 16 whose resources are
insufficient to meet his requirements is entitled to benefit; but that in
certain cases the requirements and resources of one person (for example, a
wife) are required to be aggregated with, and treated as, those of another
person (for example, her husband). However, in sharp contrast to the
contributory benefits schemes, supplementary benefit—no doubt because
it is concerned with factual need rather than legal status—for many
purposes equates the rights of "married and unmarried couples." Thus,
rules require the aggregation of the requirements and resources of
unmarried as well as married couples; and a person whose requirements
and resources are required to be aggregated is disqualified from obtaining
benefit himself.

The cohabitation rule
The application of the so-called cohabitation rule has given rise to **12–47**
much controversy; but the underlying policy is quite clear. It is simply
that where a couple live together as husband and wife the fact that they
are not legally married should not make their position either better or
worse than a couple who are in fact married. If the rule did not apply, it
would mean that an unmarried couple would be significantly better off
than a married couple, since the "requirements" of two single people
total £59.60 whereas the "requirements" of a married couple are only
£48.40.

12–48   The Act seeks to carry this policy into effect by providing that the
expression an "unmarried couple" means a man and a woman who are
not married to each other "but are living together as husband and
wife ... " In practice, there is usually no difficulty in applying this
principle; but the attempt to equate the position of an unmarried couple
with that of a married couple does involve a conceptual difficulty. This is
because marriage is a legally recognised status, and the question whether
a couple are "married" does not involve any investigation of their
personal relationship, or any resolution of the question which of the
normal incidents of such a relationship (such as the use of a common
name or the existence of sexual relations) are essential and which are
superfluous. In contrast the question whether or not a couple are "living
together as husband and wife" does involve a difficult value judgment on
that issue:

> In *Crake* v. *Supplementary Benefits Commission* [1982] 1 All ER 498, considerable
> importance was attached to the couple's intention: it is necessary first to show
> that the unmarried couple are living in the same household; but it may also be
> necessary to go on and ascertain, in so far as this is possible, the manner in
> which and why the couple are living together in the same household. Since the
> applicant in that case had moved in simply to look after a sick and incapable
> person, he was not to be held to be living with her as her husband.

It is for the authorities to prove that cohabitation is occurring, but in
practice the position may appear rather different to a claimant; for if, after
investigation, the authorities conclude that cohabitation is occurring
benefit will be withdrawn, and it will be for the claimant to appeal. In
these circumstances, guidance given in the official Supplementary
Benefits Handbook is particularly useful, all the more so since the
guidelines have been judicially approved: see for example Woolf J. in
Crake v. *Supplementary Benefits Commission* [1982] 1 All ER 498 ("admir-
able signposts").

The official practice
12–49   The Handbook states (para. 2.13) that although there is no single way
by which the issue can be decided, in every case the main criteria to be
taken into consideration are as follows:

> "(a) *Members of the same household.* The man must be living in the
> same household as the woman and will usually have no other home
> where he normally lives. This implies that the couple live together,
> apart from absences necessary for the man's employment, visits to
> relatives etc.
> (b) *Stability.* Living together as husband and wife clearly implies
> more than an occasional or very brief association. When a couple
> first live together, it may be clear from the start that the relation-
> ship is similar to that of husband and wife (for example, if the
> woman has taken the man's name and has borne his child), but in
> cases where at the outset the nature of the relationship is less clear
> it may be right not to regard the couple as living together as

husband and wife until it is apparent that a stable relationship has been formed.

(c) *Financial support.* In most husband and wife relationships one would expect to find financial support of one party by the other, or sharing of household expenses, but the absence of any such arrangement does not of itself prove that a couple are not living together.

(d) *Sexual relationship.* Similarly, a sexual relationship is a normal part of a marriage and therefore of living together as husband and wife. But its absence at any particular time does not necessarily prove that a couple are not living as husband and wife, nor does its presence prove that they are.

(e) *Children.* When a couple are caring for a child or children of their union, there is a strong presumption that they are living as husband and wife.

(f) *Public acknowledgment.* Whether the couple have represented themselves to other parties as husband and wife is relevant. However, many couples living together do not wish to pretend that they are actually married. The fact that they retain their identity publicly as unmarried people does not mean that they cannot be regarded as living together as husband and wife."

MISCELLANEOUS RIGHTS

There is, as the Law Commission pointed out in 1980 (14th Annual   **12–50**
Report 1978–1979, para. 2.32) "a growing tendency for the law to attach specific legal consequences to relationships outside marriage." However, the legal response has been rightly described as "inconsistent, piecemeal and pragmatic": Astor and Nothdurft (1985) 48 MLR 61, 65. Some examples of this approach have already been given—for example, the Inheritance (Provision for Family and Dependants) Act 1975, and the Domestic Violence and Matrimonial Proceedings Act 1976—and the only advice which can safely be given is to examine the statute book in cases in which a claim is given to a spouse to see whether a comparable claim has been given to the unmarried. This may sometimes be done in terms (as in the Domestic Violence legislation) or sometimes (as with the Inheritance (Provision for Family and Dependants) Act 1975) by making eligibility depend on a qualification—in that case being maintained by the deceased—which unmarried partners are comparatively likely to satisfy.

A striking example of a recent extension of the rights of the "unmarried   **12–51**
spouse" is to be found in the Fatal Accidents Act 1976. Under section 1 of that Act (as substituted in 1982) an unmarried person may qualify as a dependant of his or her partner, and thus be eligible in certain circumstances to sue in tort for loss of financial support if, but only if, the following conditions are satisfied:

(a) that he was living with the deceased in the same household immediately before the date of death; and

(b) had been living with the deceased in the same household for at least two years before that date; and

(c) was living during the whole of that period as the husband or wife of the deceased.

Lack of consistency in statutory definitions significant

12-52   It will be noted that this legislation imposes specific tests about such matters as the length of time for which a relationship must have existed if the applicant is to qualify. The contrast with the supplementary benefits legislation, which equates the position of an unmarried couple and a married couple if they have been "living together as husband and wife," is striking. Again—to take a less well-known example—section 3(1)(c) of the Pneumoconiosis etc. (Workers' Compensation) Act 1979 defines a dependant who is entitled to apply for compensation under that Act as including a "reputed spouse" who was residing with the person concerned, but the expression is not further defined. There may well be valid policy reasons for these different statutory definitions; but it may perhaps be thought that the diversity merely reflects the fact that English law has no consistent policy governing the circumstances in which a "marriage-like" relationship should be equated with a marriage in terms of its legal consequences.

No right to income maintenance on termination of relationship

12-53   However inconsistent and piecemeal the law relating to the unmarried family may be, there is one clear principle which remains substantially unaffected. A man has a duty to maintain his wife; and if their relationship is ended by divorce the court can and usually will exercise its wide adjustive powers to ensure that proper financial arrangements are made. In contrast, the law imposes no duty on a man to maintain the woman with whom he is living, and the court has no general power to order financial provision when the relationship breaks down.

PART III—CHILDREN AND FAMILY LAW

This part of the book deals with children and the family—who has the legal authority to bring up a child? What criteria are to be applied if there is a dispute about his upbringing? How does the law seek to protect the child whose parents are involved in divorce? What legal procedures are there for providing long-term substitute care for a child? When is the state to be allowed to interfere in parents' decisions about child-rearing? Underlying all these questions is that of parental authority—what rights do parents, or sometimes other adults, have over children? This subject is dealt with in Chapter 13; and the rest of this Part is then arranged as indicated in para. 13–18 below.

PARENTAL AUTHORITY—WHAT IT IS,
AND WHO CAN EXERCISE IT

INTRODUCTION

The traditional view of English law is that a child's parent has certain   **13-01**
rights and authority in relation to that child—for example, to control his
movements, decide where he should live, where he should go to school,
what religion he should follow, and so on—throughout the child's
minority. Moreover, at common law, those rights were vested entirely in
the father. This is vividly illustrated by the case of *Re Agar-Ellis* (1883) 24
Ch.D 317:

> Mr Agar-Ellis decided to go back on the promise he had made to his wife that
> their children should be brought up as Roman Catholics; but the wife
> nevertheless continued to take the children to Roman Catholic services. Mr
> Agar-Ellis therefore got an injunction restraining her from doing so; and he
> subsequently took his daughter Harriet (along with his other children) away
> from their mother and arranged for them to be looked after by clergymen and
> others. When Harriet was 16 she asked to be allowed to spend her holidays with
> her mother instead of being moved about from one lodging to another. An
> application was made to the court for permission for her to spend the holiday
> with her mother, and for the mother to be allowed free access to her child. The
> court refused the application. In the absence of any suggested fault on the
> father's part, the court had no jurisdiction to interfere with his legal right to
> control the custody and education of his children.

Why parental authority is still relevant

That particular case now seems (in Lord Scarman's words) "horren-   **13-02**
dous", and can (for reasons which will appear) safely be "remaindered to
the history books": *Gillick* v. *West Norfolk and Wisbech Area Health
Authority* [1986] AC 112, 183. But parental authority still exists as a legal
concept. Someone has to have the power to act on behalf of a small
child—to decide for example whether a baby should have risky but
potentially life-saving surgery. For example:

> In *Re D (A Minor) (Wardship: Sterilisation)* [1976] Fam 185 the mother of an 11-
> year-old handicapped girl was concerned about the possibility that the girl
> might be seduced and give birth to an abnormal child. Acting on the advice of a
> consultant paediatrician and gynaecologist, she made arrangements for the
> child to be sterilised. In fact, the operation was not carried out; but if it had been
> the doctors could have relied on the mother's consent as a defence to any charge
> that they had behaved illegally. The mother had the right to consent to medical
> treatment on the child's behalf.

There are two main questions:
- (a) Who is entitled to exercise parental authority?
- (b) What powers are conferred on the person who has parental authority, for how long does that authority last, and how far may the exercise of parental authority be controlled?

Who is entitled to exercise parental authority?

13-03   This question can be answered briefly and comparatively clearly:

(i) *Both parents of a legitimate child* are now (Guardianship Act 1973, s.1(1)) equally entitled to exercise parental authority over their child. Each parent can act without consulting the other unless the other parent has "signified disapproval." There is a statutory procedure whereby the parents may refer particular matters about which they disagree to the court: para. 16–32 below.

(ii) *The mother of an illegitimate child* has parental authority exclusively; if the natural father wishes to have any legal rights he must apply to the court. This rule will be preserved by the Family Law Reform Act 1987 (see Chapter 19 below) in spite of the fact that the Act abolishes most of the legal disadvantages of birth outside marriage.

(iii) *The adoptive parents of an adopted child* are entitled to exercise parental authority to the exclusion of the natural parents: Children Act 1975, Sched. 1, para. 3 (see further para. 17–19).

(iv) *If a child is a ward of court* (see para. 15–01 below) the court stands in the position of his parents. In practice of course it will delegate routine decisions to those to whom it entrusts care and control of the child.

(v) *A guardian* appointed by a parent by deed or will has parental authority after the parent's death. A guardian appointed by the court is in a similar position: see para. 17–02 below.

(vi) *A local authority* in whose favour a care order has been made under the Children & Young Person's Act 1969 or which has assumed parental rights by resolution under the Child Care Act 1980 has parental authority (subject to a number of exceptions): (see para. 18–52 below)).

But authority may be divided

13-04   A court may (and in practice often does) "split up" parental authority—thus the court in wardship proceedings itself retains parental authority over the child, but it will often delegate care and control to an individual, and give other individuals the right of access to the child. Again, the divorce court will often give "custody" (an expression whose meaning cannot be precisely defined, but which includes most of the incidents of parental authority: para. 16–16 below) to one parent, whilst allowing the other reasonable access. Moreover, the Children Act 1975 created the institution of "custodianship" under which many parental rights are given, for example, to a foster-parent, but some rights remain with the natural parents. The way in which this allocation of responsibility works in each case is best considered when we look at the different procedures involved.

May be parental responsibility without parental power

A person may come under a legal liability to support a child without   **13-05**
acquiring any parental authority over him. The clearest case is that of the
father of an illegitimate child, who may be ordered to support the child
but who will have no parental rights unless a court in wardship or
proceedings under the Guardianship of Minors Act 1971 so orders. In
practical terms, however, the more important case may be that of the step-
parent: in the absence of a specific court order he has no parental
authority at all (see *Re N (Minors) (Parental Rights)* [1974] Fam 40) but he
will almost certainly be under a contingent liability to maintain the
child—who will be a "child of the family": para. 16–03 above—if divorce
or other proceedings are taken in respect of his marriage.

What is parental authority?

This question is difficult to answer. At one time, it would have been   **13-06**
possible to make a comparatively realistic list of the "parental rights," for
example:

(i)   the right to physical possession of the child;
(ii)   the right to control the child's education and to choose his
        religion;
(iii)   the right to inflict moderate and reasonable corporal punishment
        and otherwise to discipline the child;
(iv)   the right to consent to medical treatment (as in the sterilisation
        case of *Re D (A Minor) (Wardship: Medical Treatment)* [1981] 1 WLR
        1421, see para. 13–02 above);
(v)   the right to withhold consent from a proposed marriage;
(vi)   the right to administer the child's property and to enter into
        certain contracts on his behalf;
(vii)   the right to act for the child in legal proceedings;
(viii) the right to the child's domestic services (and possibly the right to
        receive payment for work which he does for others);
(ix)   various miscellaneous rights such as the right to choose the name
        by which the child should be known.

List of rights misleading

Today the position is far less clear—it has, for example, been held that a   **13-07**
father may be convicted of the common law offence of kidnapping his
own child in spite of the fact that he has a common law right to possession
of the child: *R. v. D* [1984] AC 78; and see also *R. v. Rahman* (1985) 81 Cr
App R 349, CA. However, as Lord Scarman has pointed out in the most
recent House of Lords decision, *Gillick* at p. 176, although parental rights
are of diminishing importance they clearly do exist and do not wholly
disappear until the age of majority (now 18). In the circumstances, the
least confusing way of trying to understand the law is to set out the factors
which have led to the erosion of parental authority as an absolute
concept; and in the light of that analysis, to summarise the present scope
and extent of parental authority.

Erosion of concept of parental authority

13-08   There are three main reasons which account for much of the difficulty in providing a straightforward account of the extent of parental authority:

(a) *Welfare paramount in disputes*

13-09   It is now provided by statute (Guardianship of Minors Act 1971, section 1) that if the legal custody or upbringing of a minor or the administration of his property is in issue "the court in deciding that question shall regard the welfare of the minor as the first and paramount consideration." The dramatic effect of this acceptance on the traditional view of the meaning of parental authority can be shown by reference to decided cases which establish two principles:

13-10   (i) *Child's welfare overrides wishes of natural parents.*

In *J* v. *C* [1970] AC 668 the question was whether a 10 year old child should be returned to his natural parents in Spain, or whether he should continue to be in the care of the English foster parents who had cared for him for all save some 18 months of his life. The House of Lords upheld the decision that he should remain here. The fact that his parents were "unimpeachable" could not outweigh the fact that to return a child who had been brought up as an English boy with English ways to a strange environment and to parents who would, on the evidence, have had difficulty in coping with his problems of readjustment, would have been inconsistent with his welfare.

In *Re B (A Minor) (Wardship: Medical Treatment)* [1981] 1 WLR 1421 the parents of a new-born and severely handicapped Downs syndrome child decided to refuse their consent to the removal of a potentially fatal intestinal blockage on the basis that in all the circumstances the kindest thing would be to allow nature to take its course. The Court of Appeal had to answer the question whether the life of this child was "demonstrably going to be so awful that the child must be condemned to die". The court, reversing the decision of the judge of first instance, held that it was in the child's interests to be allowed to live.

13-11   (ii) *Child's welfare prevails over considerations of justice between parents.* Sometimes the welfare of the child may conflict with what may be regarded as the essential justice of the case. Nevertheless, the child's welfare must be decisive:

In *Re K (Minors) (Children: Care and Control)* [1977] Fam 79 the wife of an Anglican clergyman had formed an adulterous relationship with a member of the church youth group. She wanted to set up house with him, but did not want to leave the matrimonial home without an order giving her custody of the children. She succeeded because the welfare of the children (aged five and two) allowed no other solution. The father could not provide care which would outweigh the risks of separating a two year old girl from her mother. The fact that the result might seem unjust to the father could not be allowed to affect the result.

As a result of the acceptance of the welfare principle, no person can be confident that his "authority" to act on behalf of a child will not be overridden by the court. But it is important to note that the court cannot apply the principle unless and until a case is brought before it: see para. 13–17 below.

(b) *Parental authority diminishes as child becomes capable of reaching own decisions*

Not all disputes about a child come before the court. Suppose, for **13-12** example, that a 16 year-old wishes to take a Saturday job to earn pocket money. Is his father entitled to prevent him from doing so? Until recently, the answer would probably have been that the right to control the availability of the child's services was a part of the father's parental rights (see para. 13–06 above); and that this authority arose at birth and continued until the child reached majority. Of course, the law recognised that a wise parent would not in fact seek to enforce his views against the wishes of an older child; and once the child had attained the "age of discretion" the court would not assist a parent who sought to do so. Nevertheless, in the traditional view, the fact that a particular child's intellectual or emotional development was advanced was irrelevant in deciding whether or not parental authority continued, for that was a matter of law: see *R. v. Howes* [1860] 1 E & E 332 and the judgment of Parker LJ in *Gillick* v. *West Norfolk and Wisbech Area Health Authority* [1986] AC 112, 128, CA.

The Gillick decision. This traditional view has now been overturned by **13-13** the decision of the House of Lords in *Gillick* v. *West Norfolk and Wisbech Area Health Authority* [1986] AC 112:

> Mrs Gillick, the mother of four daughters under the age of 16, sought an assurance from the authority that her daughters would not be given contraceptive treatment without her prior knowledge and evidence of her consent. The authority refused to give such an assurance. Mrs Gillick therefore asked the court to declare that DHSS advice to the effect that young people could in some circumstances be given contraceptive advice and treatment without their parent's knowledge and consent was unlawful and wrong, and adversely affected Mrs Gillick's right as the children's parent. The House of Lords, by a 3–2 majority, held that her application should have been dismissed.

The basis of the *Gillick* decision is that—in the absence of an express statutory rule (for example, that requiring parental consent to the marriage of his minor child: see para. 1–07 above)—all parental authority "yields to the child's right to make his own decisions when he reaches a sufficient understanding and intelligence to be capable of making up his own mind on the matter requiring decision." (see per Lord Scarman at p. 186) The question whether a child has sufficient understanding and intelligence must be an issue of fact in each case, depending on the complexity of the issues involved, and the child's emotional and intellectual maturity. In the case of contraception, it is clear that the House of Lords considered that a very high level of maturity and understanding was to be required; less complex issues would require a correspondingly less highly developed intellectual and moral understanding. Difficult though it may be to apply this approach in practice, it is clear that the question of whether a child has capacity to take decisions for himself is not to be determined by reference to any judicially pre-ordained age level: see also *R.* v. *D* [1984] AC 778. It is also clear that a child could in appropriate circumstances give a valid consent to medical treatment even though his parents were opposed to it, or were ignorant of the fact that he was seeking it.

13–14   The implications of the *Gillick* case are potentially far-reaching, and they have not yet been worked out. But it does seem to be clear that an assertion of parental authority can now be justified only insofar as it enables the parent to perform his duties to the child and the other children in the family: Lord Fraser of Tullybelton in *Gillick* at p. 170. The important point is that, once the child is of sufficient maturity to understand what is involved, the parent no longer has authority to take decisions on the child's behalf. It will thus be for the child—assuming he understands the relevant issues—to decide whether or not he will take the Saturday job, and his parents will have no right to stop him. Again, it will be for the child—subject to the same proviso—to decide whether to live at home or with friends—and the friends will be able to ignore the father's threats that he alone is entitled to decide where the child should live.

13–15   *The welfare principle and Gillick.* The *Gillick* decision is about the scope of parental authority. It does not directly affect the power and duty of the court (see para. 13–09 above) to resolve issues which come before it by reference to the child's welfare. The result could be a conflict between the child and the court—the court saying, for example, that a particular person should have care and control of a child, the child saying that he would rather have nothing to do with that person. In practice it is most unlikely that such a conflict would ever arise since the court would obviously take the views of a mature child into account in reaching its decision; but there are nonetheless some difficult conceptual problems which remain to be worked out.

(c) *Increasing powers of state intervention*

13–16   The third and final reason why the concept of parental authority is now so elusive and attenuated is the existence of a cascade of legislation—so described by Sachs L.J. in *Hewer* v. *Bryant* [1970] 1 QB 357, 371—affecting children. This is so complex that, in his words, a "bureaucrat's paradise and a citizen's nightmare" has been created. Much of this legislation is part of an elaborate code of legislative provisions whereby the state may interfere in parents' decisions about their children's upbringing—so that, for example, a parent's right to decide about the way in which his child should be educated is now severely circumscribed: see *Re S (A Minor) (Care Order: Education)* [1978] QB 1200 (see para. 18–48 below). In certain circumstances, the local authority may itself be able to take over the parent's own rights. Again, if divorce proceedings are started the court will—whether the parties want it to do so or not—insist on looking into the arrangements that are made for the upbringing of the children: see para. 16–08 below. In the circumstances the limits of family autonomy are far more confined than was the case a century ago. But the question of precisely where they should be drawn remains a very live issue.

The present scope, extent, and relevance of parental authority—summary

(i) Certain persons have legal authority to take decisions affecting the upbringing of a child; and this authority does not altogether disappear so long as the child is under the legal age of majority—for long 21, but now 18. **13–17**

(ii) That authority diminishes as the child gets older; and is in any case now severally circumscribed—particularly by the rule that if a case is brought to court in which the child's custody and upbringing is directly in issue the court will regard the child's welfare as being the first and paramount consideration.

(iii) Parental authority remains important, however, for a number of reasons. In particular:

(a) the person who is entitled to parental authority may, in the absence of any court order to the contrary, freely take action within the scope of his authority, and this action may in practice vitally affect the child and his future: see particularly *Re D (A Minor) (Wardship: Sterilisation)* para. 13–02 above.

(b) the legal framework of child law is at the moment still expressed largely in terms of empowering the court to make orders allocating parental authority—or "the parental rights and duties" in the words of one, widely used, statutory formula (see Children Act 1975, s.85(1)). Whatever may be the limitations on the scope of this concept, we need to understand how the court may allocate or delegate parental authority to others—giving one parent, for example, the right to have the child in his daily care whilst giving another the right to access, or perhaps giving the long-term care of the child to a third party (such as a foster-parent) whilst still preserving some long term legal standing in the birth parents. Difficult though it is to explain the precise bounds of parental authority, it is nevertheless that authority and its derivatives which courts allocate to adults.

ARRANGEMENT OF PART III

In this area of family law there is at least a general principle—namely, that the welfare of the child is the first and paramount consideration. The criteria applied by the court in deciding how to resolve welfare issues are considered in Chapter 14. In many respects, however, child law is concerned with the procedures which are available in any particular case; and the clearest, if not the most logical, way of approaching the subject is to examine those procedures in turn, as follows: **13–18**

THE WELFARE PRINCIPLE

· INTRODUCTION

Application almost universal
The provisions of section 1 of the Guardianship of Minors Act 1971 (set out at para. 13–09 above) enshrine the principle that the child's welfare is "paramount"; and it has been said that the welfare principle is applied "first, last and all the time"; and that it is the "golden thread"which runs through the whole of the court's custodial jurisdiction: Dunn J. in *Re D. (Justices' Decision: Review)* [1977] Fam 158, 163. This chapter tries to summarise factors which the court takes into account in deciding what it considers to be in the child's best interests. But there are certain limitations on the applicability of the welfare principle: **14-01**

(i) The child's welfare is only required to be treated as the paramount consideration in cases in which his custody or upbringing or the administration of his property is the central issue before the court. Hence: **14-02**

> In *Richards* v. *Richards* [1984] AC 174 the House of Lords refused to allow the child's welfare principle to determine the outcome of a dispute between a couple about the right to occupy the family home: see further para. 9–06 above.

(ii) There are certain statutory procedures in which Parliament has given a different emphasis to the child's welfare—for example, the fact that adoption or the making of a care order in favour of a local authority would be in the child's interests is not of itself sufficient, since special provisions apply in those cases: see Chapters 17 and 18 below.

(iii) There are some cases in which public policy may override considerations of an individual child's welfare. For example, the court will not allow the immigration policy approved by Parliament to be subverted merely because its application can be shown to be incompatible with the welfare of a particular child (see *Re Mohamed Arif* [1968] 1 Ch 643); and in one important case the court decided that the interests of a 14-year-old girl in not being exposed to the risk of suffering psychological damage in consequence of reading accounts of the sexual predilections of her deceased father could not outweigh the wider interests of freedom of publication: *Re X (A Minor) (Wardship: Jurisdiction)* [1975] Fam 47, para. 15–27 below.

WHO DECIDES?

14-03 Opinions may well differ, even between judges who take full account of all the factors discussed later in this Chapter, about what is in the child's best interests. Indeed, the courts have recognised that two reasonable parents can perfectly reasonably come to opposite conclusions on the same set of facts: see Lord Hailsham of St. Marylebone in *Re W (An Infant)* [1971] AC 682, 700. So a crucial question is: who is to take the decision if a case comes before the court?

The trial judge—not a welfare officer
14-04 The answer is that, save in exceptional cases, the decision will be taken by the judge at first instance. First of all, although the court will often seek a welfare report the function of such a report is simply to assist the court by providing the court with factual information on which to make a decision: see *Scott* v. *Scott* [1986] 2 FLR 320, CA, (where the court welfare officers had wrongly seen their primary duty as being to produce a conciliation between the parties). The welfare report may include a recommendation; but the decision is for the judge.

Role of Court of Appeal
14-05 There is a statutory right of appeal to the Court of Appeal in most cases involving the custody, education or welfare of a minor (see Supreme Court Act 1981, s.18(1)(*h*)); but the circumstances in which that court will interfere with the order made at first instance are, as a result of the decision of the House of Lords in *G* v. *G (Minors: Custody Appeal)* [1985] 1 WLR 647 extremely restricted. In that case, the House of Lords emphasised that in deciding appeals relating to custody a court was usually faced with a situation in which a choice had in effect to be made between two wrong solutions, each of which could plausibly be represented as the better—or less disadvantageous—for the child concerned. Hence an appeal court was concerned with an appeal against the exercise of a judicial discretion; and it would thus only interfere if the first instance judge had exercised his discretion on a wrong principle, or if the decision under consideration was so plainly wrong that the judge must have exercised his discretion on the wrong basis. However, it would appear that the appellant need not go quite so far as would be necessary if he were seeking judicial review of an administrative decision: he need not satisfy the appeal court that the decision was one which no reasonable judge, having taken account of the relevant factors, could have made. The distinction is a fine one.

WHAT FACTORS ARE REGARDED AS RELEVANT IN DECIDING ON THE CHILD'S WELFARE?

Limited value of precedents
14-06 Although it may be helpful to set out a list of factors which are often

referred to in custody cases, and give some indication of the court's contemporary approach, it must be emphasised that reported cases cannot be precedents in this area; everything must ultimately depend on the court's assessment of what the child's best interests require.

Relevance of particular matters

The following list of matters often raised in custody cases should be read with that warning in mind.   **14-07**

(a) *Material advantages*

The courts frequently state that welfare is not to be equated with material advantage: "affluence and happiness are not necessarily synonymous" (Griffiths L.J. in *Re P (Adoption: Parental Agreement)* [1985] FLR 635, 637. But equally clearly the court must be satisfied that the child's material needs—for example, for adequate housing, food, and in particular continuity of care—can be met.   **14-08**

(b) *Parental conduct*

For many years the court's view of a parent's conduct was often the decisive factor in custody cases—in particular, an adulterous mother would normally not be given custody of her child. But the modern view is that matrimonial misconduct is not as such relevant; what can be relevant is the effect it may have on the child: **14-09**

> In *Re K (Minors) (Children: Care and Control)* [1977] Fam 179 (see para. 13–11 above) the clergyman's adulterous wife succeeded both at first instance and on appeal, even though the result was tantamount to granting her a judicial licence to set up an adulterous household. The father believed that the children's spiritual welfare would suffer by their being brought up in the home of an adulterous couple; but the Court held that this could not justify his being granted care and control, since the mother would in any event have had liberal access to the children (including staying access) and the truth about the mother's relationship would inevitably sooner or later have been revealed to the children.

Conduct or behaviour may of course be taken into account if it affects the child's welfare:

> In *S v. S (Custody of Children)* (1978) 1 FLR 143 CA custody of children aged 5 and 7 was given to the father; and it was a material factor in the decision that the children might be caused embarrassment and social hurt if the facts about the mother's lesbian activities became known. Again, in *May v. May* [1986] FLR 325 it was held to be relevant to take the wife's conduct into account in so far as it enabled inferences to be drawn about the likely stability of the wife's new sexual relationship.

(c) *The blood tie*

It can be said quite categorically that the existence of a biological link between parent and child is not by itself a determining factor. The leading modern case on this subject is *J v. C* [1970] AC 668 (the facts of which are set out at para. 13–10 above). The courts refused to order the return of a   **14-10** child who scarcely knew his natural parents, notwithstanding the fact that the natural parents were "unimpeachable". To do so might have been disastrous. But, an even more dramatic illustration of the irrelevance of a purely biological link can be given:

> In *A* v. *C* (1978) [1985] FLR 445 CA a man entered into a "sordid commercial bargain" with a prostitute. She was to bear his child by AID, and then hand the child over to him. During the pregnancy she changed her mind and refused to do so. The father applied for access; and at first instance the judge held that he should have it: a parent should in principle have access to his child unless there was a very good reason to the contrary. The Court of Appeal held that this was wrong: the only factor justifying access on the facts of the case was the biological link, and that was insufficient.

14–11   This does not mean that the wishes of the natural parents will be ignored. The courts accept that a home with a natural parent is usually the best option, provided that the circumstances are right and a loving relationship exists; and this factor will often lead to the court trying to preserve a parental link where that is of value to the child (Lord Scarman in *Re E (SA) (A Minor) (Wardship)* [1984] 1 All ER 289, 292). The courts accept a degree of parental autonomy; and this may mean that the "natural parents have a strong claim to have their wishes considered; first and principally, no doubt, because normally it is part of the paramount consideration of the welfare of the infant that he should be with them, but also because as the natural parents they have themselves a strong claim to have their wishes considered as normally the proper persons to have the upbringing of the child they have brought into the world." (Lord Upjohn in *J* v. *C* at p. 724).

(d) Continuity of care

14–12   The courts are now well aware that young children need security; and Ormrod LJ said (*Re B (A Minor)* (1983) 13 Fam. Law 176, 177) that the fundamental rule of child care is that stability is all important and the maintenance of some sort of routine crucial. If a child has been in the care of one parent for a long period of time, a change of care and control should be contemplated with caution; and the courts show themselves anxious to avoid the disruption which would be caused by changing the child's present residence. It can be said that it is usually in the child's interests to preserve the status quo, because there is likely to be an emotional trauma of a significant kind if relationships and environment are changed on the transfer of a child from one parent to another. But the question is always one of fact:

> In *Allington* v. *Allington* [1985] FLR 586 the child was a girl aged 22 months at the date of the hearing. For the first 18 months of her life she had been at home with both her parents, but the mother then left her home and baby to live with another man. The parents established a routine under which the baby continued to spend a lot of time with the mother, and although the baby lived and slept at the father's home the child's bond with the mother was not materially impaired. The judge decided that although the "status quo" had not

lasted for very long, he should not take the risk of altering it. He accordingly made an order that the father should continue to have care and control of the child. On appeal, the court held he had been wrong to do so. In view of the short time which had elapsed there was not really a "status quo"; and nothing had happened which made it inappropriate for the mother to continue to bring up her daughter. The child was therefore to be transferred to the mother's care.

(e) *Mother best?*

14-13

Statements will be found in the reports that as a general rule it is better that very young children should be in the care of the mother, and that older boys should be in the care of their father, and girls with their mother. Although these are not principles or rules but rather judicial statements of general experience, whose application depends on the facts of every case, it does seem that judges usually accept that very young children should be with their mother unless some reason to the contrary can be shown: *M* v. *M (Custody of Children)* (1982) 4 FLR 603, 609. Indeed, *Allington* v. *Allington* (the facts of which have been summarised above) was much influenced by the view that a baby girl prima facie needs the care of her mother.

14-14

Nevertheless, it must be repeated that the test is one of the child's welfare, and that this is essentially a question of fact and judgment:

In *B* v. *B (Custody of Children)* [1985] FLR 166 a father who had decided to live on social security so that he could care for his 4 year old child was held to be entitled to custody. At first instance the trial judge had said that a father's primary role was to work and generate resources to provide support for himself and the child. The Court of Appeal held that it was wrong thus to show more concern for the welfare of the public purse than for the welfare of the child. Oliver L.J. pointed out the difficulty which would confront a father if it were held that a man who did not take paid employment to the limit of his capacity was not fit to care for his child. A father who did take paid employment would be unable to care for his child.

In *May* v. *May* [1986] 1 FLR 325 the court gave care and control of children aged 8 and 6 to the father, who had made arrangements with his employers to work hours which enabled him to take the children to school and be at home when they returned. The crucial factor was that the judge thought it to be in the best interests of the children to be brought up with the father's standards—which involved emphasis on fostering academic achievement and discipline—rather than to be exposed to the different and more free and easy standards which prevailed in the mother's household.

(f) *Brotherly love?*

14-15

Similar considerations apply to the supposed "principle" that siblings should not be separated. The court will give considerable weight to the support which children will give one another by living and growing together: see *Adams* v. *Adams* (1984) 5 FLR 768, CA; but that is merely one factor in determining how the child's welfare would best be served.

(g) *Religion*

14–16   Custody disputes were (as Scrutton L.J. put it in *Re J M Carroll* [1931] 1 KB 317, 331) for long primarily concerned, not with the body, but with the soul of a child. Today the court may still attach considerable importance to the continuance of religious education if a child has already embarked on it, but will usually refuse to pass judgment on the beliefs of parents; the only relevant question will be whether adherence to a particular sect (such as the Jehovah's Witnesses) will lead to the child's social isolation or other psychological damage or to the possibility of his suffering physically (for example, because of a risk that he may not be given a necessary blood transfusion).

14–17   The case of *Re B and G (Minors) (Custody)* [1985] FLR 134 is a recent reminder that religion may still determine the outcome of a case; for (in the judge's words) scientology was at the centre of the dispute about what was best for children aged 8 and 10. The mother had made agreements under which the father was to have custody of the children; and he still had the children in his care more than five years later. So far the balance would lie emphatically with not disturbing the status quo. But Latey J. (whose decision was upheld by the Court of Appeal: [1985] FLR 493) held that care and control should go to the mother, and that she be allowed to take the children to live with her abroad. The father was a practicising scientologist; the mother had broken with what the judge found on detailed examination to be an immoral, pernicious, socially obnoxious, corrupt, sinister and dangerous cult. It was obviously particularly relevant that the judge found that scientology set out to capture children and impressionable young people, and "indoctrinate them so that they became the unquestioning captives and tools of the cult, withdrawn from ordinary thought, living and relationships with others."

(h) *The child's wishes*

14–18   The court will take into account the wishes of the child; but the best way of ascertaining those views will often be by means of an interview with a skilled welfare officer. The traditional view is, however, that the decision must clearly be seen to be taken by the parents or the court, so that the responsibility does not rest with the children. As Dunn L.J. put it in *Adams* v. *Adams* [1984] FLR 768, 772:

> The children should not be allowed "to feel that they have to take the decision as between the father and the mother, with which of them they shall live. The pressures on children are quite sufficient when the marriage has broken down and one of the parents has left home without putting on them the additional burden of being made to feel that they have to decide their own future."

14–19   But it is at least arguable that, as a result of the *Gillick* decision [1986] AC 112 (see para. 13–13 above) the wishes of a child who can be shown to understand the issues involved should be allowed to determine the question of where he is to live; and it will be interesting to see whether the courts' practice in dealing with elder children will change in any way.

Certainly it would seem odd to find decisions like that in *Williamson* v.
Williamson [1986] 2 FLR 146, CA, where (so far as appears from the
report) the first instance judge seems to have paid little attention to the
expressed wishes of children aged 14 and 15 that they did not wish to live
with their mother. The issue is a difficult one, not least because judges are
reluctant to state with clarity matters which may well have influenced
their judgment, but which could further exacerbate already disrupted
family relationships.

The balancing exercise

By definition, the above list of factors taken into consideration cannot   **14-20**
be exhaustive, and it would be dangerously misleading to treat it as a
catalogue of relevant matters. The court must take all the relevant facts,
relationships, and claims and wishes of parents into the balance and
weigh them up in an attempt to reach the decision which will most serve
the child's welfare. "That," said Lord MacDermott in *J* v. *C* [1970] AC 668,
711, "is the first consideration because it is of first importance and the
paramount consideration because it rules upon or determines the course
to be followed."

Chapter 15

THE WARDSHIP PROCEDURE

INTRODUCTION

15-01   Most procedures involving children are subject to some conditions or restrictions—for example, that the child's parents are divorcing (see Chapter 16) or that a local authority believes that certain statutory conditions justifying the making of a care order are satisfied. Wardship is unique in not being subject to pre-conditions of this kind. Any child can be made a ward of court by issuing a summons under the provisions of section 41 of the Supreme Court Act 1981. Thereafter no important step in his life can be taken without the leave of the court, so long as the wardship continues. In deciding the issues which come before it the court will apply the principle that the child's welfare is paramount. The result is that in any case involving a child the lawyer will have to ask whether wardship should be invoked in preference to some other procedure.

The wardship jurisdiction is of great antiquity; but its flexibility, and the wide range of the powers and remedies at the court's disposal make wardship a remarkable example of the adaptation of a long-standing institution to modern circumstances.

CHARACTERISTICS OF WARDSHIP

Any person may make a child a ward of court
15-02   Any person may issue a summons making a child a ward of court (and in cases of urgency orders can be made before the summons has been issued by a judge sitting at his home, or even over the telephone). Proceedings have, for example, been started by:

15-03   (i) A concerned neighbour or friend, as in *Re D (A Minor) (Wardship: Sterilisation)* [1976] Fam 185, the facts of which have been given at para. 13–02 above.

15-04   (ii) A relative or other person who has no standing under any of the various statutory procedures dealt with in Chapters 16 and 17 of this book:

In *B v. W (Wardship: Appeal)* [1979] 1 WLR 1041 a wealthy grandfather who hoped that his grandson would succeed him in the business he had built up arranged for the grandson to go to boarding school. The boy's mother (who resented her father's domination and regarded him as seeking to gain control over the son's upbringing) decided after about three years to take him away from the school. The grandfather made the boy a ward; and it was held that he had behaved properly in so doing. "Where there is serious conflict between

166

grandparents and their children and they are unable to agree as to what will be in the best interests of the grandchildren" wardship may be the only way to secure a satisfactory solution, said Viscount Dilhorne.

Again, wardship may in exceptional cases be invoked if a person who is officially involved in local authority child care procedures considers that a decision not to pursue them is a serious error detrimental to the child's welfare:

In *Re JT (A Minor) (Wardship: Committal to Care)* [1986] 2 FLR 107, CA a local authority removed a child at birth from his mother (who had been sentenced to imprisonment for wounding his elder brother) and started care proceedings (see para. 18–36 below). However, the authority decided to try to rehabilitate the child with his mother. The guardian *ad litem* appointed by the court (see para. 18–87 below) was dismayed that such a decision had been taken, and made the child a ward of court, thereby causing the whole issue to be reviewed by the High Court. The judge expressed strong approval of the guardian's "very brave" action in warding the child.

(iii) A man who has inseminated a woman artificially, with the **15-05** intention that she should be a surrogate mother, bearing a child to be handed over at birth:

In *Re C (A Minor) (Wardship: Surrogacy)* [1985] 0 FLR 846 the applicant was an American whose wife was unable to bear children. He contacted an agency in America and entered into a contract whereby the agency, in return for a cash payment, undertook to find a surrogate mother who would bear his child and hand it over to the applicant and his wife for them to bring up. The court held that the methods used to produce the child were irrelevant; and that it would be best for the baby that her care and control be given to the applicant and his wife. They were accordingly given leave to take the child out of the country. (For an earlier surrogate parenting case, see *A v. C* (1978) (1985) FLR 445, para. 14–10 above).

(iv) A local authority may institute wardship proceedings if its statutory **15-06** powers (dealt with in Chapter 18 below) are inadequate to secure the welfare of the child—for example, if it cannot establish a sufficient ground on which to base a parental rights resolution (see, *e.g. Crosby (A Minor) v. Northumberland CC* (1982) 12 Fam 92; *Lewisham LBC v. Lewisham Juvenile Court Justices* [1980] AC 273) or if it has failed in an application for a care order under the Children & Young Persons Act 1969: *Re C (A Minor) (Justices' Decision: Review)* (1979) 2 FLR 62. The local authority may also invoke wardship in aid of its statutory powers and duties in respect of children in care—for example, to obtain an injunction restraining a person from going within a specified distance of the child's home or establishing any contact with him: see *Re B (A Minor) (Wardship: Child in Care)* [1975] Fam 36: para. 18–73 below.

(v) The fact that there are no formal restrictions on the institution of **15-07** wardship proceedings may sometimes lead to abuse. In *Re Dunhill* (1967) 111 SJ 113, a night club owner made a 20-year-old girl a ward of court largely for publicity purposes. The procedural rules were changed so that it is now necessary for the applicant to state his relationship to the minor; and the proceedings will be dismissed if they are an abuse of the process of the court.

All important issues affecting a ward must be referred to the court

15–08   Once a child has become a ward the court exercises an extensive and, if necessary, detailed control over him. In the exercise of this jurisdiction the court's powers are very wide; and in deciding what is to happen the court will not necessarily confine itself to considering the course of action proposed by the parties, because the court has the ultimate responsibility for the child's future: *Re E (SA) (A Minor)* [1984] 1 All ER 289 (where the House of Lords decided to take a course of action which had not been considered in the courts below in an attempt to prevent a final break between the child and the natural parents.)

15–09   No important step in the child's life can be taken without the court's consent and all important issues affecting the ward must be brought before the court. Amongst the issues which the court has decided are:

15–10   (i) whether a new-born child should be taken to live abroad by a couple who had made a surrogate parenting agreement: *Re C (A Minor) (Ward: Surrogacy)* (above);

15–11   (ii) with whom should a child live? Probably the commonest issue in wardship is who should have the care and control of the child—should he live with his mother, or a foster-parent, or his grandparent, should he be placed for adoption, etc., But the court has complete control:

> In *Re F (orse. A) (A Minor) (Publication of Information)* [1977] Fam 58 the court made an order that a 15 year old ward should not be harboured by a "very bad character" of 28 who was one of a hippy gang doing no work but squatting in empty premises and taking drugs.
> In *Re CB (A Minor) (Wardship: Local Authority)* [1981] 1 WLR 379 a local authority was rebuked for moving a child from one foster-parent to another without leave of the court.

15–12   (iii) whether an abortion should be carried out on a ward—

> In *Re P (A Minor)* [1986] 1 FLR 272 the ward, Shirley, who was 15, had a baby (born when Shirley was only 13) for whom she was caring in a mother and child unit with schooling facilities. Shirley became pregnant again, and wanted an abortion. Shirley's parents were against this on religious grounds, and also because they thought Shirley would live to regret having her child aborted. They offered to care for the existing baby so that Shirley could herself care for the new-born child. The court, applying the principle that the ward's welfare was paramount, decided that Shirley's pregnancy be terminated. If it were not, Shirley's own growing-up as a child would be endangered, and there would be a risk of injury to her mental health.

(iv) Whether any other medical treatment or examination should take   **15–13**
place:

In *Re B (A Minor) (Wardship: Medical Treatment)* above the court had to decide
whether a severely handicapped baby should be allowed to live or die. The
court decided in favour of life: see para. 13–10 above.

The wardship court has wide and effective powers

Once a child becomes a ward certain consequences automatically   **15–14**
follow. For example, it is a contempt, without leave of the court, to marry
the ward or to remove any child named in a wardship summons from the
country.

The court also has a wide range of powers to enforce its orders by
injunction, breach of which will be a contempt. Thus, it was once
common for parents to make their daughter a ward in an attempt to bring
to an end an association of which they disapproved; and the court would
in a proper case grant an injunction restraining the girl from communicating with the man in question.

The wardship court has much more extensive and flexible powers than   **15–15**
are available in most civil proceedings. For example, it is a general rule
that an order can only bind the parties to proceedings; but:

In *X County Council* v. *A and another* [1985] 1 All ER 53 the court held that it had
power to grant an injunction, operating against the world at large, prohibiting
publication of facts which would have revealed that the ward's mother was
Mary Bell (a person who at the age of 11 had been found guilty, after a trial
involving much publicity, of killing two small boys).

Evidence in wardship cases will be on affidavit, supported by oral
evidence at the hearing. The reliance on affidavit evidence stems
originally from the practice of the Chancery Court which used to exercise
the jurisdiction; but the practice is found to be helpful in helping to ensure
that the issues are clearly formulated, and that all those concerned are
given notice of the matters in dispute.

Wardship proceedings are not subject to the normal rules of evidence   **15–16**
and procedure applicable to ordinary litigation (where the judge is simply
an arbiter between two parties, and need only consider what they choose
to put before him). The judge may see the child and perhaps one or other
or both parents in private if he considers it desirable to do so. It is the
practice to admit hearsay evidence if that is the best available; and the
judge may take into account the contents of a confidential report (*e.g.* by
the Official Solicitor who sometimes represents the ward) without
disclosing those contents to the parents, even though the ordinary rules of
natural justice might require the disclosure of any adverse allegations
against them.

ANCILLARY POWERS

15–17   Although most of the powers of the court are inherent, these powers have been supplemented by a number of statutory provisions. The more important are:

Maintenance
15–18   Under the Family Law Reform Act 1969 the court has power to order either parent of a ward of court to pay periodical sums to the other parent or to any other person having the care and control of the ward or to the ward himself. The payment may be continued until the ward attains 21.

Care and supervision orders
15–19   The usual order in wardship proceedings is to grant care and control to one of the parties, and continue the wardship. The Family Law Reform Act 1969 extended the powers of the wardship court in two important respects:
(a) the court has power to commit a ward who is under 17 to the care of a local authority (see para. 18–57 below) if there are "exceptional circumstances making it impracticable or undesirable" for him to be or to continue to be under the care of either of his parents or of any other individual.
(b) the court has power, if there are "exceptional circumstances" to make a supervision order (see para. 18–55 below) in favour of a local authority or welfare officer.

15–20   However, these statutory powers to make orders are subject to a number of conditions; and it has been held that they do not cut down the inherent powers of the court:

In *Re SW (A Minor) (Wardship: Jurisdiction)* [1986] 1 FLR 24 a 17-year-old girl stole jewellery from her mother, ran away from home on a number of occasions "after some of which she returned very much the worse for drink and showing clear signs of having indulged in sexual intercourse," had her hair shaved, and was tattooed. The statutory power to commit her to care did not exist since she was too old; but the judge held that the court retained its inherent power to place her in the care and control of the local authority, and that the court could if appropriate give directions that she be accommodated in secure accommodation.

THE COURTS WITH JURISDICTION

15–21   Traditionally, the wardship jurisdiction was exercisable only in the High Court; and it is still only the High Court which can make an order that a minor be made a ward of court, or that a ward of court should cease to be a ward. However, the judges of the High Court no longer have a monopoly over wardship cases:

(i) The Matrimonial and Family Proceedings Act 1984 enables the High   **15–22**
Court, either of its own motion or on the application of any party to the
proceedings, to transfer wardship proceedings to a county court. (It must
be emphasised that the proceedings must still be started in the High
Court). A *Practice Direction (family business: transfer between High Court
and county courts)* [1986] 2 All ER 703 gives some guidance about the
allocation of cases—the general principle is that wardship, in common'
with other family proceedings, may be dealt with in the county court, but
that some classes of case (for example, where a local authority is or
becomes a party) should normally be dealt with in the High Court. It is
too early to say how these powers of transfer to the County Court (which
only came into force on April 25, 1986) will in practice be exercised. They
may lead to some reduction in the number of wardship cases because
there seems little doubt that the experience and specialist knowledge of
the Family Division judges was one of the reasons which accounted for
the increasing use of wardship.

(ii) Even if the case is still being dealt with in the High Court, that   **15–23**
jurisdiction (as a result of the flexible system introduced by the Courts Act
1971) may be, and in some parts of the country is in practice, often
exercised by a circuit judge sitting as a High Court judge, and indeed it
may sometimes be exercised by a barrister sitting as a deputy High Court
judge.

Duration of Wardship

Although a child becomes a ward of court automatically on the making   **15–24**
of an application to that effect, he will cease to be a ward unless an
appointment for the hearing of the summons is made within 21 days.
   A child ceases to be a ward on attaining his majority—*i.e.* 18—and no
order can be made in respect of a person who has attained 18.
   The High Court may at any time, either on application by a party or of
its own motion, order that wardship shall cease.

Welfare Paramount—First, Last, and (Nearly) All the Time

One of the great advantages of wardship has always been that it is   **15–25**
characterised by the "golden thread" as Dunn J. described it in *Re D (A
Minor) (Justices' Decision: Review)* that the welfare of the child is
considered "first, last and all the time". The court is not limited to
deciding the particular dispute which may have precipitated the proceedings: its duty (to quote Lord Scarman in *Re E (SA) (A Minor) (Wardship:
Court's Duty)* [1984] 1 WLR 156 is to act in the way best suited to serve the
true interest and welfare of the child, whose welfare is its paramount
concern. However, the principle that the child's welfare is paramount is

not entirely without exception (see para. 14–02 above), and there are two particular qualifications on the principle in the context of wardship:

15-26   (i) The fact that a child is in the care of a local authority under the statutory child care code (see Chapter 18 below) does not in principle mean that the wardship jurisdiction is for all purposes ousted or abrogated. The local authority may itself make the child a ward of court (as in the abortion case, *Re P (A Minor)* discussed at para. 15–12 above) and the court may exercise its powers to assist the local authority by granting injunctions etc. in support of its statutory duties. But it has been firmly laid down by the House of Lords (*A* v. *Liverpool City Council* [1982] AC 363; *Re W (A Minor) (Wardship: Jurisdiction)* [1985] AC 791) that it is not for the courts to allow the wardship jurisdiction to be used to exercise a supervisory or reviewing role over the merits of decisions taken by local authorities within their statutory powers. Attempts to use the wardship jurisdiction to question local authority decisions about parental access and other matters have thus been decisively rejected. This important question is further discussed at para. 18–72 below.

15-27   (ii) In deciding whether (and how) to exercise its powers over a child who has become a ward there will be occasions when the court must consider not only the child's interests but also the rights of outsiders and the public interest. For example:

In *Re X. (A Minor) (Wardship: Jurisdiction)* [1975] Fam 47 the defendants proposed to publish a book containing explicit descriptions of the sexual predilections and behaviour (variously described as "bizarre," "salacious," "scandalous" and "revolting") of the deceased father of a 14-year-old girl. It was accepted that if she were to read the book or hear about it from others it would be psychologically grossly damaging to her. At first instance an injunction was granted to prevent publication, on the basis that this was necessary to prevent injury to the ward. On appeal, however, it was held that the interests of the child should not prevail over the wider interests of freedom of publication.

Chapter 16

CHILDREN IN FAMILY BREAKDOWN—THE LEGAL PROCEDURES

Introduction

A parent whose relationship is breaking up may want the security of a   **16-01**
court order to regulate the allocation of parental authority over the
children between him and his partner; and he may want an order that his
partner provide financially for the children. Numerically most of these
cases now end up in the divorce court—which, in any event, will consider
custody matters whether or not the divorcing parents want it to do so. So
the first part of this Chapter deals with children in divorce. The second
part briefly outlines the other private law procedures which may be
invoked to deal with custody of children and related matters. The variety
is somewhat bewildering; but the different procedures each have their
distinctive characteristics.

Children in Divorce

The scale of the problem

A large number of children are involved in divorce. In 1984, 83,530   **16-02**
divorcing couples had one or more children aged under 16. In that year,
148,600 children under 16 were involved in their parents' divorce. 43,909
of those children were under five years old; and 56,810 were aged
between 5 and 10. It has been estimated that, if present trends continue,
one in 22 children will experience their parents' divorce by the age of five,
and one in five children will experience their parents' divorce before
turning 16: see J. Haskey, "Children of Divorcing Couples" (1983)
Population Trends, No 31.

In an attempt to mitigate any adverse effects divorce may have on the
large number of children involved, the court has been given exceptionally
wide powers to make orders for custody and financial matters. Perhaps of
greater significance is the fact that the court—in contrast to its traditional
role in civil litigation—has been given a wide inquisitorial and protective
role in an attempt to ensure that satisfactory arrangements are made for
children before the marriage is finally dissolved.

Before dealing with the court's powers we must analyse the definition
of the children over whom the court's powers can be exercised.

Children over whom court's powers exercisable

The court's powers can be exercised over any *"child of the family"*; and   **16-03**
there are restrictions on the courts' powers to grant final decrees if the
couple have such children. The Matrimonial Causes Act 1973, s.52(1)
provides that:

"child of the family,' in relation to the parties to a marriage, means—
(a) a child of both of those parties; and
(b) any other child, not being a child who has been boarded-out with those parties by a local authority or voluntary organisation, who has been treated by both of those parties as a child of their family."

16-04   *This definition is extremely wide.* All children of both parties to the marriage—whether they be legitimate, legitimated, illegitimate, or adopted—are included within it; but the definition goes much further, and makes the existence of a biological—or even a formal legal relationship (such as adoption)—between the child and the parties irrelevant. A child will be within the definition if he has simply been "treated" as a child of the family by both parties. A child who is being looked after by relatives on a long term basis will thus be a child of their family; as will a child who is privately fostered by them. (A child who is boarded out by a local authority is excluded, no doubt because it was thought that the local authority would make appropriate arrangements in such a case.)

16-05   A *step-child* living with the spouses will also be within the definition—and if his parents' previous marriage was ended by divorce he will also remain a child of their family. The definition thus accurately reflects the erosion of traditional kinship patterns incidental to increasing divorce and remarriage, as a result of which a child may have links (biological and/or factual) with several different marriages.

16-06   *But not an unborn child.* It has been held to be impossible to treat an unborn child as a child of the family: if a man marries a woman who is pregnant by someone else the baby will be a child of his family if he treats it as such after birth—even if the wife has deceived him into thinking that he was the father. But if the relationship breaks down before the birth the child will be outside the definition, whatever the husband may have said about his intentions to treat the baby as his own: see *A v. A (Family: Unborn Child)* [1974] Fam 6.

Safeguarding the Welfare of Children in Divorce

16-07   The policy of the divorce legislation is to emphasise the importance of the welfare of the children. First, the court is now directed to give first consideration in considering the exercise of its financial powers to the welfare of children of the family. This provision has already been discussed: see paras. 11–54 above. Secondly, a procedure has been developed in an attempt to ensure that proper custody and access arrangements are made for the children, and that these are considered by the court. Thirdly, the court has available a number of special powers designed to ensure that investigations can be made and that the court should have the information it needs. Finally, the orders available to the court in relation to custody and access are wide-ranging and flexible.

1. The judicial appointments procedure

Section 41 of the Matrimonial Causes Act 1973 is intended to ensure that the court does not overlook the question of the interests of the children. Its effect is that the court must not make a decree absolute unless it has made a so-called *declaration of satisfaction* to the effect that the arrangements for the welfare of every child of the family who is under 16 (or older and still in education or training) are "satisfactory or are the best that can be devised in the circumstances," or that it is impracticable for such arrangements to be made. (The court may also make the decree absolute if there are circumstances making it desirable that the decree should be made absolute without delay). If the court fails to make such a declaration any final decree will be void (with the result that any subsequent marriage by either party would itself be void). However, inaccuracies in a declaration do not affect its validity.   **16-08**

Special procedure cases
A decree nisi can be obtained under the special procedure (see para. 3–09 above) without the parties having any personal contact with a judicial officer; but a judge will look into arrangements for the children at a special "children's appointment." (It is no doubt significant that this function is reserved to a judge, whereas a Registrar can make financial orders in even the most complex cases.) The appointment will normally be for the day on which the judge has pronounced the decree nisi in the case; and research suggests that usually only one of the parents attends; and that the hearing is often short—the average time taken in a sample at Bristol was only 10 minutes.   **16-09**

The Booth Committee made a number of proposals for increasing the effectiveness of the procedure—for example by using a detailed question-naire—in an attempt to involve both parents at an early stage and to emphasise their continuing joint responsibility for their children. The Committee appreciated the argument that the court's duty under section 41 "is not an adjudicative function and that it smacks of paternalism". But it concluded that the matter was of such general importance that it could not consider recommending repeal without proposing the substitution of some practicable alternative; and the Committee noted that they had not received any suggestion as to what that could be: para. 2.24.   **16-10**

2. Power to make inquiries—welfare reports

The court may at any time refer to a court welfare officer for investigation and report any matter arising in matrimonial proceedings which "con-cerns the welfare of a child." (Matrimonial Causes Rules 1977, r.95(1)), and extensive use is made of the power. Surveys have found that a report   **16-11** was called for in more than half of contested custody cases, and also in a significant number of uncontested cases. The court has a complete discretion as to whether it should order a report or not; but it is common to do so even in uncontested cases—if, for example, the child has not been in the care of the same person between separation and petition, or if a change in the child's residence seems to be in issue. The mere fact of contest often leads the court to order a welfare report. Sometimes, the reference will specify particular matters on which a report is required; but this must not prevent the reporting officer from bringing to the notice of the court any other matters which he considers that the court should have in mind: *Practice Direction (Divorce: Welfare Report)* [1981] 1 WLR 1162.

What the welfare officer does

16–12   The primary function of the welfare officer is to assist the court by providing the court with the factual information on which to make a decision: *Scott* v. *Scott* [1986] 2 FLR 320. The officer (who may be a member of a specialist team, or a probation officer doing other work as well) has power to inspect the court file. He will then usually interview all the parties; and his report should contain a statement of their different proposals for the future care of the children. It should also contain—

   a statement of the conditions, both material and otherwise, in which the children are living or in which it is proposed that they should live;
   a reference to, or summary of, any relevant reports on the family and the children by independent persons such as doctors, school teachers, social workers, probation officers and police records;
   a statement of the relations of the children with each of their parents, including, when the children are old enough, a summary of their own views about their respective parents and their homes, and their own wishes as to the future.

Confidentiality

16–13   The report can be inspected by the parties, but it is to be treated as confidential and should not be shown to anyone other than the parties and their legal advisers. The court may if it thinks it appropriate order the officer to attend the hearing and submit himself to cross-examination by the parties.

Recommendations

16–14   The report may (and usually will) contain a recommendation; and this may be of great significance because it has been held (*Clark* v. *Clark* (1970) 114 SJ 318) that if courts do differ from the welfare officer's report, it is essential for them to explain why they have done so. However, the decision is for the court, not for the welfare officer.

3. Orders which can be made

Independent of outcome of dispute between parents

Although the divorce court's wide and flexible powers can only be **16–15** invoked if divorce or other proceedings have been started, once that has been done the policy of the legislation is to make the exercise of the court's powers substantially independent of the result of the litigation between husband and wife. Hence section 42(1) of the Matrimonial Causes Act 1973 empowers the court to make such orders as it thinks fit for the custody (which includes access) and education (which includes training) of any child of the family who is under the age of 18, either on granting the decree or before or after it—in practice the court may well make interim orders before the granting of the decree nisi, but the hearing of the main custody issue will usually be deferred until after the decree. Even if the suit is dismissed, the court can still make orders either at once or "within a reasonable period after the dismissal."

What is custody?

The court is primarily concerned with the making of "custody" orders; **16–16** but unfortunately it is not entirely clear what that expression means. For some 50 years it was generally assumed that "custody" in a divorce court order referred to what Sachs L.J. (in *Hewer* v. *Bryant* [1970] 1 QB 357, 373) described as "a bundle of rights and powers" extending beyond the right to have physical possession of the child to such matters as giving consent to medical treatment, choosing education and religion, and so on. Hence the divorce court would sometimes make so called "split orders" giving custody to H and care and control to W—the understanding being that W would have the child in her daily care but that H would retain the right to make long term decisions, for example about education.

The decision in *Dipper* v. *Dipper* [1981] Fam 31, CA has cast doubt on **16–17** this view. In that case, the court said that it was "a misunderstanding" to think that a parent who had a custody order in his favour could control the child's education. Secondly the court said that whatever custody order had been made neither parent had any "pre-emptive right" with respect to education or any other major matter. Both were entitled to know and to be consulted, and if there is a disagreement either may bring the matter before the court.

Possibly the least unsatisfactory interpretation of the decision in *Dipper* is that although a parent who has custody may in principle take decisions, yet he should not do anything of major importance without consulting the other and either obtaining his agreement or bringing the matter to the court. However it is impossible to be confident about the precise effect of the decision; whilst the decision in *Gillick* v. *West Norfolk and Wisbech Area Health Authority* [1986] AC 112, HL, para. 13–13 above, adds yet further uncertainty to the analysis of custody rights. Whatever the position may be as a matter of strict law, research carried out by Priest and Whybrow on behalf of the Law Commission (Supplement to Working Paper No 96, para. 5.20) suggests that those involved in divorce generally (if errone-ously) equate sole custody with "complete control" subject to a number of exceptions—for example, concerned with the right to change the child's name: see para. 16–19 below—and (wrongly) assume that a custody order is final and irrevocable.

4. Orders which are made

16–18 Against this background of uncertainty, it seems best to outline the seven types of order which are in fact made by the court; and (so far as is possible) explain their effect:

(1) Custody to wife, access to husband
16–19 In practice, this is the order which is most frequently made by the divorce court. The Judicial Statistics record that 63,540 out of a total of 82,059 custody orders made in matrimonial cases in county courts were in favour of the wife (Table 4.10); and Priest and Whybrow (see above) conclude that at all age groups mothers were more likely to be granted sole custody, on average at a ratio of 10 to 1: para. 4.24. Again, access orders are made in a high proportion of cases—83% of those in which the order gave custody to the wife: Priest and Whybrow, Table 11.

What is the legal meaning and effect of these orders?

(a) *Custody*
It can be said with certainty that under such an order the custodial parent is entitled to have the child reside with her, but it is not clear how far she is entitled to take decisions about such matters as medical treatment or schooling without consulting the other parent: see para. 16–17 above.

One particular problem which troubled the courts was the choice of surname by which the child should be known. In particular, if the mother remarried she might well wish that the child be known by her new husband's name, whereas the child's father might wish the child to retain his name as a symbolic assertion of the child's links with his paternal family. This has now been dealt with by a Rule of Court: orders for custody or care and control provide that no step (other than the institution of proceedings in a court) be taken by the parent which would result in the child being known by a new surname except with the leave of a judge or the consent in writing of the other parent (MCR 1977, r. 92(8)).

(b) *Access*
16–20 The question of access gives rise to considerable problems in practice. The English courts have not adopted the doctrine eloquently advocated by Goldstein Freud and Solnit in *Beyond the Best Interests of the Child* that continuing access by the non-custodial parent is against the child's interests. English courts will usually consider it to be in the child's interests that his natural father should be able to preserve his links with the child; and Priest and Whybrow suggest that the large number of

access orders made reflects judicial concern that access should be encouraged. If the custodial parent is recalcitrant over access, the court is likely to stress the importance of contact for the child's welfare, as well as a matter of the child's entitlement; and several judges in the Survey took active steps to resuscitate access: para. 6.13.

But the factor which determines whether or not access will be ordered is the child's welfare; and in some cases (3.9% of all access orders made: Priest and Whybrow para. 6.18) access will be refused. For example:

> In *Re BC (A Minor) (Access)* [1985] FLR 639 the court denied a father access to his child on the ground that his behaviour caused his former wife genuine anxiety which might affect her own capacity to care for the child. This factor could be taken into account even though the conduct complained of had no direct effect on the child.

Types of access order. The simplest type of access order merely provides that the non-custodial parent have *reasonable access* to the child and it is then for the parents to agree on how that is to be arranged. The order may, however, be more specific. In particular, it may provide that the non-custodial parent is to have *staying access;* that is to say the right to have the child to stay with him, for example at weekends or during holiday periods. Sometimes the court is asked to *define access;* and such orders may be extremely detailed, specifying precisely the time and place at which visits are to take place, the arrangements for the child's return, and so on. Sometimes the court may order that access be *supervised.* Finally, *conditions may be imposed* on an order giving access, for example, that a child be not brought into contact with a named person.

(2) Custody to husband, care and control to wife

The divorce court has power to make *split orders* giving custody to one parent, and care and control to the other. However, such orders are made very rarely indeed—none of the judges interviewed by Priest and Whybrow (see para. 5.40) recalled having made such an order. The judicial view that such orders are generally undesirable (*Dipper* v. *Dipper* [1981] Fam 31, CA, and *Williamson* v. *Williamson* [1986] 2 FLR 146, CA) is partly based on the fact that split orders can give rise to serious difficulties—for example, the parent with "custody" and thus with the right to take decisions on important issues such as medical treatment might not be available when a decision is urgently needed. But there is no inviolable rule against the making of a split order: once again the fundamental question is simply whether in all the circumstances such an order would be best from the point of view of ensuring the welfare of the child: Purchas L.J. in *Williamson* (above) at p. 150. Thus:

16-21

> In *Jane* v. *Jane* (1983) 4 FLR 712, CA there was no dispute that the mother should have the care and control of the child; but her religious beliefs taught her that it was against God's law for a child to have a blood transfusion. In those circumstances, the court, exceptionally, made a split order giving the father custody and the mother care and control. Such an order would enable the father to authorise a blood transfusion if an emergency arose.

(3) Custody to husband and wife jointly, care and control to wife (or husband)

16-22   This is what English lawyers call a ⌈*joint custody order.*⌉ (In some countries, the expression refers to an arrangement whereby the child divides his time between the two parents.) A joint custody order in the English sense recognises that both parents retain their right to be consulted on any major decisions affecting the child's upbringing, whilst accepting that he will normally have his home with only one parent. The Booth Committee pointed out that an order vesting custody in one parent alone could be seen as carrying with it the termination of the other parent's role in the children's lives; and expressed the wish that joint orders should be made wherever that is in the best interests of the children. The Committee hoped that this would come to be in the vast majority of cases: para. 2.27.

The Judicial Statistics record that in 1985 10,607 joint custody orders were made (out of a total of 82,059 orders): Table 4.10; and Priest and Whybrow (see para. 16–17 above) suggest that the proportion of joint orders has increased significantly—from some 5.2% of all custody orders in 1974 to 12.9% in 1985. But the overall increase masks considerable regional variation—in Oxford joint orders formed 43% of the total, but in Romford only 4% (see Priest and Whybrow, Table 8). There are a number of factors influencing this divergence of practice; and it seems clear that there is no consensus judicial attitudes—for example, about the symbolic impact of such orders, and whether they are more or less likely to reduce discord.

16-23   *Does a joint custody order mean anything?* As a matter of strict legal theory it may be questioned whether a joint custody order confers any additional rights on the parent who does not have day to day care of the child: see the Booth Report para. 4.131. This is because, according to *Dipper* v. *Dipper* [1981] Fam 31, para. 16–17 above, both parents are entitled to be consulted on major matters such as education even if only one of them has custody. But the emotional impact of a joint order may be considerable; and joint orders may thus (as the Booth Committee hoped) emphasise to parents that they continue to have joint responsibilities for their children even though they have ceased to be husband and wife.

(4) Custody to a third party

16-24   The divorce court may give custody or care and control to a third party—for example, a grandparent—but this is only done in a statistically insignificant number of cases—possibly 400 each year: Priest and Whybrow (para. 16–17 above) para. 72

(5) Supervision orders

16-25   ⌈Section 44 of the Matrimonial Causes Act 1973⌉ empowers the court to place a child under the supervision of a local authority or welfare officer whilst it is in someone's care, but only if there are "exceptional circumstances making it desirable that the child should be under the supervision of an independent person." The limitation of the power to "exceptional" cases reflects the belief that the state should be hesitant to intervene in the private sphere of family life; but this belief may seem difficult to reconcile with the increased readiness to regard divorce as being a fact which justifies the state in interfering in the family's autonomy—for example, by requiring the court to consider the arrangements agreed by the parents whether they want it to or not. But criticism is possibly academic since the courts will normally be able to find that "exceptional circumstances" exist in any case in which it is desired to make an order—and supervision orders are in fact made in over 2,000 cases each year: Priest and Whybrow (para. 16–17 above) Table 14.

The legislation does not lay down the supervisor's duties and in practice   **16–26**
the supervision may be of a very informal kind, involving perhaps annual or twice yearly visits to the child. Moreover the supervisor is given no powers (except to apply to the court for directions.)

(6) Care orders
The court may make an order committing the child to the care of a local   **16–27**
authority if it appears that there are exceptional circumstances making it impracticable or undesirable for the child to be entrusted to either of the parties to the marriage or to any other individual.
So long as a care order is in force, the child continues in the care of the local authority notwithstanding any claim by a parent or other person; but the effect of a care order made in divorce proceedings is rather different from the effect of a care order made in care proceedings—in particular, the divorce court retains powers to give directions to the local authority on such matters as access: see para. 18–58 below.

(7) Other orders
The final group of orders are rarely made: **16–28**

(a) *Wardship proceedings*
The court may instead of making a custody order, if it thinks fit, direct   **16–29**
that proper proceedings be taken for making the child a ward of court. It is not clear what useful purpose is served by this power.

(b) *Declaration of unfitness*
The divorce court can make a declaration that a party to the marriage is   **16–30**
unfit to have custody of the children of the family. The effect of such an order is simply to prevent that parent automatically becoming entitled to the child's guardianship or custody on the other parent's death: see para. 17–02 below. Such orders are made very occasionally—for example, where the parent has sexually abused the child.

OTHER CUSTODY PROCEDURES

16–31   There may be a dispute about a child's upbringing even though no divorce proceedings have been started, and the law provides a variety of methods whereby such matters can be brought before the court. Of these, the most important in conceptual terms is wardship, dealt with in Chapter 15 above. The other procedures—some of which are very widely used—are statutory. No attempt is made to give a full account of these procedures; but they can be summarised::

(1) Application by a parent to resolve a particular issue

The consequence of giving mothers parental rights
16–32   The Guardianship Act 1973 conferred the same parental rights and authority on a mother as the common law conferred on the father, and made those rights exercisable by either parent without the concurrence of the other. In the result a mother now has as much right as a father to decide whether a child should undergo medical procedures, what school he should attend and so on. But by conferring the rights on two people the Act introduces the possibility of conflict: what is to happen if they disagree? The Guardianship Act 1973 also provided a solution to the problem which it had created. It provides (s.1(3)) that if a minor's father and mother disagree on any question affecting his welfare, either of them may apply to the court for its direction and the court may make such order regarding the matters in difference as it may think proper.

Court can only resolve particular issue
16–33   What the court cannot do on an application under the Guardianship Act 1973 is to make any order regarding the legal custody of a minor or his parents' right of access to him. Hence, the result is that if there is a disagreement between the parents as to how the parental rights should be exercised by them, either can apply to the court to have that particular issue resolved under the provisions of the Guardianship Act 1973. If, however, orders for custody, access or financial provision are sought, application must be made under the Guardianship of Minors Act 1971, which is dealt with below, or in divorce, wardship, or other proceedings.

(2) Application by a parent for legal custody, access, etc. under the Guardianship of Minors Act 1971
16–34   This Act is widely used: some 10,000 applications a year are made annually in magistrates' courts, and applications are also made in the High Court and County Court. The Act enables the mother or father of a child to apply to the court for orders regarding legal custody, access and maintenance. Its main attributes are as follows:

(a) *Only mother and father can apply for custody, etc.*
16–35   Only the child's mother and father can apply under this Act for custody or

financial orders. Grandparents, foster-parents or others who want custody cannot apply for custody under this Act (although a grandparent may now apply for access if a parent has died or there have already been custody proceedings). Grandparents, etc., may be eligible to apply for a custodianship order (see para. 17–06 below); or they can make the child a ward of court and seek care and control.

(b) *Child's welfare is sole issue for court*

A parent does not have to make out any ground to justify his invoking **16–36** the court's jurisdiction. He applies for an order, which the court will grant if (but only if) it is for the child's welfare to do so. The Act is thus particularly useful to parents whose marriage has broken down, but who cannot or do not wish to take other matrimonial proceedings.

Indeed, applications by spouses are in practice usually only made in a situation of marital breakdown. This is because, although a parent may apply to the court whilst still residing with the other, the court cannot give legal custody to both parents, and orders made cease to have effect if the parents continue to live with each other in the same household, or resume living with each other, for a continuous period exceeding six months.

The father of an illegitimate child may apply for custody etc. under this Act, and many applications are made to the court by fathers who seek access to their illegitimate children. Where the applicant's paternity is disputed, that issue must be resolved before the court can consider the merits of the case: *Re O (A Minor: Access)* (1984) 6 FLR 716.

(c) *The orders that can be made*

The court has power to make orders for legal custody, access and **16–37** maintenance. It may also, if there are "exceptional circumstances" make a care order committing the child to the care of a local authority and a supervision order. There are powers to make interim orders. "Legal custody" means "such of the parental rights and duties as relate to the person of the child"—a concept introduced by the Children Act 1975 in an unsuccessful attempt to clarify the law. For present purposes it suffices to note that it includes the "right" to physical possession of the child, and the "right" to consent to medical treatment; it does not include the right to administer the child's property.

The court may also make orders for periodical payments or for a lump sum (not to exceed £500 in the case of magistrates' orders) against a parent excluded from actual custody.

(3) Application by a spouse in matrimonial proceedings in magistrates' court

The procedure under which either party to a marriage can apply to the **16–38** magistrates' domestic court under the Domestic Proceedings and Magistrates' Courts Act 1978 for financial and other orders has been explained at paras. 10–24 to 10–38 above. Once such an application is made the court must not dismiss or make a final order until it has decided whether to exercise its powers under the 1978 Act to make orders for legal custody, access and maintenance in respect of any child of the family (an expression which has the same meaning as under the divorce legislation, explained at para. 16–03 above.) The powers can be exercised even if the application is dismissed, and whether or not either parent has asked the court to make orders relating to the children: the exercise of the court's powers depends on the initiation of proceedings, not on success in those proceedings.

16–39   The orders which the court can make in respect of children are similar to those available under the Guardianship of Minors Act 1971; and it is worth drawing attention to two matters which may influence the choice of procedure:

(i) Under the Guardianship of Minors Act it is not necessary to allege any "ground"; under the 1978 Act a ground must be alleged in the summons, but it is immaterial for this purpose, whether or not it is made out.

(ii) Under the Guardianship of Minors Act, only the mother or father of a child can apply but they need not be married to one another, or indeed to anyone; under the 1978 Act the applicant must be a party to a marriage, but orders can be made in respect of any "child of the family" in relation to that marriage.

Chapter 17

LONG TERM ARRANGEMENTS FOR SUBSTITUTE PARENTING

INTRODUCTION

Chapter 16 was concerned with four procedures which may be used in a situation of family breakdown to deal with custody and other arrangements. This Chapter deals with three procedures—Guardianship, Custodianship and Adoption—which are primarily associated with the making of long term arrangements for a child in cases which will often not be connected with family breakdown in the sense in which that expression is normally used. The reader should however be warned that the distinction thus made between the short-term (or at least freely variable) procedures used in breakdown situations on the one hand, and the more long term procedures used in other cases is somewhat arbitrary, and may in some respects be misleading. Again, adoption and custodianship are now often used in the context of local authority care for children, which is a subject somewhat artificially divided and dealt with in Chapter 18.

17-01

GUARDIANSHIP

The concept of guardianship is imprecise; but for present purposes it suffices to note that a guardian has virtually all the powers and responsibilities of a parent. (For a detailed analysis of the guardian's position, reference should be made to the Law Commission's Working Paper No 91, pp. 49–63.) Guardianship is significant today primarily because it enables a parent to decide who is to be entitled to step into his position in the event of his death during his child's minority—for example, a couple may decide to prefer one set of grandparents to the other to act as their child's guardians.

17-02

Appointment
There are two main ways in which a guardian may be appointed: (i) by the parent's deed or will; (ii) by the court:

17-03

(i) *Appointment by parent's deed or will*
Either parent of a legitimate child may by deed or will appoint any person to be guardian of the child after the parent's death: Guardianship of Minors Act 1971, s.4. Such a guardian will act jointly with the surviving parent—and there are complex provisions dealing with what is to happen if there are disagreements. If both parents appoint guardians they will after the death of the surviving parent act jointly; and, again, there are provisions for resolving disputes between joint guardians.

17-04

185

(ii) *Appointment by the court*

17-05   The Guardianship of Minors Act 1971 empowers the court to appoint a guardian for a child if the child has no parent, guardian of the person or other person having parental rights with respect to him. The application will be made by the intended guardian; and this power is obviously useful if, for example, a child has been orphaned as the result of an air crash killing both his parents.

This power cannot be used if there is anyone who already has "parental rights" over the child. Hence, if the child's parent is still alive this procedure is not available to a foster parent who may have cared for the child for a long time. "Parental rights" means rights acquired by some formal legal process such as the making of a custody order: a step-parent does not as such have parental rights for this purpose even though he may have cared for the child for many years, nor does the father of an illegitimate child.

There are two other cases in which the court may appoint a guardian (although it seems likely that they are comparatively rarely invoked). First, if one of the child's parents dies without having appointed a guardian, the court may appoint a guardian to act jointly with the surviving parent. Secondly, the court may appoint a guardian to act jointly with the surviving parent if a testamentary guardian appointed by a deceased parent dies or refuses to act.

CUSTODIANSHIP

Introduction

17-06   The concept of custodianship stems from the Report of the Houghton Committee on Adoption of Children (Cmnd. 5107, 1972) which identified two particular concerns about the working of the law. First, the Committee thought that adoption—which, as we shall see, involves a complete and irrevocable severance of the legal link between a child and his birth parents—was being inappropriately used by relatives and by step-parents. The Committee was concerned that adoption in such cases could distort family relationships and sometimes resulted in concerned relatives being frozen out from a proper involvement in the child's life. Secondly, the Committee pointed out that, with the exception of wardship, there was no procedure whereby foster-parents and others caring for a child on a long-term basis could obtain formal legal recognition of their relationship with him, and protection against a claim by the natural parent. Such people had no legal status in relation to the child in their care. The Committee accordingly recommended that relatives (particularly step-parents) and foster-parents who were caring for a child should be entitled to apply to the court for "guardianship" of the child under the Guardianship of Minors Act 1971. The Children Act 1975 instead created the new legal institution of custodianship.

What is a custodianship order?

The Children Act 1975 (s.33(1)) defines a custodianship order as "an   **17–07**
order vesting the legal custody of a child in the applicant, or . . . in one or
more of the applicants . . . "; and legal custody means (s.86) "so much of
the parental rights and duties as relate to the person of the child
(including the place and manner in which his time is spent"). The
custodian is therefore to be entitled (subject to intervention by the
court—see below) to have the child in his care and to take decisions about
such matters as medical treatment and education; but he is not (it would
seem) entitled to change the child's name, to administer any property he
may have, or to change his religion, because those rights are not within
the definition of "legal custody." In effect therefore a custodianship order
transfers the right to care for and control the child to the custodian whilst
leaving intact his legal status as the issue of his natural parents. The result
is that the child's nationality and his right to succeed on his natural
parents' intestacy, for example, are unaffected.

Who can apply for custodianship?

The Act contains some rather complex provisions. First, certain people   **17–08**
are *debarred from applying* because there are other procedures available to
them:

(i) *Neither the mother nor the father* (and this expression probably
includes the natural father of an illegitimate child) can apply for
custodianship. They should use the Guardianship of Minors Act
1971 or other legislation.

(ii) *A step-parent cannot apply if (in effect) the child has been the object of
the divorce court's custody jurisdiction.* Custody applications in such
cases should continue to be dealt with in the divorce court. But a
step-parent can apply if the marriage of the child's parents was
ended by death.

Subject to those restrictions, *an application may be made:*   **17–09**

(a) by any person with whom the child has had his home for a period
or periods before the making of the application amounting to three
years in all (or 12 months if a person with legal custody of the child
consents), which period must include the three months preceding
the date of the application; or

(b) by a relative or step-parent of the child with whom the child has
had his home for the three months preceding the making of the
application, provided that a person with legal custody of the child
consents to the application. For this purpose, relative includes a
grandparent, brother, sister, uncle or aunt.

Joint applications

It is possible for an order to be made in favour of "one or more persons."   **17–10**
There is no restriction on the age, sex, or relationship between applicants.
A brother and sister could apply for an order, as could a lesbian or other

homosexual couple. In contrast an adoption order (see para. 17–35 below) may only be made in favour of a couple who are married.

Significance of length of care period

17-11   The Children Act 1975 (s.87(3)) defines the expression "has his home"; but it cannot be said that the definition is helpful; but see *Re S (A Minor) (Care: Wardship)* (1986) 17 Fam Law, CA. This is unfortunate, since it is a crucial concept in the custodianship scheme. Although, as we shall see, the child's welfare is the first and paramount consideration in deciding whether to grant an application for a custodianship order, the application cannot be made in the first place unless the child has spent the relevant period of time with the applicants. A foster-parent who has only had the care of the child for 10 months cannot apply for custodianship however desirable it may be that he keep the child in his care. If such a foster parent wants an order to that effect he must make the child a ward of court and seek care and control.

Protection against removal of child

17-12   What is to stop the natural parent simply retaking his child before the foster-parent has started proceedings? The answer depends on the circumstances. If the child has been committed to the care of a local authority the parent will have no right to retake him without their leave: see para. 18–52 below. Moreover, the Children Act 1975 provides (s.41), that where the child has had his home with a foster-parent for a period (whether continuous or not) amounting to at least three years and the foster-parent has instituted an application for custodianship, no one is entitled without the leave of the court to remove the child from the foster-parent's custody without the foster-parent's consent. This provision does not of course give any protection against the sudden removal of a child before proceedings have been started; but it does enable a foster-parent to resist a decision to remove the child by the local authority which has boarded the child out. This may be an important right, because the foster-parent would find the wardship court unsympathetic to an application designed to question the local authority's decision: see para. 18–72 below.

Significance of parental agreement

17-13   Parental agreement is not a pre-condition to the making of a custodianship order, but is relevant (if at all) only to the period for which the applicant must have cared for the child in order to qualify to make an application. In deciding whether to make an order against the wishes of the parents the court will be guided by the welfare principle, discussed below.

What factors will the court take into account in deciding whether to make an order?

17-14   The Children Act 1975, s.33(9), declares that the court, in deciding applications for custodianship orders, must regard the welfare of the child as the first and paramount consideration. The applicant must give notice of the application to the local authority for the area where the child resides; and the authority must then in every case arrange for a full and detailed report to be prepared in accordance with the Custodianship (Reports) Regulations 1985, SI No. 792. The contents of this report (which will include a recommendation as to whether the order should be made, and if not suggestions for alternatives) will help the court in deciding what is in the child's best interests. Medical certificates are also usually required. These provisions are much more akin to those applied in adoption rather than other custody cases—where generally it is left to the court to decide whether or not it needs a report—and perhaps emphasise the fact that although a custodianship order is revocable, it is to be seen as normally providing a long term solution.

Effect of a custodianship order

A custodianship order is intended to give the custodian legal security in   **17–15** his relationship with the child. So long as it remains in force he has in most day to day matters full authority over the child's upbringing. But four important points must be noted:

(i)   A custodianship order vests legal custody in the custodian. This does not give the custodian the right—to which many long-term foster parents attach importance—to change the child's name.

(ii)   The child's birth parents (and his grandparents) may apply for access to the child at any time while the order is in force.

(iii) A custodianship order, unlike an adoption order, only suspends the rights of the natural parents. Hence the court is given power to revoke a custodianship order on the application of the child's birth parents. It is true that there are provisions designed to prevent the same applicant repeatedly making unsuccessful applications; but the custodian's position is not and cannot be wholly secure.

(iv)   Points (i) to (iii) suggest that custodianship is not advantageous to those seeking a secure long-term legal relationship with the child. But the fact that custodianship does not sever the legal link between the child and his parents has one possibly advantageous consequence for the successful applicant—the court can order the parents to make periodical payments or a lump sum payment in respect of the child. (Local authorities are also given a discretionary power to make financial contributions towards the custodian's expenses in providing accommodation and maintenance for the child: Children Act 1975, s.34(6)).

Custodianship orders made in adoption proceedings

The Houghton Committee thought that adoption was inappropriate to   **17–16** govern the legal relationship between step-parents, relatives, and children for whom they were caring; and effect was given to that policy by provisions of the Children Act 1975 (dealt with at para. 17–39 below) requiring the court hearing an adoption application made by such persons to consider the alternative of making a custodianship order.

The merits of custodianship

17-17   The case for a procedure whereby foster-parents can be given adequate legal security, and an assurance that their care of the children will not be unreasonably interfered with is obviously strong; and the official view (as expressed in DHSS LAC 85/13) is that custodianship can provide "security and stability to children and to those who care for them as parents," and that it also gives local authorities "a new option in planning for children in care"—as discussed in Chapter 18 below.

17-18   There were, before the Custodianship provisions were brought into force on December 1, 1985 a number of judicial suggestions that custodianship would have been a preferred solution had it then been available: see for example *Re H (A Minor) (Adoption)* [1985] FLR 519 CA and *Re F (A Minor) (Adoption: Parental Consent)* [1982] 1 WLR 102 CA and:

> In *Re V (A Minor) (Adoption: Consent)* [1986] 1 All ER 752, CA the child had been with the foster-parents for three years ever since it was 21 months old. Although the mother had at one time said that she would allow the foster-parents to adopt the child, she changed her mind. The Court held that the mother's decision could not be over-ridden, and that the child should remain as a ward of court in the care and control of the foster-parents. Oliver L.J. suggested that custodianship (which was not then available) might have been the right solution, since it would provide a greater formality and degree of permanence than the care and control order; and that the "more imposing title" might help to "supply a psychological gap."

17-19   It has also been suggested (Balcombe L.J. in *Re C (A Minor) (Adoption Order: Condition)* [1986] 1 FLR 315, CA) that custodianship might be used in cases in which the birth parent opposes adoption because he wishes to preserve a link with the child, and that its availability might reduce the number of contested adoption cases.

In this view, therefore, custodianship has a role as an alternative to adoption if adoption is not available, or only available as the possible outcome of potentially traumatic contested proceedings to dispense with parental agreement: see para. 17–48 below. Examples of other cases in which custodianship might be thought appropriate have been given by the DHSS (see LAC 13/85, para. 13). These are, first, the older child who has ties with his birth parents which should not be severed; and secondly, the handicapped child to whom foster parents are willing to make a commitment for their own lifetimes, without feeling able to accept any future responsibility on behalf of their own children or other relatives such as might be implied by adoption which would make the child legally a full member of their family.

17-20   It is too early to form a reliable picture of the working of the custodianship legislation in practice; and it is still therefore difficult to predict whether or not custodianship will prove to have a valuable part to play. There are certainly some who consider that the changing nature of adoption (see para. 17–24 below) has made custodianship a superfluous and needlessly complex legal institution; and this view may derive support from research which suggests that many foster-parents would regard custodianship as a very inadequate substitute for adoption, particularly in view of the fact that a custodianship order is always revocable and confers no right to change the child's name. Conversely, there may be circumstances in which the flexibility of wardship provides a more satisfactory outcome:

> In *Re J* (1986) 17 Fam Law 89, the question was whether an order should be made in favour of Jehovah's Witnesses, who would not be prepared to give their consent should the child ever need blood transfusions. Sheldon J. pointed out that there was no power to impose conditions in a custodianship order, and once an order had been made the court would have no power to give directions as to how the custodian should exercise his rights and duties—for example, in relation to medical treatment. The fact that the court had no power to restrict the making of repeated access applications by the birth parents was also a relevant factor in pointing to the continuance of wardship as a better solution than custodianship.

ADOPTION

Preliminary note. The Adoption Act 1976 ("AA 1976" hereafter) is a **17-21** consolidating measure, bringing together statutory provisions to be found in the Adoption Act 1958, the Children Act 1975, and other legislation. It is not yet in force, but it provides the easiest source of reference for student use, and it is therefore referred to in this book. Unless the contrary is indicated all the provisions referred to are in force in other statutes.

Introduction—law and practice
In English law the legal theory of adoption is simple and dramatic. An **17-22** adoption order made by the court irrevocably transfers a child from one family to another. It does this by vesting the "parental rights and duties" (an expression defined by Children Act 1975, s.85(1) as "all the rights and duties which by law the mother and the father have in relation to a legitimate child and his property") in the adopters, and extinguishing the parental rights and duties of the birth parents and others (AA 1976, s.12(1)). The child is thenceforth treated as if he had been born as a child of the adopters' marriage, and not as the child of anyone else; and the legislation prevents an adopted child from being treated as illegitimate: AA 1976, s.39. In principle, therefore, the adopted child is treated for succession purposes as a member of his adopted family and not of his birth family; and a child adopted by a British citizen becomes a British citizen if he was not one already: British Nationality Act 1981, s.1(5).

There are certain statutory modifications of the general principle—for **17-23** example, the prohibited degrees of marriage between the child and his birth family are unaffected; and although he is put within the prohibited degrees to his adoptive parents these prohibitions do not extend to other members of his adoptive family—so that an adopted child may legally marry his adoptive sister, for example. But the general principle is clear enough.

Changing concepts of adoption

17-24   This concept of adoption—with its corollary of a complete severance between the old family and the new (and until 1975 the preservation of secrecy so that there was no way in which the child or his birth parents could ever regain contact) may have reflected the social realities when the legal institution of adoption was first created in English law by the Adoption Act 1926, and possibly for many years thereafter. It evidently filled a need: the number of adoption orders made each year increased steadily to a peak of 26,986 in 1968. At that period, it seems that adoption was seen primarily as a method whereby a healthy, white, and usually illegitimate baby would be placed with a childless couple who would bring him up as their own child.

17-25   Adoptions of this kind are no longer typical: in 1984 only 681 adoptions were made in respect of illegitimate children aged under six months in favour of adopters neither of whom was a parent. Moreover, in recent years there has been a sharp and fairly steady decline in the total number of orders made each year: in 1984, only 8,648 orders were registered. It seems clear that the purposes for which adoption is used are changing; and in particular it is often now seen as the appropriate solution for children in care, and in particular for those who have traditionally been regarded as difficult to place—for example because they were handicapped or had emotional or behavioural problems. As part of the same trend, adoption is now often used for older children: in 1972, 12 per cent. of adoption orders were in respect of children aged 10 or over; in 1984 the comparable figure was 26 per cent. and nearly three-quarters of all adoptions were of children aged two or over. Adoption services are being integrated with local authority social services; and although provisions of the Children Act 1975 (AA 1976, ss.1, 2) requiring local authorities to establish a comprehensive adoption service have not been formally brought into force, the days when adoption was virtually the exclusive preserve of specialist voluntary agencies have long since gone.

Links with birth family

17-26   The courts have recognised that an adopted child—and particularly one who is no longer a baby—may continue to have links with his birth family. An adoption order cuts the legal tie, but it does not necessarily cut the factual tie. The essential effect of an adoption order is that it puts the adoptive parents in full legal control: it will be for them to decide if and when access to the birth family is to take place. But it is wrong to use adoption if links with the birth family are thought to be necessary for the child's welfare: *Re V (A Minor) (Adoption)* [1986] 1 All ER 752. It is wrong to make continued access a condition of an adoption order in other than exceptional circumstances (*Re GR (Adoption: Access)* [1985] FLR 643); and indeed it is wrong to impose any legal fetter on the rights of the adoptive parents:

> In *Re C (A Minor) (Adoption Order: Condition)* [1986] 1 FLR 315 CA the child's mother was a schizophrenic and quite incapable of looking after the child who went into local authority care. The child's father was deeply attached to her, and had access for some time until the Local Authority terminated access (see para. 18–67 below) on the basis that the visits were disturbing to her. When the foster-parents applied to adopt the girl (who had come to look on them as her natural parents) the father asked the court to impose a condition on the order which would require the adoptive parents to provide annual reports about the child's welfare and progress which could be forwarded to him. The Court of Appeal held that it would be wrong to do so. Such a condition would be contrary to the basic concept of adoption, and contrary to the interests of the child, since it could undermine the adoptive parents' sense of security.

Confidentiality versus the right to know

In many cases, of course, there will be no continuing link between the child and his birth family; and there is a procedure enabling adoptive parents to conceal their identity from the birth parents. The general principle of the legislation is still that it should not be possible for the child, or his birth or adoptive parents to be identified or for his pre- and post-adoption identity to be linked: DHSS LAC 84(3), para. 107. But it has for long been regarded as good practice for a child to be brought up in the knowledge of his true parentage and the circumstances leading up to his adoption; and adoptive parents are given written background information about the child and his birth family in an attempt to help them bring up the child in the knowledge of his adoption from an early age: see Annex C to DHSS LAC 84(3); and see also para. 17–32 below. Moreover on attaining the age of 18, an adopted child now has a statutory right of access to his birth records which will reveal his original name and true parentage insofar as that is recorded: AA 1976, s.51.

17-27

The child's welfare

The legislation provides that in reaching any decision relating to the adoption of a child, a court or adoption agency shall have regard to all the circumstances, "first consideration being given to the need to safeguard and promote the welfare of the child throughout his childhood; and shall so far as practicable ascertain the wishes and feelings of the child regarding the decision and give due consideration to them, having regard to his age and understanding." (AA 1976, s.6).

17-28

The precise effect of this provision is not easy to state; but it is clear that it was intended to make a deliberate contrast with the requirement imposed on the court under section 1 of the Guardianship of Minors Act 1971 (discussed at para. 13–09 above) to regard the child's welfare as the "first and paramount" consideration in dealing with custody issues. It seems that in adoption matters the child's welfare is to be given greater weight than other considerations, but that it need not necessarily prevail over them: see *R. v. Avon CC ex parte K and others* [1986] 1 FLR 443, para. 18–16 below. The extent to which the child's welfare is a relevant consideration in justifying an adoption against the will of its birth parents is discussed in para. 17–53 below.

Courts and agencies—respective roles

17-29   It is only the court which can make an adoption order; but much vital work is now done by adoption agencies, whose duties are prescribed by rules. It is essential to have some understanding of this framework, and of the interrelationship between law and practice.

(a) *Independent placements prohibited*

Until 1982 there was nothing to stop private individuals such as matrons of maternity homes from arranging adoption placements; but it is now (subject to some exceptions) a criminal offence for anyone other than an adoption agency to make arrangements for the adoption of a child or to place him for adoption: AA 1976, s.11.

(b) *What is an adoption agency?*

An adoption agency is either a local authority, or an adoption society approved by the DHSS. Such societies are usually described as "voluntary agencies".

(c) *The agency's duties*

We have already noted the statutory requirement that in reaching any decision relating to an adoption of a child the agency must have regard to all the circumstances, first consideration being given to the need to safeguard and promote the welfare of the child throughout his childhood. Agencies are also specifically required "so far as practicable" to ascertain the wishes and feelings of the child regarding the decision and give due consideration to them, having regard to his age and understanding: AA 1976, s.6. This general duty is elaborated in the specific procedures laid down by the Adoption Agencies Regulations 1985:

17-30   (i) *Investigation, reports and counselling.* The agency has extensive duties to obtain reports about the child, his birth parents, and the prospective adopters. For example, it must obtain a health history covering the birth parents and their family and giving details of serious or inherited and congenital disease. The agency must also find out the birth parents' wishes and feelings about adoption. The agency must make a very full investigation of the prospective adopters, including their financial position, and their previous experience of caring for children. There must be an assessment of their ability to bring up an adopted child throughout his childhood and a medical report, which will even include details of any daily consumption of alcohol, tobacco and habit-forming drugs. The child will be medically examined, and a detailed account produced dealing with such matters as his personality and social development, educational attainment, the extent of his relationship with his birth family and his wishes and feelings in relation to adoption. The agency must also provide a counselling service for the birth parents, the child, and prospective adopters. (For an example of what this may mean in practice see *Re T (A Minor) (Adoption: Parental Consent)* [1986] 1 All ER 817).

(ii) The adoption panel. The agency must establish a panel including **17-31** social workers, a medical adviser, and at least two independent members. The panel must consider proposals for placement. It considers all the information and reports referred to above, and may seek other relevant information; and it must obtain legal advice about each case. It is then for the panel to recommend whether adoption is in the best interests of the child, whether a prospective adopter is suitable to be an adoptive parent, and whether he is suitable to be the adoptive parent of the particular child. The agency can only take decisions on these matters after taking account of the panel's recommendations.

(iii) Placement. If, but only if, an agency has decided in accordance with **17-32** these procedures that a prospective adopter would be a suitable adopter for a particular child, it may make written proposals to the prospective adopter for a placement. This proposal will be accompanied by written information about the child, his personal history and background, (including his religion and cultural background) and his health history and current state of health. If the prospective adopter accepts the proposal, the child may be "placed for adoption." This is a technical term: in many cases the child will already be in the care of the prospective adopters—for example because he has been fostered with them—and it may be that in such cases the prospective adopters will be confused by the well-intentioned but undeniably complex procedures. Indeed, the recent case of *Re T (A Minor) (Adoption: Parental Consent)* [1986] 1 All ER 817 suggests that agencies may not themselves always be clear as to the technicalities and their legal consequences.

Once the placement proposal has been accepted, the agency must give notice to all concerned in accordance with the rules. Perhaps fortunately, it has been held (*Re T*, above) that these provisions are directory rather than mandatory. Failure to comply with them will not invalidate the adoption application.

The agency also has duties to supervise the placement and to give advice and assistance. It is for the prospective adopter to apply to the court for an adoption order; and if an order has not been made within three months of the placement the agency must review the placement.

(d) *The application to the court*

An adoption order may be made by an "authorised court"—in cases **17-33** not involving a foreign element either the magistrates' domestic court, the county court, or the High Court: AA 1976, s.12(1). (The great majority of applications—85 per cent. in 1984—are made to the county court).

The court will be supplied with a detailed report by the adoption agency, dealing with the child his natural parents and the prospective adopters—for example, the report must comment on the stability of the prospective adopters' marriage, give particulars of their home and living conditions and details of income and living standards, the prospective adopters' reasons for wishing to adopt the child, and their "hopes and expectations for the child's future": Adoption Rules 1984, Sched. 2. Medical reports will also be before the court.

If it appears that a parent is unwilling to agree to the application (or there are special circumstances) the court may also appoint a guardian ad litem to investigate and report.

Position where no agency involved
17-34   There are still cases in which no agency is involved—for example, where foster-parents or relatives apply for adoption of a child not placed with them by a local authority. In these cases, a local authority will be notified, and will perform investigatory and reporting functions along the lines described above.

Who may adopt and be adopted
17-35   The legislation contains certain basic rules about the age and status of adopters:

    (i)   An adoptive parent must be at least 21 years of age.

    (ii) An adoption order may be made in favour of a married couple but with that important exception an adoption order may not be made on the application of more than one person. The result is that it is not possible for a brother and sister, or an unmarried cohabiting couple jointly to adopt a child.

    (iii) An adoption order may be made in favour of a sole applicant, although in practice the great majority (8,567 out of 8,648 in 1984) of adoptions are joint. If a sole applicant is married an order can only be made if the court is satisfied that his spouse cannot be found, or is incapable by reason of ill health of applying, or that the spouses have separated and are living apart and that the separation is likely to be permanent.

17-36   In practice, in the exercise of their discretion in arranging placements, adoption agencies are likely to apply very much more demanding tests. The law does not, for example, set an upper age limit for adopters, but in practice few agencies will consider for a first baby a couple where the wife is over 40, and frequently nowadays the limit is set as low as 35.

The Act (AA 1976, s.12(5)) provides that the person to be adopted must never have been married and must be under 18 years of age. It is not a bar to adoption that the child has been previously adopted.

Adoption by relatives and step-parents
17-37   The legislation contains three provisions designed to prevent adoptions

by relatives and step-parents unless there are circumstances making such an adoption desirable in the interests of the child's welfare:

(a) *Applications by mother or father alone*

At one time it was not uncommon for a mother to adopt her own   **17-38**
illegitimate child; but it is now provided that if an adoption application is made by the mother or father of a child alone, the court must dismiss the application unless it is satisfied that the other natural parent is dead or cannot be found, or that there is some other reason justifying the exclusion of the other natural parent. If such an order is made the court must record the reason: AA 1976, s.15(3).

(b) *Step-parent applications*

Where an adoption application is made by a step-parent, either alone or   **17-39**
jointly with a natural parent, the court shall dismiss the application if it considers that issues affecting the child's custody would be better dealt with under the divorce court's matrimonial jurisdiction: AA 1976, s.14(3). This provision is concerned with adoption applications in respect of a step-child who has been a "child of the family" in English divorce proceedings: see para. 16–03 above. If the custodial parent remarried after the divorce, it might seem a good idea to use adoption legally to integrate the child into that reconstituted family—in 1976, before the introduction of this new rule, over 40 per cent. of adoptions were step-parent cases. The attractions of adoption included the fact that adoption would ensure that the child had the same name as his step-father and other members of the new family; but of course this and other advantages of legal integration were only achieved at the price of legally severing the link with the other birth parent and his relatives.

As a result of the provisions of section 14(3), the court must now compare the legal consequences of adoption with those of a custody order in divorce (see para. 16–18 above), and it should refuse to make an adoption order if satisfied that a custody order would be the better solution: *Re D (A Minor) (Adoption by Step-Parent)* (1980) 2 FLR 102; contrast *Re S (Infants) (Adoption by Parent)* [1977] Fam 173. The Report supplied to the court by the adoption agency will state why a step-parent applicant prefers adoption to an order relating to the custody of the child; and the reporting agency will give its view on the relative merits of adoption and custody.

Research has shown a considerable variation in the way in which this   **17-40**
rule has been applied by the courts; but orders are now made in a significant number of step-parent cases—in 1984 more than half of all adoptions involved a parent. For example:

An order was made in *Re D* (above) where children, aged 13 and 10, had ceased to regard their birth father as their real father and felt that adoption would make the step-father their "proper Dad."

An order was made in *Re S (A Minor)* (1974) 5 Fam Law 88 where the father had only seen his four year old son once shortly after birth. The real father-figure in the child's life since he was six months old had been the step-father; and an adoption order thus gave legal recognition to the factual situation. But the court will not make an order where the advantages are "vague and uncertain" and adoption might effectively cut out a real link with the birth family: *Re S* (above).

(c) *Applications by relatives*

17-41   The Act contains a more general provision requiring the court to consider the alternative of custodianship (see para. 17–06 above) in all adoption applications by step-parents and relatives—a term which is widely defined to include a grandparent, brother or sister, and uncle or aunt: AA 1976, s.72(1). If the court—although satisfied that the birth parents agree to adoption or that it would be proper to dispense with their agreement: para. 17–48 below—is nevertheless satisfied that the child's welfare "would not be better safeguarded and promoted by the making of adoption order in favour of the applicant than it would be by the making of a custodianship order" in his favour, and that it would be appropriate to make a custodianship order, it will treat the adoption application as an application for custodianship.

This provision requires the court to consider the competing advantages for the child of adoption as compared with custodianship. If after a full investigation the court considers that the balance of advantage lies with custodianship then a custodianship order can be made; and if it lies with adoption the adoption application will go ahead. If the balance is exactly equal (so the Court of Appeal has held in *Re S (a Minor) The Times*, December 31, 1986) the adoption application will proceed—in effect the court will not impose custodianship on an adoption application unless custodianship would clearly be better for the child.

17-42   In practice the courts have seen advantage in adoption as providing better prospects for long term legal security. The leading case is now *Re S (a Minor), The Times,* December 31, 1986:

An illegitimate child born to a 19 year old girl had been placed six months after his birth in 1982 with the girl's father and his second wife. The grandfather and his wife brought the child up as their own son, and in due course—with the mother's agreement—applied to adopt him. However, the local authority report (see para. 17–34 above) said that adoption would not enhance the quality of the relationship which the boy and the applicants already had, and could confuse existing relationships; and that custodianship would be an appropriate option. The Court of Appeal rejected this view; it saw two advantages tipping the scales in favour of adoption. First, an adoption order would give greater legal security for the actual relationships on which the child was by now totally reliant, and would minimise the risk of those relationships being disrupted by the mother or anyone else. Secondly, the fact that the adoption order would confer the legal status of the applicants' own child would (so the court thought—contrast the views of the Houghton Committee, paras. 17–06 and 17–13 above) reduce rather than increase the risk of emotional confusion or the onset of insecurity when the boy was introduced to the facts about his birth parentage. An adoption order was made.

Again:

> In *Re W (A Minor) (Adoption by Grandparents)* (1980) 2 FLR 161 the trial judge refused to make an adoption order in favour of the grandparents who already had custody of a seven year old boy under a divorce court order because the child would be no better off; but the Court of Appeal reversed this decision. If the grandparents adopted their grandson they could appoint a testamentary guardian (see para. 17-04 above), and thus control his long term future. They could not appoint a guardian under the divorce court order—nor could they have done so under a custodianship order.

The fact that adoption alone puts the applicants fully in legal control   **17-43**
has increasingly been seen as an important factor: see for example *Re D (A Minor) (Adoption by Grandparents)* [1985] FLR 546 and *Re M (Adoption: Parental Agreement)* [1985] FLR 664 in both of which adoption was for this reason seen as the right solution on applications by grandparents.

On the other hand, there may be cases in which the legal link established by birth should not be irrevocably severed, particularly where there is a real prospect of a reunited family at a later date: see, *e.g. Re V (A Minor) (Adoption: Consent)* [1986] 1 All ER 752. In the words of the Houghton Committee (Cmnd. 5107, para. 113)—whose recommendations led to this legislation—custodianship can be used to "protect a child from removal by a young unstable mother without distorting relationships, and would leave the way open for variation of the order if in later years this was for the welfare of the child. Family circumstances may change, and a mother whose relationship with her child has not been distorted by adoption may later be able to offer him a stable home."

The provision dealing with relative adoptions will also apply to step-   **17-44**
parent applications, but most of these will effectively be disposed of under the specific rule discussed at para. 17-39 above. Exceptionally, the present provision will be relevant if, for example, the child's birth parents' marriage ended by death so that the divorce court custody jurisdiction is not available.

Conditions for making of adoption order
(a) *Child must have lived with the applicants before the making of the order*
Although, as we have seen at para. 17-29 above, the court is going to   **17-45**
depend very much on the detailed enquiries into all the circumstances which will have been made by the adoption agency, the legislation (AA 1976, s.13) stipulates that an adoption order must not be made unless the child is at least 19 weeks old, and has at all times during the preceding 13 weeks had his home with the applicants or one of them. If the child has not been placed with the applicants by an adoption agency (for example, if he is their foster-child) a longer period of 12 months is required, unless the applicant or one of the applicants is a parent, step-parent or relative. These periods are laid down to allow a period for the child to settle in the home, for the applicants to adjust to their new role as parents, and for the court to be able to assess the suitability of the placement; and there is an

overriding rule that no order may be made unless the court is satisfied that the adoption agency has had sufficient opportunities to see the child with the applicants together "in the home environment": AA 1976, s.13(3).

17-46   *Removal of child from prospective adopters.* What is to stop a parent exercising his parental authority by removing the child from the prospective adopters, and thus preventing their satisfying the condition that the child should have his home with the applicants? There are three relevant provisions:

(i) A parent or guardian who has once agreed to the making of an adoption order (even informally: *Re T (A Minor) (Adoption: Parental Consent)* [1986] 1 All ER 817) is not entitled, so long as an adoption application is pending, to remove the child from the person with whom the child has his home without leave of the court: AA 1976, s.27(1).

(ii) If an application to free a child for adoption (see para. 17–49 below) is pending, no parent or guardian of the child may remove the child from the custody of the person with whom he has his home against that person's will without the leave of the court: s.27(2). This provision (in contrast to (i) above) applies even where there has never been any parental consent to the freeing.

(iii) If a child has had his home with a person for five years, and that person starts adoption proceedings or gives written notice of his intention to do so, the child must not be removed without leave of the court: AA 1976, s.28. This provision is widely drawn: for example, it would even prevent the local authority which has boarded the child out from removing him from foster-parents whose adoption application it does not support. (There are comparable provisions where a custodianship application has been started by someone who has had the child with him for three or more years: Children Act 1975, s.41; see para. 17–12 above.)

17-47   The new "freeing for adoption" procedure (para. 17–49 below) will possibly minimise the need for these provisions because it will ensure that in many cases the issue of parental agreement will be disposed of before the child is even placed for adoption. But it will not make them unnecessary since, apart from anything else, many adoptions—for example, those by a private foster-parent or many by relatives—will still not involve an adoption agency.

(b) *Parental agreement or dispensation necessary*

17-48   Although the welfare of the child is the first consideration in adoption, it is not the paramount consideration (see para. 17–28 above); and in principle an adoption order is not to be made unless each parent or guardian of the child "freely, and with full understanding of what is involved, agrees unconditionally to the making of the adoption order" (AA 1976, s.16(1)(*b*)). The court does have power to dispense with parental agreement, but the grounds upon which it may do so are restricted. There is a clear difference of legal concept between adoption on the one hand and other methods of providing long-term substitute care for children:

(i) An adoption order is permanent and irrevocable; other orders dealing with custody can be varied.

(ii) Adoption severs the legal family ties with the natural parents and their relatives. In exceptional cases (see *Re V (A Minor) (Adoption: Consent)* [1986] 1 All ER 752 CA, para. 17–26 above) there may still in practice be some continued access after adoption; but this will be a matter for the adopters to decide: see *Re GR (Adoption: Access)* [1985] FLR 643. The birth parent has no statutory right even to apply for access.

(iii) Adoption affects legal status. It therefore affects the child's citizenship and his succession rights; a custody order does not.

Freeing for adoption. Until 1984 a parent could only consent to a specific **17–49** adoption and that consent could be withdrawn after the child had been placed with the prospective adopters and at any time up to the making of the final order. As a result, local authorities who feared that there would have to be a traumatic contest about dispensing with the birth parent's agreement may have been reluctant to place children for adoption. The fact that an agreement once given could nevertheless be withdrawn may well have encouraged indecisiveness on the part of the birth parents; and it certainly seems likely to have made the waiting period very tense for almost all prospective adopters.

In an attempt to deal with this problem it is now provided (AA 1976, s.18) that the court may, on the application of an adoption agency, make an order declaring a child "free for adoption"; and an adoption order may then subsequently be made without further evidence of parental consent. The court will of course only make a freeing order if it considers it to be in the interests of the child (AA 1976, s.6; para. 17–28 above); and it must be satisfied in the case of each parent or guardian of the child that "he freely and with full understanding of what is involved, agrees generally and unconditionally to the making of an adoption order," or that his agreement should be dispensed with on one of the grounds considered at paras. 17–50 to 17–60 below.

"Freeing for adoption" is thus a procedure under which the issue of parental agreement is decided before the hearing of the adoption application; and often before the child has been placed for adoption—indeed, it has been held that an agency should start freeing proceedings as soon as practicable after they have decided that adoption is the right course, and in the usual case the agency need not at that stage have any particular prospective adopters in mind: see *Re PB (A Minor) (Application to Free for Adoption)* [1985] FLR 394.

Dispensing with agreement

There are six grounds on which the court may dispense with the parent or guardian's agreement to adoption:

201

(a) *He cannot be found or is incapable of giving agreement*

17–50   This provision will normally apply to cases where the whereabouts of the person whose agreement is required are unknown and cannot be discovered, or where he lacks the mental capacity to give agreement. But it has been held that a person "cannot be found" for the purposes of this section if there are no practical means of communicating with him, even if his physical whereabouts are in fact known:

> In *Re R. (Adoption)* [1967] 1 WLR 34 the parents lived in a totalitarian country and any attempt to communicate with them would involve embarrassment and danger. The court dispensed with their agreement.

(b) *He is withholding his agreement unreasonably*

17–51   The leading case on the interpretation of this provision is *Re W (An Infant)* [1971] AC 682 in which the House of Lords laid down a number of principles. The case law now seems to establish:

17–52   (i) *Child's welfare not only factor.* There is a clear distinction between adoption and custody cases; and the legal relationship of parent and child is not to be sundered lightly and without good reason. The fact that the court is required by statute (AA 1976, s.6, para. 17–28 above) to give "first consideration" to the child's welfare has not altered that principle: *Re P (An Infant) (Adoption: Parental Consent)* [1977] Fam 25. A parent may, in deciding whether or not to agree to adoption, reasonably take into account not only the welfare of the child, but also his own wishes and welfare, and the welfare of other persons affected such as siblings and grandparents. For example:

> In *Re V (A Minor) (Adoption: Consent)* [1986] 1 All ER 752 CA the mother had left her 21-month-old daughter with foster parents. At one time the mother agreed that the foster parents should adopt the child, but she changed her mind; and by the time of the hearing (when the child had been with the foster parents for nearly three years) she had decided that in the long term she wanted the child back to live with her and her two younger children. The Court of Appeal held that the court should not have dispensed with the mother's agreement. It was not unreasonable for the mother to hope to reunite her family. The foster-parents should continue to have the care of the child; but the mother should have access.

17–53   (ii) *Child's welfare relevant to extent that reasonable parent would so regard it.* In the words of Lord Hailsham (*Re W*, above, para. 17–51, at p. 699):

> " . . . the fact that a reasonable parent does pay regard to the welfare of his child must enter into the question of reasonableness as a relevant factor. It is relevant in all cases if and to the extent that a reasonable parent would take it into account. It is decisive in those cases where a reasonable parent must so regard it."

In practice, this way of looking at the issue enables the court to attach considerable importance to its assessment of how far adoption would promote the child's welfare. For example:

> In *Re F (A Minor) (Adoption: Parental Consent)* [1982] 1 WLR 102 a two year old

child who had been ill-treated and neglected by his mother was placed with foster-parents in whose care he remained at the hearing of their adoption application three years later. The mother accepted that the child should remain in the care of the foster parents, but nevertheless genuinely thought that it would be beneficial to the boy that she should continue to have some contact with him in the future. On this basis the President of the Family Division held that a reasonable mother could reasonably conclude that she should withhold her agreement to adoption, and refused to dispense with the mother's agreement. On appeal, however, it was held that there were in fact no reasonable prospects of the mother re-establishing contact with the child, and that a reasonable parent would have accepted that it was wrong to deny the child the security of eliminating the uncertainty implicit in fostering arrangements.

It would seem that the crucial distinction between this case and that of *Re V* (above) is in the likelihood of a successful resumption of the link with the birth parent: see also *Re H and W (Adoption: Parental Agreement)* (1982) 4 FLR 614, CA.

(iii) Test is reasonableness not culpability. Since the test to be applied is   **17-54** the reasonableness of the parent's decision, the court may dispense with agreement even though the parent has been wholly innocent of any breach of parental duty and is in no way responsible for the state of affairs which has led to the adoption application:

In *Re El-G (Minors) (Wardship and Adoption)* (1982) 4 FLR 589 the mother had been struck down by what Slade L.J. aptly described as "a series of terrible blows which destroyed her health and prevented her from fulfilling her maternal role in spite of her desire to do so." Her inability to care for her children had been entirely the result of misfortune, but the court nonetheless dispensed with her agreement.

(iv) Court must not substitute its own view as to what is reasonable for that   **17-55** *of parent.* It has been stressed that the court should not substitute its own view for that of the parent. This is because (to quote Lord Hailsham, in *Re W* at p. 700, (above, para. 17-51) again):

"Two reasonable parents can perfectly reasonably come to opposite conclusions on the same set of facts without forfeiting their title to be regarded as reasonable. The question in any given case is whether a parental veto comes within the band of possible reasonable decisions and not whether it is right or mistaken. Not every reasonable exercise of judgment is right, and not every mistaken exercise of judgment is unreasonable. There is a band of decisions within which no court should seek to replace the individual's judgment with its own."

In effect, therefore, a decision should only be held to be unreasonable if no reasonable parent could have taken it. In practice, however, it is difficult for the court to avoid applying its own standards, for it is exceedingly difficult to be objective about hypothetical people with hypothetical minds and decide whether they are looking at matters reasonably. As Slade L.J. put it, a parent who loves her children and is not a lawyer may well find it difficult to understand how she could ever be said to be acting unreasonably if she refuses to agree to an adoption which would deprive her of any right to maintain contact with them: *Re El-G (Minors) (Wardship and Adoption)* (1982) 4 FLR 589, 601.

17–56   *Difficulty of applying reasonableness test in freeing cases.* In deciding whether a parent's withholding of agreement is unreasonable the court has to consider the reactions of a hypothetical reasonable parent, and it has often been the attractions of a specific adoption—in terms of the links that the child has formed with the prospective adopters, the quality of the life they can provide for him and so on—which have enabled the court to say that a parent who refused consent was unreasonable in withholding his agreement. It may be more difficult to dispense with agreement on this ground in an application to free a child for adoption (see para. 17–49 above) because it will often be difficult to say that the hypothetical reasonable parent would be unreasonable in withholding his agreement to an adoption by persons about whom he has no information, and who have as yet had no opportunity to form links with the child.

(c) *Has persistently failed without reasonable cause to discharge the parental duties in relation to the child*

17–57   In order to satisfy this ground two conditions must be fulfilled. First, there must have been a persistent failure. This apparently connotes a permanent abrogation of responsibility (see *M* v. *Wigan MBC* [1980] Fam. 36, para. 18–30 below)—has the parent "washed his hands" of the child? Secondly, the failure must be "without reasonable cause":

> In *Re M (An Infant)* (1965) 109 SJ 574 it was held that an unmarried mother's wish to conceal the birth from her parents was a sufficiently reasonable cause.

But *Re M* should be contrasted with:

> *Re P (Infants)* [1962] 1 WLR 1296 where the mother had simply given up the children soon after birth and had no excuse for not having them with her or at least visiting them in their foster home. (This case also establishes that the parental duties include both the natural and moral duty of a parent to show affection, care and interest towards his child, and the legal duty of a parent to maintain him—the mother had collected welfare benefits in respect of her children but not supported them to any significant extent.)

(d) *Has abandoned or neglected the child*

17–58   For this purpose the word "abandoned" has to be construed in its context of neglect or persistent ill-treatment, and thus means such conduct as would expose a parent to the sanctions of the criminal law. It seems that there are few acts (short of leaving a child on a doorstep) which will satisfy the restrictively interpreted ground:

> In *Watson* v. *Nikolaisen* [1955] 2 QB 286 a mother had given her illegitimate child over to foster-parents who wanted to adopt it, and in whom she had confidence. The child was in the foster-parents' care for some two years, and during that time the mother made no contribution to her support—indeed, she kept the Family Allowance paid for the child—and saw her only once. The court

held that she had not abandoned the child since she genuinely wanted the child to remain hers and not be adopted.

A similarly restrictive interpretation has been given to the word "neglected."

(e) *Has persistently ill-treated the child*

If this condition is to be satisfied the ill-treatment must be persistent: **17–59** see for example:

> *Re A (A Minor) (Adoption: Dispensing with Consent)* (1979) 2 FLR 173 where there had been severe and repeated assaults on an 11 month old child over a period of three weeks.

But a single attack (however grave) cannot suffice. Moreover, it is the child who must be shown to have been ill-treated:

> This condition was not satisfied in *Re F (T) (An Infant)* [1970] 1 WLR 192 where the father had killed the child's mother and been convicted of manslaughter.

Again, it would seem that the court could not dispense with the parents' agreement to the adoption of one child on this ground merely because the parent had persistently ill-treated another child in the same family.

(f) *Has seriously ill-treated the child, and (whether because of the ill-treatment or for other reasons) the rehabilitation of the child in the parents' household is unlikely*

In contrast to the ground of persistent ill-treatment discussed above **17–60** there is no need to show a course of conduct: a single act of ill-treatment may suffice provided that it is sufficiently serious. However, the proviso (that agreement cannot be dispensed with on this ground unless, whether because of the ill-treatment or for other reasons, the rehabilitation of the child within the household of the parent or guardian is unlikely) is important not least because it is independent of the first condition: it would thus apparently suffice if it is the parents' deteriorating mental or physical condition, or even the lack of proper housing which makes rehabilitation unlikely.

The court's decision

The fact that there is parental agreement to the adoption, or that the **17–61** court has decided that it could properly dispense with that agreement, does not necessarily conclude the issue. The court has a discretion whether or not to make the adoption order; and in exercising that discretion it must have regard to all the circumstances, first consideration being given to the need to safeguard and promote the child's welfare throughout his childhood: AA 1976, s.6. Specifically, the court may now make a custodianship order in favour of the applicants if it is of opinion that it would be more appropriate to do so: Children Act 1975, s.37(2).

This provision (which is in addition to the provisions considered at **17–62** paras. 17–41 to 17–44 above dealing with adoption applications by step-parents and relatives) is not very happily drafted: the jurisdiction which it confers to make a custodianship order on an adoption application only arises if the parents have agreed to adoption or if the court has decided that it could dispense with that consent. That may be a sensible rule in those cases in which the parents have agreed to adoption, since the court may in such a case perfectly reasonably take the view that their decision should not prevail. But the rule produces absurd results where the parent has refused his agreement to adoption. If in such a case the court is to dispense with agreement it will often have to find that no reasonable parent could have refused agreement to the adoption (see para. 17–55 above); but if it is to make a custodianship order it will then have to find that it would nonetheless be more appropriate to make such an order rather than an adoption order. It is difficult to believe that such a result could have been intended; but the legislation, however bizarre in content, seems clearly drafted, and the Court of Appeal has interpreted it accordingly: *Re M (A Minor) The Times*, October 13, 1986. In practice, however, the drafting defects may be comparatively unimportant since (as already pointed out: see para. 17–42 above) the courts see advantages in adoption as promoting the long-term security of the child; and in *Re A (A Minor) (Adoption: Parental Consent)* [1987] 1 WLR 153, 160, CA, it was said that the onus is on an objector to adoption to satisfy the court that a custodianship order would better safeguard and promote the child's welfare or would be more appropriate than an adoption order.

Birth Certificates
17-63   If an adoption order is made, appropriate entries are made in the Adopted Children's Register. A certified copy—the short form of which will contain no reference to the child's parentage or to the fact that he has been adopted—in effect replaces the child's original birth certificate. For the adopted child's right to trace the original birth particulars, see para. 17–27 above.

Chapter 18

THE CHILD, THE FAMILY AND THE STATE

Boundaries of state intervention

The state has always assumed some duties to orphans and other **18-01** deprived children—for many years primarily through the Poor Law—but the scope and extent of these duties was limited. In 1948 as part of the creation of the modern welfare state after the Second World War, the Children Act imposed a general duty on local authorities to provide care for children deprived of a normal home life; and local authorities, acting primarily through their Social Services Committees, now offer a wide range of services for children in need. In most cases, of course, there is no question of court proceedings or other formalities; but sometimes compulsion may be involved, and the law has to decide when the state should be allowed (or perhaps even required) to intervene in the upbringing of a child. There is little dispute that such intervention is required when a child is being physically abused, for example; but where is the boundary to be drawn? How far is the state to be entitled to override the views of a parent about the way in which a child should be brought up? This chapter is concerned with such issues.

Open to Review?

This chapter is also concerned with the related question of how far **18-02** decisions taken by local authorities about children in their care can be questioned, whether in the courts or in some other way, by those affected. Is an authority to be free to decide that a parent should not be allowed to visit his child—perhaps because the authority considers that the child's interests would best be served by his being placed for adoption? Is a local authority foster parent to be entitled to question a decision to return the foster-child to his birth parents, or to place him with other foster parents? Is a local authority's decision to close a children's home for financial reasons to be open to question on the grounds that the closure will harm the children in its care? Such issues have given rise to much controversy in recent years.

The law can most easily be considered under three heads: **18-03**

(a) What duties do local authorities have to provide for children in need?
(b) When can a local authority exercise compulsion—for example to remove a child from its parents?
(c) How far are the powers and discretions conferred on local authorities subject to appeal, judicial review and other formal scrutiny?

207

A. THE DUTY OF LOCAL AUTHORITIES TO PROVIDE FOR CHILDREN IN NEED

1. The Local Authority's Duty to Provide Care

18–04   The Children Act 1948—the provisions of which are now to be found in section 2 of the Child Care Act 1980 (hereafter CCA 1980)—imposed a duty on an authority to receive into its care any child in their area under the age of 17, if it appeared:

> "(a) that he has neither parent nor guardian or has been and remains abandoned by his parents or guardian or is lost; or
> (b) that his parents or guardian are, for the time being or permanently, prevented by reason of mental or bodily disease or infirmity or other incapacity or any other circumstances from providing for his proper accommodation, maintenance and upbringing; and
> (c) in either case, that the intervention of the local authority under this section is necessary in the interests of the welfare of the child."

No power to take into care
18–05   This provision imposes a duty to receive, not a power to take, into care; an authority has no power under these provisions to compel a parent to place his child in care. An authority which removes a child from his parents without a court order etc under the provisions discussed at paras. 18–21 to 18–59 below is acting illegally: see *Havering LBC v. S* [1986] 1 FLR 489 where a local authority improperly removed a new born child from his mother.

Voluntary care—the duty to return the child to his parents
18–06   The so-called "voluntary" principle was fundamental to the scheme of the 1948 Act; and it is specifically provided (CCA 1980, s.2(3)) that nothing in section 2 authorises a local authority to keep a child in its care under that section if any parent or guardian desires to take over the care of the child. There are, of course, cases in which the authority will decide that it needs to override the parent's wishes; and the law provides machinery, discussed in Part B below, whereby a local authority may acquire parental authority. But the legislation is careful to preserve the principle that a parent is not to be deprived of his rights without having the opportunity to bring the issue before a court where he will have an opportunity to be heard before any order is made: Lord Scarman in *Lewisham LBC v. Lewisham Juvenile Court JJ* [1980] AC 273, 307.

The duty to rehabilitate
18–07   When a child is in voluntary care, the local authority is under a positive duty to seek to rehabilitate the family unit so far as this is consistent with the child's welfare: CCA 1980, s.2(3).

Effect of child's being in care on parent's legal position

Although it is a fundamental principle of the law that reception into **18-08**
care should have no direct effect on the parents' legal rights to custody,
the fact that a child has come into care may have an important indirect
effect on the parents' legal position:

(a) *Authority not under absolute duty to return*

A local authority is not obliged physically to return a child to the parent **18-09**
merely because that is what the parent wants:

> In *Krishnan* v. *London Borough of Sutton* [1969] 3 All ER 1367 a 17-year-old girl,
> who was in voluntary care, refused to return to her father. The court refused his
> application for an order that the authority should return her to him. This is
> consistent with the modern notion of parental authority (see para. 13–12
> above): the local authority had no legal right to keep the girl in their care, but
> since she was of an age to take decisions for herself they were not obliged to
> compel her to return to her father.

(b) *Authority may take steps to authorise retention*

A child remains "in care" until he is actually removed from the physical **18-10**
control of the authority: *Lewisham LBC* v. *Lewisham Juvenile JJ* [1980] AC
273. In consequence, the authority remains under the statutory duty
imposed by CCA 1980, s.18(1) (see para. 18–16 below) to give first
consideration to his welfare. If the authority considers that the child's
return would not be in his interests, they should consider the legal
techniques available to enable them to retain him.
These include:

(i) *Wardship.* The authority may issue a summons making the child a **18-11**
ward of court. Thereafter, no important step in his life (e.g. changing his
residence) may then be taken without leave of the court:

> For example, in *Havering LBC* v. *S* [1986] 1 FLR 489 where the local authority
> had illegally removed a baby from its mother the court nonetheless refused to
> order that the baby be returned to her until there had been a full hearing. In
> appropriate circumstances the court can in wardship proceedings make a care
> order in favour of the authority: see para. 18–57 below.

(ii) *Parental rights resolution.* The authority may, if grounds exist (see **18-12**
para. 18–21 below), pass a resolution assuming parental rights over the
child. The fact that the child has been in their care for three years is a
sufficient ground: CCA 1980, s.3(1)(*d*).

(c) *Notice of intended removal sometimes required*

Once a child has been in care for a period of six months, a parent must **18-13**
give the authority 28 days' written notice before he removes the child.
This gives the authority time to consider whether return is in the child's
interests. If not, it will be able to take action as summarised above: CCA
1980, s.13(2) as amended.

(d) *Foster parent may be able to retain child pending adoption or custodianship hearing*

18-14   If a foster-parent with whom the child has had his home for the relevant period (three years in custodianship, five in adoption) starts proceedings, the child must not be removed without leave pending their determination: see paras. 17–12, 17–46 above.

Powers in relation to children in care

18-15   Local authorities are given a number of specific statutory powers—for example, to help parents with the expenses of visiting—in relation to children in their care: see CCA 1980, Part III. Accommodation and maintenance for a child in care should so far as practicable be near the child's home (CCA 1980, s.21(1)(*c*); see para. 18–65 below); and may be provided either by boarding the child out (*i.e.* placing him with foster-parents who agree to provide a temporary home) or placing him in a residential institution (a "community home" run by the authority or a "voluntary home" run by a charity, another organisation, or a private individual). Boarding-out with foster-parents has traditionally been favoured where possible; and there are detailed regulations governing such matters as the selection of foster-parents, and medical examination of children. Foster-parents are required to sign an undertaking, in a specified form, to care for the child and bring him up as they would their own child, encourage him to practise his religion, look after his health, and permit him to be visited. In particular, they are required to undertake to allow the child to be removed when the authority requires.

The general duty to children in care

18-16   In reaching any decision relating to a child in care the authority must give "first consideration" to the need to safeguard and promote the child's welfare throughout his childhood. So far as practicable the child's wishes and feelings must be ascertained; and the authority must give "due consideration to them, having regard to his age and understanding": CCA 1980, s.18(1):

> In *R v. Avon CC ex parte K and others* [1986] 1 FLR 443 the Council decided to close a community home. In reaching that decision, they failed to consider the needs of any of the children who were resident there, nor were they told that the children were opposed to closure. The decision was quashed because the Council was in breach of the duty imposed by section 18. They had not given first consideration to the welfare of each individual child, and in particular they had not had regard to the child's views on closure.

2. Avoiding the Need for Children to Come into Care

Prevention better than care

18-17   Although many children come into care during a short-term emergency (such as illness) in a satisfactory home, and return when that emergency ends, it is clearly usually desirable to keep families together. CCA 1980, s.1(1) therefore imposes a duty on every local authority "to make available such advice, guidance and assistance as may promote the welfare of childen by diminishing the need to receive children into or keep them in care . . . ." In particular, the Act enables provision to be made "in kind or, in exceptional circumstances, in cash."

Use of preventive powers

Local authorities use these extremely flexible powers, for example to   **18–18** help overburdened mothers by admitting young children to day care and older children to after-school play schemes. Financial help may range from paying the price of a railway ticket to enable a relative to come and look after the family while the mother is in hospital to paying off rent arrears in order to keep a roof over the family's head. In particular, an authority may provide housing for a family if the children would otherwise stand in peril of being received into care: *Attorney-General ex rel. Tilley* v. *Wandsworth LBC* [1981] 1 WLR 854.

Authorities' duty to consider

The decision of the Court of Appeal in the *Tilley* case makes it clear that   **18–19** the legislation imposes a positive duty on authorities; and accordingly they must consider, in the light of the facts of each individual case, how to exercise their discretion in order to perform that duty. Wandsworth's general policy of refusing assistance to families who had become "intentionally homeless" within the meaning of the Housing Act 1985 was thus invalid, because it prevented the authority from considering the individual circumstances of families whose children would in the result come into care.

B. Compulsion—How a Local Authority may Acquire Parental Rights Over Children

Why compulsory powers necessary

An authority may wish, in the child's interests, to be able to exercise   **18–20** parental rights and duties without the risk of interference from the child's own parents. It may, for example, want to remove a child "at risk" from the care of parents who claim to be wholly innocent; or it may wish to make long-term plans for a child to have a more secure future than can be provided by its own parents. This may involve stopping the parents from having access to the child, and placing the child with long-term foster parents or with prospective adopters. There are two main statutory procedures:

(i) If the child is already in care, the authority may in certain circumstances pass a *parental rights resolution*;
(ii) The court may make a *care order*.

There are also *emergency procedures* available which can be used to authorise the removal of a child considered to be at risk to a place of safety; and it should be remembered that the local authority may make a child a *ward of court,* and obtain orders from the court relating to the care and upbringing of the child.

1. Parental Rights Resolutions

18-21   Section 3 of the Child Care Act 1985 provides an essentially administrative procedure (originating in the Poor Law) whereby a local authority may by resolution acquire parental rights and duties in relation to a child who is in voluntary care, and remove the parent's statutory right (discussed in para. 18–06 above) to have the child returned to him. Such a resolution gives the authority wide powers, but it does not override the parent's rights in relation to adoption; nor does it allow the authority to change the child's religion.

There are two main requirements for the exercise of this power:

(i) *The child must already be in the authority's care* "under section 2 of this Act." This clearly means that the authority has no power to "take" a child who is not in care from its parents. If it wishes to remove a child it must use one of the procedures discussed below; and

(ii) it must "appear" to the authority that *one or more prescribed conditions* are satisfied. These are set out in the following paragaphs.

(1) The child's parents are dead and he has no guardian or custodian

18-22   A person qualifies as a custodian only if a court order has been made, and as a guardian only if he has been formally appointed: see para. 17–02. The natural father of an illegitimate child is not a parent for the purpose of this provision unless—after the coming into force of the Family Law Reform Act 1987: see Chapter 19 below—he has a court order giving him the right to actual custody.

(2) The child has throughout the three years preceding the passing of the resolution been in the care of a local authority

18-23   This provision was introduced by the Children Act 1975 in an attempt to lessen the problem of children lingering in local authority care because the natural parents might unreasonably obstruct the making of long-term plans (such as adoption or long term fostering). It was and is controversial.

(3) One of the child's parents is unable or unfit, within the meaning of one of five specific provisions of section 3(1)(*b*) of the Child Care Act 1980, to have the care of the child

18-24   The five provisions in question have been restrictively interpreted; removing parental rights can only be justified if the parent's conduct is "culpable, and culpable to a high degree" (Waterhouse J. in *Wheatley* v. *Waltham Forest LBC* [1980] AC 311, 316). They are:

(a) *The parent has abandoned the child*

18-25   A parent is deemed to have abandoned the child if the parent's whereabouts have remained unknown for 12 months after the child has been received into care. Otherwise, the ground is only satisfied if the parent's conduct would make him liable to prosecution—

In *Wheatley* the mother was feckless and irresponsible, but had left the child with its grandparents and had continued to visit the child after it had been received into care. The condition was not satisfied.

(b) *The parent suffers from some permanent disability rendering him incapable of caring for the child*
This rarely used head requires not only that the disability be permanent, but also that it render the parent actually incapable of caring for the child.   **18-26**

(c) *The parent, while not falling within sub-paragraph (ii) suffers from a mental disorder (within the meaning of the Mental Health Act 1983) which renders him unfit to have the care of the child*
In mental illness cases the condition need not (in contast to head (ii), disability) be permanent, but it must make the parent unfit to care for the child—for example, because his doing so is likely to cause psychological damage to the child.   **18-27**

(d) *The parent is of such habits or mode of life as to be unfit to have the care of the child*
There is little case law on the interpretation of this (quite frequently used) head. Vagrancy, violence, drunkenness, drug addiction or prostitution are apparently often the conditions involved.   **18-28**

(e) *One of the child's parents has so consistently failed without reasonable cause to discharge the obligations of a parent as to be unfit to have the care of the child*
The considerable body of case law on this widely used ground establishes a basic principle that a parent cannot be said to have failed to discharge the parental obligations unless his behaviour can be shown to be "callous, blameworthy, reprehensible" (Sir J. Arnold P. in *O'Dare* v. *South Glamorgan CC* (1980) 3 FLR 1, 4). A parent who co-operates with social workers in attempting to establish a proper relationship with the child has not in this sense failed to discharge the parental obligations: *W* v. *Nottinghamshire CC* [1982] 1 All ER 1. A parent who is psychologically and emotionally inadequate may not be "culpable": *O'Dare* (above.)
There are four questions to be asked: **18-29**

(i) *Has there been a failure to discharge the obligations of a parent?* Not providing adequate housing could be an example of such a failure (*W* v. *Sunderland MBC* [1980] 1 WLR 1101); but the obligations of a parent are not limited to legal duties (for example, to maintain the child) and extend to the natural and moral duty of a parent to show affection, care and interest towards the child. A failure to visit the child or to establish a proper relationship with him is therefore capable of constituting failure to   **18-30**

213

discharge parental obligations for this purpose: Sir J. Arnold P. in *W v. Sunderland MBC* [1980] 1 WLR 1101, 1109, and:

> In *M. and Another v. Wigan Metropolitan Borough Council* [1980] Fam 36 it was held to be relevant that the parents of a child had deliberately abandoned an agreement that the father should have a vasectomy even though the mother's repeated and difficult pregnancies prevented her from establishing a satisfactory relationship with her children who had repeatedly to be received into care.

18-31 *(ii) Has the failure been consistent?* It is not necessary that the failure be persistent (compare para. 17–59 above), but simply that it establishes a pattern—of rejection, for example.

18-32 *(iii) Has the failure been without reasonable cause?*

> In *Wheatley v. Waltham Forest LBC* (above) the local authority had allowed the mother to visit her child only once weekly for three hours; and this was a reason for her failure to relate to the child. In contrast, a callous or self-indulgent failure to visit—for example because the mother prefers to travel rather than look after her child—could, of course, satisfy the statutory condition.

18-33 *(iv) Is the failure such as to render the parent unfit to have the care of the child?* This is a distinct requirement which has been said to emphasise the gravity and drastic consequences of the decision to divest a parent of the parental rights and duties: Waterhouse J. in *Wheatley*, above, at p. 316.

(4) A resolution is in force under s.3(1)(*b*) of the Child Care Act 1980 in relation to one parent of the child who is, or is likely to become, a member of the household comprising the child and his other parent

18-34 A parental rights resolution on one of the heads discussed above only transfers to the authority the rights of the parent "on whose account the resolution was passed." If, for example, the authority assumed rights over the child of a drug addict mother, that resolution would not affect the parental rights of her husband, who might be legally entitled to remove the child from care and bring him back to live with the mother. The present provision is intended to allow the local authority to prevent such a situation by assuming the father's rights in such a case.

Challenging a parental rights resolution

18-35 The parent must be given written notice of the resolution. He may then challenge it by serving a counter-notice on the authority. The authority then has 14 days to start proceedings in the juvenile court, which may uphold the resolution if three cumulative conditions are satisfied:

(i) that the grounds on which the local authority purported to pass the resolution were made out when the resolution was passed; and

(ii) that at the time of the hearing there continue to be grounds—not necessarily the same—on which a resolution could be founded; and,

(iii) that it is in the interests of the child that the resolution remain in force.

2. Care Proceedings

The Juvenile Court has power under the Children and Young Persons Act   **18-36**
1969 ("C & YPA 1969" hereafter) to make orders in respect of a person
aged under 17 if, first of all, any one of a number of primary conditions is
proved. If, but only if, a primary condition is proved the court must ①
consider as a separate matter whether the "care and control" test (that the
child is in need of care or control which he is unlikely to receive unless the ②
court makes an order) is satisfied. Finally, the court must consider
whether in all the circumstances it is right to make an order. It is ③
important to understand at the outset that these conditions are cumulative, and that no order can be made unless all three are satisfied:

> In *D (A Minor)* v. *Berkshire County Council* [1987] 1 All ER 20, HL a child had
> been born to a drug addict. As a direct result of the mother's deliberate and
> excessive taking of drugs during pregnancy, the baby was suffering from drug
> withdrawal symptoms and needed intensive hospital care. Both mother and
> father remained addicted to hard drugs. The question was whether the juvenile
> court could make a care order; and the issue which was fought up to the House
> of Lords was whether the primary condition that the child's proper develop-
> ment was being avoidably prevented or neglected or her health avoidably
> impaired or neglected: C & YPA 1969; s. 1(2)(a) (para. 18–37 below) had been
> established. The House of Lords held that it had been; and, there being no
> dispute that the other two requirements were satisfied on the facts of the case,
> the care order was upheld.

But this case does not mean that a mother who smokes or drinks during
pregnancy, and whose baby is said in consequence to have suffered some
developmental damage, will necessarily be at risk of having her child
removed from her care. Even if the primary condition referred to above
were satisfied (which is by no means certain: see para. 18–39 below), the
court would still have to find that the "care or control" condition
(para. 18–48 below) was satisfied, and to decide in the exercise of its
discretion that it would be appropriate to make an order. It is
inconceivable that it would or could do so when faced with a remorseful
mother aware of the harm she had done and able and willing properly to
care for the child.
    With this in mind, we summarise the three requirements:

(1) The primary conditions

(a) *The child's "proper development is being avoidably prevented or neglected
or his health is being avoidably impaired or neglected or he is being ill-
treated": C & YPA 1969, s.1(2)(a)*
This condition covers cases of child abuse in its broadest sense; and it is   **18-37**
frequently used in practice. In many cases the question is whether a
parent has been responsible for physical injury to the child; but emotional
or psychological deprivation suffices.

215

18–38   *'Avoidable.'* It is sometimes suggested that harm is only avoidable if the parent could by an act of the will have prevented it, so that if (for example) the harm is the result of the parents' physical disabilities the condition would not be satisfied. There is no authoritative guidance on this point. But it does seem clear that moral culpability is not required: care orders can be made if the parent refuses to provide medical treatment of a kind to which he objects (*e.g.* blood transfusions).

18–39   *Apprehended neglect insufficient.* This ground is not established merely on the basis that the child is "at risk." There must be something which is happening at the moment which results in the proper development of the child being affected. Thus:

> In *Essex County Council v. T.L.R. and K.B.R.* (1978) 143 JP 309 the child was in voluntary care, well cared for by foster-parents. The child's father, a serving soldier, informed the foster-parents that he was going to Hong Kong to marry a Chinese girl, and that he would then want to take the children with him on a posting to Northern Ireland. The local authority considered this would not be in the child's interests, but failed in an application for a care order based on "avoidable neglect."

But both past and future may be relevant in deciding whether situation now exists.

> In *D (A Minor) v. Berkshire County Council* HL—the facts of which have been given at para. 18–36 above—the House of Lords rejected arguments that the statutory conditions no longer existed at the time of the proceedings, because the only time when the child's health was being impaired was when the mother was taking drugs during pregnancy, that this had ceased when the child was born, and that consequently the only impairment was either in the past or merely apprehended. The Law Lords emphasised that the requirement that the child "is being" ill-treated etc. is a continuing rather than an instant state of affairs; and they held that the relevant time for determining whether or not the condition was satisfied was the moment when the statutory preventive machinery was put into operation—in this case, by the local authority obtaining a place of safety order see para. 18–59 below. In considering whether the relevant situation existed at that time the court could properly look to the past, even before the child's birth, and it could also look to the future as part of the process of determining whether, in the absence of intervention, the situation would have been likely to have continued. For example, the condition would be satisfied if the child had been cruelly beaten in the past and there was a likelihood that such treatment would have been repeated in the future, even if at the date of the hearing the child was in a secure and loving foster-home.

It is important to emphasise that this condition will not be made out if the conduct in question can be shown to be entirely a thing of the past: it would seem that if the mother in *D v. Berkshire County Council* (above) had irrevocably given up drugs before the child was born the condition would not have been satisfied. The damage would have been done; but the child's health was not *being* avoidably impaired at the relevant time: see *per* Lord Goff of Chieveley. Nor is it sufficient to look solely to the future: the *Essex*

County Council case [above] was correctly decided because an order could not be founded solely on apprehensions about the future.

(b) *It is probable that condition (a) above "will be satisfied in his case, having regard to the fact that the court or another court has found that condition is or was satisfied in the case of another child or young person who is or was a member of the household to which he belongs" (C & YPA 1969, s.1(2)(b)*

This condition is intended to deal with the case where there is evidence   **18–40**
that one child in a family has been abused; and the court considers that in the circumstances there is a risk of harm to the others.

Previous care proceedings not necessary. Although the court must be   **18–41**
satisfied that another child of the household has already suffered, it is not necessary for this fact to have been established in previous legal proceedings:

> In *Surrey CC v. S. and Others* [1974] QB 124 the child's sister had died. Her father had been acquitted of her murder. It was held that the magistrates should have heard evidence intended to show that the dead girl had in fact been abused. From that history the court could infer that it was probable the surviving child would be harmed.

Same "household." The child who has already suffered harm must be or   **18–42**
have been a member of the same household as the child now before the court. "Household" is widely construed:

> In *R. v. Birmingham Juvenile Court, ex parte N* (1984) 5 FLR 683 two children were held to be in the same household for this purpose, notwithstanding the fact that one of them was in care and had never lived in the same building as the other. It is the persons in the group comprising the household rather than the physical locality which is significant; and in this case the children's mother was the unifying element since she would be concerned with the children's care.

(c) *It is probable that condition (a) will be satisfied in his case, having regard to the fact that a person who has been convicted of certain serious offences against children is, or may become, a member of the same household as the child before the court: C & YPA 1969, s.1(2)(bb)*

Under this—in practice little used head—the court must be satisfied of   **18–43**
three matters. First, that there has been a conviction of a specified offence (for example, causing actual bodily harm to a child). Secondly, the person convicted must be a member of the same household as the child, or there must be a probability that he will become a member of it. Thirdly, in the result, there must be a probability of damage to the child in respect of whom the order is sought.

(d) *The child is exposed to moral danger: C & YPA 1969, s.1(2)(c)*

This condition may be satisfied in cases where the child is taking drugs,   **18–44**
or is promiscuous, involved in prostitution, or the victim of incest or other sexual misconduct. But the court must take into account the parties' background and way of life. A court might well decide that a 13-year-old English girl who was persistently having sexual intercourse with a 26-

year-old man who had suffered from venereal disease was in moral danger:

> But in *Alhaji Mohammed* v. *Knott* [1969] 1 QB 1 it was held that a care order should not have been made on this ground in respect of a 13-year-old Nigerian Muslim girl living with her 26-year-old husband.

(e) *He is beyond the control of his parent or guardian: C & YPA 1969, s.1(2)(d)*

18-45   A parent can no longer now himself start care proceedings, but he can ask the local authority to do so on this ground. If the authority does not do so within 28 days, the parent can apply to the court for an order directing the authority to act.

This ground can of course be used against the parent's will and even if he believes he is controlling the child. Children under 10 cannot be prosecuted, and care proceedings may be used if they misbehave.

(f) *He is of compulsory school age and is not receiving "efficient full-time education suitable to his age, ability and aptitude": C & YPA 1969, s.1(2)(e)*

18-46   Parents who fail to send their child to school may be prosecuted; but in many cases the child's truancy will be symptomatic of emotional problems rather than a direct result of any failure on the parent's part. If a care order is made, the result will be that the local authority can take the child into a community home and ensure his attendance at educational classes.

(g) *He is guilty of an offence, excluding homicide: C & YPA 1969, s.1(2)(e)*

18-47   This provision was intended to enable care proceedings to be used in place of the prosecution of juvenile offenders. However, since the provisions of the C & YPA 1969 which were designed to restrict prosecution in such cases were never brought into force, this head is of little practical importance. Prosecution (or cautioning) is almost always used.

(2) The care or control test

18-48   It is quite clear that the court must treat the "care and control" condition (see para. 18–36 above) as a separate matter. Proof of a primary condition alone does not suffice to justify the making of an order. However, the clarity of the distinction is blurred to some extent by a decision of the Court of Appeal:

> In *Re S. (A Minor) (Care Order: Education)* [1978] QB 120 the parents of a well-behaved, well-disciplined and respectful 11-year-old boy deliberately kept him away from school because they were opposed to comprehensive education. (They apparently hoped that the local authority would pay for the child's education at an independent boarding school.) In the circumstances, there could be no doubt that the primary condition of section 1(2)(e) was satisfied; but had it been proved that the child was in need of care and control? The Court of Appeal rejected the view that a child was only in need of care and control if he was being neglected in respect of his day-to-day physical or emotional needs. The Court took the view that the provision of education was a component of the care

which a child needed. If he was being denied a proper education he was therefore in need of care, and the care or control condition was satisfied.

The result of this decision may be that courts will too readily allow proof of the need for care or control to be inferred from proof of a primary condition; but the dangers of this lax and incorrect approach should not need to be emphasised. If proof of a primary condition alone were to suffice, the care legislation could become the means of in effect punishing a parent for past failures by removing his child; and that is clearly not the policy to which Parliament intended to give effect.

The court should also ask itself whether the making of an order is the   **18–49** only way of ensuring that the child receives the care he needs, or is any other way of dealing with the case likely to provide a solution? Perhaps the parents will agree to co-operate with caring agencies; or perhaps relatives can take over the care of the child. Of course in practice these issues may well have been explored before the authority decided to bring the proceedings as the only solution.

(3) Disposal—the orders that can be made
If the court is satisfied about these matters, it will find the complaint   **18–50** proved; and it will at that stage consider social work reports in order to decide what action to take. The court has a discretion (in exercising which it must have regard to the child's welfare: C & YPA 1933, s.44(1)) whether or not to make an order; and this may sometimes be a difficult decision:

> In *Re S. (A Minor) (Care Order: Education)* (above, para. 18–48) for example the court had to decide whether it would be better for the boy to stay with his parents at home and not receive any education at all, or to be taken from them in order to ensure that he was educated.

If the child is mentally ill, the court May make a hospital or   **18–51** guardianship order under the Mental Health legislation. In other cases it may (but in practice almost never does) order the parent to "enter into a recognisance" in a specified sum—which can be forfeited if there is a breach—to take proper care of and exercise proper control over the child. In most cases, the choice will lie between a care order and a supervision order.

(a) Care orders   CORE ORDER
A care order commits a child to the care of a local authority which is   **18–52** thereby put under a duty to receive the child into their care and to keep the child in care notwithstanding any claim by his parent or guardian: CCA 1980, s.10(1). The authority cannot give the parental consent which is a prerequisite to adoption, or alter the child's religion; but with those exceptions it is given the same powers and duties with respect to the child as his parent or guardian would have had over him: CCA 1980, s.10(2). The local authority will also have the powers discussed at para. 18–15

above over the child; and his welfare should be the first consideration in reaching decisions: CCA 1980, s.18.

18-53   The authority's powers included the right to restrict or even terminate all parental access to a child. This is often done as a preliminary to an adoption placement; but legislation now gives a parent whose access is terminated the right to apply to a juvenile court for an access order: see para. 18–64 below.

Conversely, authorities often try to rehabilitate the child in the family unit by allowing him to be "home on trial". In the light of disquiet about this practice expressed by the Committee of Enquiry into the death of Jasmine Beckford (1985) the Children and Young Persons (Amendment) Act 1986 envisages the making of regulations to require consultation and medical and other supervision in such cases.

18-54   *Discharge of care orders.* The court has power to discharge a care order; but must not do so where the child still appears to be in need of care and control unless the court is satisfied that, whether through the making of a supervision order (see para. 18–55 below) or otherwise he will receive that care or control. Although this provision (C & YPA 1969, s.21(2A)) gives no guidance to the weight to be attached to the perhaps competing interests of the child's welfare and his parents' fitness it has been said (Ormrod J. in *re W (A Minor)* (1982) 2 FLR 360, 367) that "unwrapping the language, what that really means is that they have to show that there is no risk of the child being ill-treated if returned."

In order further to minimise the risk of a care order being discharged in inappropriate circumstances the court now has power to order that the child be separately represented by a guardian ad litem in any case in which it considers there may be a conflict of interest between the child and his parent; and separate representation is mandatory if the discharge application is unopposed—presumably because in other cases the local authority in opposing the application can be relied on to put the child's case: see further para. 18–87 below.

(b) *Supervision orders*

18-55   A supervision order places the child under the supervision of a local authority (or in certain circumstances of a probation officer) whose function is to "advise, assist and befriend" the supervised person: C & YPA 1969, s.14. Such an order may impose requirements (for example, that the child reside with a particular person in a particular place, or receive treatment). However, the supervisor has no power to give legally effective directions about the upbringing or conduct of the child.

(c) *Interim orders*

18-56   If the court before which a child is brought in care proceedings is not in a position to decide what order, if any, ought to be made, the court may make an interim order, *i.e.* a care order containing provision for the order to expire with the expiration of 28 days or some shorter period. The legislation contains no guidance as to the basis on which an interim order may be made; and the statute seems to permit the making of such an order without any evidence having been heard.

There is no statutory limit on the number of interim orders which may be made; but it has been held that it is the duty of the local authority to deal expeditiously with care proceedings, and that the legislation does not envisage successive applications for interim care orders: *R. v. Birmingham Juvenile Court, ex parte N* (1984) 5 FLR 683.

Committal to care in wardship, matrimonial and other proceedings

The court has statutory powers to commit a child to the care of a local **18-57** authority in the exercise of its wardship, guardianship, and divorce jurisdiction, and in proceedings under the Domestic Proceedings and Magistrates Courts Act 1978. In each case, the only condition which has to be satisfied is that there are "exceptional circumstances making it impracticable or undesirable" for the child to be under the care of a parent or an individual. In practice, it is not difficult to satisfy this condition:

> In *Lewisham LBC* v. *M* [1981] 1 WLR 1248, for example, the child's foster parent could only manage with the help of a boarding out allowance which could not be paid unless the child was in care. The court made the order.

A care order made in such proceedings is in almost all respects com- **18-58** parable to a care order made under the C & YPA 1969 by the Juvenile Court. The only significant difference is that the court may give directions about the child's accommodation and welfare: *J* v. *Devon CC* [1986] 1 FLR 597. Hence a divorce court which has made a care order can, for example, order that the child live with a specified relative or make an order about parental access: *Re Y (A Minor) (Child in Care: Access)* [1976] Fam. 125. In practice the court would no doubt be reluctant to exercise these powers, but the fact that it has power to do so in an appropriate case is important. In contrast, the Juvenile Court in care proceedings has no power to make orders governing the future treatment of the child; the local authority is put completely in control, subject only to the limited rights considered at para. 18-60 below to question its decisions. It is because wardship is so flexible, and that no important decision affecting the child can be taken without the approval of the court (given after hearing all those with legitimate interests in the outcome) that it will often be a preferred option even for parents who accept that their child will have to go into care. For example:

> In the drug addicts' baby case, *D (A Minor)* v. *Berkshire County Council*, HL (para. 18-36 above) the baby's parents, and the guardian ad litem appointed to safeguard the baby's interests, all agreed that a care order was necessary. For the reasons stated above, however, they opposed the making of such an order by the Juvenile Court. They thought that the order should have been made in wardship, in particular because they feared that the authority if given the wide and effectively unsupervised powers conferred by a Juvenile Court order (paras. 18-52 to 18-53 above) might decide to programme the child for early adoption without the parents being given an adequate opportunity to resist that course: *per* Lord Brandon of Oakbrook.

In addition to these statutory powers, the High Court and County Court have wide inherent powers over wards of court: see Chapter 15 above.

In *Re SW (A Minor) (Wardship: Jurisdiction)* [1986] 1 FLR 24 (see para. 15–18 above) the court held that these powers included power to commit to care a rebellious and delinquent 17-year-old girl. No statutory powers were available because the girl was over 16: see para. 15–20.

3. Emergency procedures

18-59   Care proceedings take time. Legislation therefore contains a number of provisions intended to safeguard children in case of emergency. For example, if it is suspected that a child is being neglected a magistrate can grant a search warrant (C & YPA 1933, s.40) authorising the police to search for the child, and to enter specified premises (if need be by force), and to remove the child to a "place of safety"—*i.e.* a community home, police station, hospital "or other suitable place": C & YPA 1933, s.107. Again, a magistrate may make a "place of safety order" authorising the child's detention in a place of safety for a period of up to 28 days if the applicant has reasonable cause to believe that one of the primary conditions specified in the C & YPA 1969 (and discussed at paras. 18–37 to 18–47 above) is satisfied or in certain other circumstances: see C & YPA 1969, s.28(1).

The place of safety order is a powerful weapon for facilitating speedy action in case of emergency; but there are those who think that it is sometimes used unnecessarily as a routine method of starting care proceedings even in cases where it is not really necessary to remove the child before the hearing. Consider, for example, the facts revealed by the report of *Re W (A Minor) (Wardship: Jurisdiction)* [1985] AC 791 where parents asked the local authority to take their daughter into care, and yet the authority applied for and obtained a place of safety order.

C. QUESTIONING LOCAL AUTHORITY DECISIONS

18-60   A parent or other person may want to dispute the local authority's right to take decisions affecting the child, or he may want to question particular decisions (for example, to deny or restrict access to the child as a preliminary to placing him for adoption, or to close a particular establishment in which the child has been living). In many cases, of course, there will be informal discussions—and recently there has been some emphasis on the part which elected members of the authority can play in this area: see DHSS LAC (84)(5)—but there are five formal procedures which may be available: (i) appeal; (ii) application for an access order; (iii) making the child a ward of court; (iv) judicial review; (v) investigation by the Local Government Ombudsman:

(1) Appeal

(a) If a *parental rights resolution* has been confirmed by the Juvenile   **18-61**
Court (see para. 18–35 above), any parent or guardian may appeal to the
Family Division of the High Court. There are then further rights of appeal
to the Court of Appeal and House of Lords. (The local authority may also
appeal against the juvenile court's refusal to confirm the resolution): CCA
1980, s.6.

(b) A child may appeal against the making of an order in care   **18-62**
proceedings; or against a refusal to discharge a care order. (This right may
be exercised by the child's parent on his behalf, unless a separation order
has been made because of conflict of interest: see para. 18–87: *A-R* v. *Avon
CC* [1985] Fam 150. If there has been a separation order the parent will
have his own right of appeal once the relevant provisions of the Children
and Young Persons (Amendment) Act 1986 have been brought into
force.)
    The appeal is to the Crown Court—which is primarily concerned with
serious adult crime—and takes the form of a rehearing of the case.
Thereafter there is a right of appeal to the Family Division of the High
Court, but judicial regret has been expressed that the initial appeal is not
to the Family Division: Purchas L.J. in *W* v. *Nottinghamshire CC* [1986] 1
FLR 565, 575.
    The local authority has no right of appeal against a refusal to make a
care order. In this, as in other respects, the criminal overtones of the
legislation are apparent: a prosecutor cannot appeal against sentence,
so why should a local authority be able to appeal in care proceedings?
However, if the local authority believes the failure to make an order
exposes the child to risk, it may invoke the wardship jurisdiction.

(c) Any party may appeal to the Court of Appeal from decisions of the   **18-63**
High Court or County Court in the exercise of the wardship or statutory
jurisdiction referred to at para. 18–57 above. The appeal court will only
interfere in exceptional circumstances: see para. 14–05 above.

(2) Access to children in care; application to juvenile court for access order

The juvenile court in care proceedings has no power to impose   **18-64**
conditions requiring that access to a child be given to his parents or others
concerned for him; and the fact that the destiny of a child over whom a
local authority had obtained parental rights was so completely in the
hands of the authority (which in practice often seemed to mean in the
hands of a few social workers) became a matter of controversy. The
Health and Social Services and Social Security Adjudications Act 1983
introduced two measures in an attempt to deal with these problems. First,
the Minister is under a statutory obligation to issue a code of practice
dealing with access to children in care. Secondly, a parent has a right to

apply to the juvenile court if access to his child has been refused or terminated.

(a) *The Code of Practice*

18-65   The Secretary of State is required to prepare a code of practice with regard to access to children in care, and lay it before Parliament. Either House may require it to be withdrawn; and it has been suggested that the contents may therefore be taken as reflecting Parliament's view of the interpretation of the relevant legislation: see Cumming-Bruce L.J. in *Re M (A Minor) (Wardship: Jurisdiction)* [1985] Fam 60, 70 but contrast the approach of the Divisional Court in *R. v. Bolton MBC, ex parte B* [1985] FLR 345. It seems reasonable to suppose that departures by local authorities from the terms of the code will need justification if the reasonableness of the decision comes into question under the procedures discussed at paras. 18–67 to 18–71 below.

The original code was laid before Parliament on December 16, 1983, and has not yet been revised. Its purpose is to set out basic principles on which authorities should operate in promoting and sustaining access (which is to be accepted as a positive responsibility on their part) and in handling decisions to restrict or terminate access where it is decided that access is not in the child's interests—for example, because it is damaging the child or because it is recognised that there is no realistic hope of rehabilitation and that the child's future lies with a substitute family.

18-66   The Code emphasises, amongst other matters, the need to explain and discuss decisions about access with the parents and others affected. It stresses the need to establish adequate procedures to enable parents and others affected to pursue complaints about access and to ask for such decisions to be reviewed. It also deals with the practicalities of access (for example, the internal organisation and timetable of residential homes should not make visiting difficult, and arrangements for visiting must be flexible.)

The Code stresses the need to keep full and clear records to enable access to be monitored, and to provide a basis for understanding the decisions which have been taken and the reasons for them; and states that all decisions and agreements about access arrangements, and any changes to the arrangements, and the outcome of all formal and informal reviews of access, should be confirmed in writing to the parents. Decisions to terminate or refuse access should be considered by the authority's Director of Social Services personally.

(b) *Access orders*

18-67   A local authority must not terminate arrangements for access to a child who is in its care under certain specified statutory provisions without first giving the parent notice in a prescribed form of termination or refusal. The notice will inform the parent of his right to apply to a juvenile court for an access order.

On such an application, the court is to regard the welfare of the child as the first and paramount consideration. Access should only be given if it is in the interests of the child; the court should not be influenced by the conception that a fit and proper parent has a right to access to the child: Sir J. Arnold P. in *Hereford and Worcester CC v. JAH* [1985] FLR 530, 533, (affirmed [1986] 1 FLR 29).

The juvenile court may order the local authority to allow the parent access to the child "subject to such conditions as the order may specify with regard to commencement, frequency, direction or place of access or to any other matter for which it appears to the court that provision ought to be made in connection with the requirement to allow access." This provision empowers the court to make very detailed orders—in contrast to the stark simplicity of a care order which can do no more than commit the child to care.

An appeal lies to the High Court against any decision of the juvenile court.

This well-intentioned provision was intended to provide for a simple and swift hearing before the local juvenile court (Wood J. in *R. v. Bolton MBC* [1985] FLR 343) but experience has highlighted certain problems:

(i) There is no right to apply for an access order unless the authority has   **18-68**
"terminated" or refused to make arrangements for access: CCA 1980, s.12B(1). There is no right to apply to a juvenile court if access is merely restricted; and the question whether access has been so restricted that it has in reality been terminated may have to be litigated. It has been held that an authority considering whether to terminate access must take the decision urgently; but in some cases the necessary enquiries and investigations will take time: *R. v. Bolton MBC* (above).

(ii) The right to apply for access orders only arises if the child is in care   **18-69**
under the specified provisions (CCA 1980, s.12A(1))—broadly speaking under a care order or parental rights resolution. There is no right to apply if the child is in voluntary care—no doubt because in theory the parent retains his common law rights to access and could in any case remove the child from care. In practice, however, things may be rather different; and a parent may find himself without any formal means of redress.

(iii) The only persons who can apply for access are the child's parents or   **18-70**
a formally appointed guardian or custodian. Grandparents (see *Re W (A Minor) (Wardship: Jurisdiction)* [1985] AC 791), siblings, and step-parents have no right to apply. The Code of Practice (above, para. 8) instructs local authorities to pay attention to the child's "wider family"; but there is at present no way in which such persons may bring the issue before a court if the authority refuses to give them access: *Re W* (above).

The natural father of an illegitimate child had no right to apply under this provision; but it appears that he could apply for access under the provision of the Guardianship of Minors Act 1971, s. 9; see para. 16-34 above, and *R. v. Oxford Justices, ex parte D* [1986] 3 All ER 129. It does not, of course, follow that the court would be prepared in the exercise of its discretion to make an order intended to affect the father's access to a child who was in fact in local authority care. The Family Law Reform Bill annexed to the Law Commission's *Second Report on Illegitimacy*, Law Com. No 157, 1986 which is before Parliament as this book goes to press apparently confers all the rights of a father under the access order provisions—including the right to be notified of a decision to terminate access and the statutory right to apply for an access order on the child's natural father, irrespective of whether he already had a court order giving him rights over the child (see clause 2(1)(*f*)).

18-71   (iv) The question of access will often be part of the wider issue of the arrangements to be made for the child's long term future. In particular, a decision to terminate access may be a preliminary to preparing the child for adoption. An authority which decides to terminate access with a view to adoption may now start proceedings in the magistrates' court to free the child for adoption (see para. 17–49 above); and in *M. v. Berkshire* CC [1985] FLR 257 it was suggested that the fact that this procedure is now available means that the court has adequate powers to deal with the issue as a whole. However, the freeing application will be heard by the Domestic Court; and there is nothing to stop a parent starting access proceedings in the juvenile court. Moreover, the adoption proceedings may be started in the High Court or County Court perhaps by the foster parents with whom the child has been living (see para. 17–46 above for the rights of such persons):

> In *Southwark LBC* v. *H.* [1985] 2 All ER 657 the Divisional Court suggested that where such a situation arose the question of access between parent and child should be disposed of first. This may have the paradoxical result that a juvenile court—the lowest court in the judicial hierarchy—could, by granting access to the parents, not only overturn the local authority's plan for the child's future but effectively pre-empt the decision of the High Court about whether adoption was in the child's interests. If that were to happen the local authority could seek to make an expedited appeal to the High Court; and to consolidate the adoption application with the appeal: RSC Ord. 4, r. 9. However, the situation is far from satisfactory.

(3) Wardship

18-72   In wardship proceedings, as we have seen (para. 15–25), the question which the court asks is: "what course of action would best serve the child's welfare?" for that question is (to repeat a quotation which bears repetition) considered "first, last and all the time" in wardship: Dunn LJ in *Re D (A Minor) (Justices' Decision: Review)* [1977] Fam 158, 163. Hence, persons dissatisfied with local authority decisions often tried to invoke the wardship jurisdiction as a means of questioning the decision, on the basis that in such proceedings the welfare of the child would be assigned its proper place. For example:

In *A* v. *Liverpool CC* [1982] AC 363 a mother made her child, who was the subject of a care order, a ward of court in an attempt to challenge the local authority's decision to reduce her access to him from once weekly to once monthly. The House of Lords—influenced to some extent by the cost and delay caused by excessive use of the wardship jurisdiction—held that the courts should not exercise that jurisdiction in order to review the merits of the authority's decision. This was because Parliament had in the child care code marked out an area in which, subject to the enacted limitations and safeguards, decisions for the child's welfare were removed from the parents and from supervision by the courts.

This restrictive approach was reinforced by the House in *Re W (A Minor) (Wardship: Jurisdiction)* [1985] AC 791:

Grandparents and other relatives wanted to get care and control of a child whom the local authority intended to free for adoption. They issued a summons making her a ward, but the House of Lords held that it would be wrong to use the wardship jurisdiction in such a case. Decisions about where the child was to have its home had been entrusted by Parliament to the local authority. It was irrelevant that the relatives had no right to be heard in freeing, access, or other legal proceedings.

The result seems to be that the wardship jurisdiction can no longer be invoked as a way of questioning local authority decisions, save perhaps as an alternative to judicial review in certain exceptional circumstances considered below.

Circumstances in which wardship used

This does not mean that wardship is irrelevant in the context of local **18–73** authorities' powers over children. On the contrary local authorities are encouraged to have recourse to the wardship jurisdiction when their powers are inadequate to ensure that the welfare of the child is properly safeguarded. Hence, the court has been prepared to exercise its jurisdiction if:

(i) the child is in voluntary care, and there is a risk that he will be removed by the parent in circumstances in which the child's welfare may be endangered: *Lewisham LBC* v. *Lewisham JJ* [1980] AC 273; para. 18–10 above.

(ii) the local authority cannot establish a sufficient ground for the passing of a parental rights resolution, or if it has been unsuccessful in establishing one of the conditions for the making of a care order or if a care order has been discharged.

(iii) A local authority exercising its statutory powers and duties over a child in care needs the assistance of the court—for example, by way of injunction prohibiting a person from seeking to ascertain the whereabouts of the child, or from going within a specified distance of his home or from establishing any contact with him, or publishing any information about him or his parentage: see *X CC* v. *AB* [1985] 1 All ER 53 para. 15–13 above.

(iv) the case is one of exceptional difficulty, as for example *Re C (A Minor) (Wardship: Surrogacy)* [1985] FLR 846 where the question was the future of a new-born baby conceived in performance of a surrogate parenting agreement.

This seems to give all the advantages to a local authority, who may thus use the wardship jurisdiction in circumstances in which a private individual could not do so. Indeed, it has been held that the local authority may, if it thinks fit, waive the right to object to the wardship court assuming jurisdiction:

> In *A. v. B and Hereford and Worcester County Council* [1986] 1 FLR 289 a 15 year old mother asked the local authority to receive her new-born baby into care. The child's 16 year old putative father started wardship proceedings in which he asked that care and control of the baby be given to its maternal grandmother. As a matter of law, the local authority's decision about the placement of a child in its care was one which could not have been questioned in wardship against its will (*A v. Liverpool CC* (above)); but since the court would have acceded to a request to use wardship from the authority even if the case were one in which it would not permit wardship to be used by an outsider it was held to be wrong to refuse to hear the case since the authority did not object to the court doing so.

Is it therefore the case that a local authority can use wardship whenever it pleases? In principle it is not clear why this should be regarded as objectionable; but it has, rather enigmatically, been questioned whether the court has an unfettered discretion to permit such use: Purchas L.J. in *Re DM (A Minor) (Wardship: Jurisdiction)* [1987] 2 FLR 122, 133; see also Stephen Brown L.J. in *D (A Minor) v. Berkshire CC* [1987] 1 All ER 20, CA.

(4) Judicial review

18-74   The remedy of judicial review is available to question local authority decision-taking relating to children on the usual grounds of illegality, irrationality, or procedural impropriety (to follow Lord Diplock's classification in *CCSU v. Minister for the Civil Service* [1985] AC 374):

(a) *Illegality*
For example:

18-75   In *R. v. Bolton MB ex parte B* [1985] FLR 343 the authority had misunderstood its duties under the access legislation and by failing to give statutory notice of termination (see para. 18–67 above) had deprived parents of their right to bring the issue to the juvenile court. The Divisional Court in judicial review proceedings made an order of mandamus requiring the authority to perform its statutory obligations.

(b) *Irrationality*
18-76   Is the decision so irrational that no reasonable authority properly directing itself could have taken it: see *R v. Bolton MBC*, above? In many cases, the ground of complaint may be a failure properly to consider the relevant factors: for example:

> In *Re D. (A Minor)* (1978) 76 LGR 653 the local authority passed a parental rights resolution, but the relevant committee acted on the basis of a written report which inadequately set out the factual material necessary for a proper exercise of its discretion.

It may be that the publication of the statutory code of practice governing access will be of great importance in this context since a failure to comply with the code might indicate that the authority had not properly directed itself to the relevant considerations.

(c) *Procedural impropriety*
For example:

In *Re L(AC)* [1971] 3 All ER 744 the local authority had misled the mother about   **18-77**
her statutory rights to object to the passing of a parental rights resolution; and there was also evidence that the relevant committee had not directed its mind to the appropriate matters. The decision was thus open to review (albeit, in that case, in wardship).

Limited scope of judicial review. Judicial review is not appropriate if there   **18-78**
is a right of appeal: *R. v. Slough JJ ex parte B* [1985] FLR 384; *Southwark LBC v. H* [1985] 2 All ER 657; and it must be remembered that it is concerned with the legality of the process whereby the decision which is in issue has been reached, not with the question whether that decision is right or wrong: *R. v. Slough JJ* (above) following Lord Brightman in *Chief Constable of North Wales Police* v. *Evans* [1982] 1 WLR 1155.

Judicial review embodies a number of safeguards for the authority whose decision is in issue—for example, leave of the court is necessary, and the applicant must state specifically the statutory duty breach of which is alleged and the manner in which the breach is alleged to have taken place: Purchas L.J. in *Re DM (A Minor) (Wardship: Jurisdiction)* (above) at p. 133. Judicial review is thus obviously less satisfactory than wardship to parents and others wishing to question local authority child care decisions not only because of the comparative narrowness of the grounds upon which the court will intervene and the procedural obstacles which must first be surmounted, but also because the result of a successful application is simply that the decision in question will be quashed and the case remitted to the authority. In contrast, in wardship the court would take control of the case.

(5) Local government ombudsman

The Local Government Act 1974 provides that a Local Commissioner   **18-79**
for Administration may investigate complaints made by or on behalf of members of the public who claim to have suffered injustice in consequence of maladministration; however, it is provided that no investigation shall be made if the person aggrieved has or had a remedy by way of proceedings in any court of law.

This procedure may be invoked to question decisions taken by local authorities in the exercise of their statutory powers. In practice, however, this remedy may not be satisfactory since the Commissioner only has limited powers. If he considers that injustice has been caused by maladministration his report must be considered by the local authority, which must then notify the Commissioner of the action they have taken or propose to take. However, the Commissioner cannot order the authority to take any specific action; and the sanctions available against a recalcitrant authority are limited to making a second report. In practice, only a small proportion of complaints made under this procedure relate to local authority social services; but the procedure can be of value where the person aggrieved has no other way of getting at the truth—for example, where an authority has suddenly changed its attitude without explanation.

CONCLUSION—REFORM OF THE LAW

18-80 Child welfare has come to be a major concern of the welfare state; and there is now a vast code of legislation evidencing this concern. Unfortunately, the legislation is not governed by consistent and coherent principles. It is to be found in many different enactments, inspired by different philosophies; and the result is confusion, complexity, technicality and subtlety.

In 1984 the House of Commons Social Services Committee recommended that a working party be set up by the DHSS with a view to the production of a simplified and coherent body of law; and in 1985 that Working Party produced a Report to Ministers ("the Review"). In 1987 the Goverment published a White Paper, *The Law on Child Care and Family Services* (Cm. 62) setting out its proposals for a major overhaul of child care law; but in the meantime the complexity of the statute book had been yet further increased by the enactment of the Children and Young Persons (Amendment) Act 1986—a private member's bill which attempts to deal with some of the more pressing inadequacies of the law. The provisions of the 1986 Act have not been brought into force; but the Government has said that it intends to introduce legislation "as soon as the Parliamentary timetable allows" to give effect to the more comprehensive White Paper proposals. Those proposals are designed to "rationalise, clarify and where possible simplify the law, above all in the interests of children whose well-being is the primary objective of child care law" (Cm. 62 pp. iv and 22).

The complex issues involved in any reforms of the law are fully discussed in the Review, to which reference may usefully be made. They include the following:

(1) On what grounds should the state be entitled to interfere in the autonomy of the family unit?

18-81 At present the wardship jurisdiction can be invoked simply on the basis that the child's welfare so requires; but care orders and parental rights resolutions can only be used if specific and in some respects narrowly worded conditions are satisfied.

The Review rejected the view that these grounds should be replaced by a broad welfare test. If applied literally such a broad test would lead to a substantial proportion of the child population being taken into care on the basis that the children would be "better off' with foster parents. It would give rise to varying and subjective interpretations, and would accordingly fail to provide sufficient statutory protection against unwarranted interference.

The Government has accepted the Review's recommendation that the **18-82** court should be empowered to make an order only if each of three elements is present:

(i) Evidence of harm or likely harm to the child; which is—

(ii) attributable to the absence of a reasonable standard of parental care or to the child being beyond parental control; provided that—

(iii) the order proposed is the most effective means available to the court of safeguarding the child's welfare (Cm. 62, para. 59).

These changes will enable the court to act in cases of apprehended harm (contrast *Essex CC v. TLR and KBR*, para. 18–39 above) and they will thus reduce the need for local authorities to invoke the wardship jurisdiction. (This appears to have been the objective underlying a number of the White Paper proposals).

If a child has been abandoned, the court will be able to make a guardianship order under the Guardianship of Minors Act 1971 (see para. 17–05 above): Cm. 62, para. 25.

Time will tell whether the proposed reformulation provides the right degree of protection against unwarranted interference; and there are those who think that the conditions should be far more specific—for example, intervention might be justified on the ground (amongst others) that the child has suffered, or there is a substantial likelihood that he will suffer, an injury causing disfigurement, impairment of bodily functioning or severe bodily harm: see *Care Cases: Proposals for Legal Reform* (Family Rights Group 1985) which are heavily influenced by the views of M. Wald (1976) 28 Stanford L.Rev.

(2) Should it be possible for authorities to obtain parental powers by administrative procedures?

At present local authorities can assume parental rights over a child in **18-83** care by parental rights resolution: para. 18–21 above. However, the Government has accepted the philosophy that transfer of parental powers and responsibilities should only be effected by a full court hearing following due legal processes; and accordingly local authorities will have to seek an order in care proceedings if they are concenred about the arrangements to be made for the child and cannot reach agreement with the parents: Cm. 62, paras. 5, 25.

The Government also propose (para. 22) that, in line with the concept of voluntary partnership, authorities should no longer be able to require a period of 28 days notice before a parent can recover a child who has been in care for more than six months: contrast para. 18–13 above. There will be those who think that this proposal will seriously erode the protection currently given to children in voluntary care; and that it can only—contrary to the general policy of the White Paper—lead to an increase in recourse by local authorities to the wardship jurisdiction to prevent removals of children who would otherwise be at risk.

(3) Procedural rules

18-84   The Children and Young Persons Act 1969 was drafted on the basis that care proceedings would be the normal method for dealing with delinquent children as well as those in need of protection. But the legal framework appropriate for the delinquent may not be appropriate in protection cases. For example, the child accused of delinquency is entitled to be protected by strict rules of evidence, whereas the child in need should not be put further at risk by insistence on rigid technicality. Again, in proceedings based on delinquency the central issue must be the culpability of the child. The behaviour of the child's parents will usually be irrelevant, and it will often be sensible to look on them as representing their child if they so wish. But in "protection" proceedings it is very often the behaviour of the parents which is in issue: it is they who are "in the dock" because they are accused of having neglected their child. In such circumstances the parents should obviously have a right to defend themselves; and it would be absurd to allow them to represent the child whose interests may be very different from their own.

The 1969 Act could not adequately provide for the two different kinds of case, and unfortunately usually followed the "delinquency" model, with results which were all the more unfortunate since care proceedings were in fact very rarely used in delinquency cases. Various piecemeal reforms have been made, but the situation is still unsatisfactory. The White Paper proposes sweeping changes, made possible by recognising that care proceedings should no longer be founded on the commission of a criminal offence. The main difficulties in the present law, and the reforms which are proposed, are:

(a) The parties to the proceedings

18-85   The child is the respondent in care proceedings. Under the 1969 Act, the parents could not be parties to the proceedings; but they could be required to attend the court, and were given the right to meet any allegations made in the course of the proceedings by calling or giving evidence, and the right to cross-examine any witness.

This left the parents' position in many respects obscure; and the Children and Young Persons (Amendment) Act 1986 would (if it were to be brought into force) require the parents to be made parties whenever the court decided that there was a conflict of interest between parent and child.

Although this change would improve the position of parents—for example, by giving those who were joined the right to object to the admission of evidence—it would not by itself resolve all the difficulties stemming from the fact that care proceedings ae still (see Lord Bridge of Harwich in *Re W (A Minor) (Wardship: Jurisdiction)* [1985] AC 791) in form adversarial. In particular, there would often be other persons with a vital interest in the proceedings (for example, foster-parents, grandparents and other members of the wider family: see *Re W (A Minor) (Wardship: Jurisdiction)* [1985] AC 791, para. 18–72 above) who would not be parties to the proceedings, and who would thus have at best only restricted rights to take part in them by making representations.

The 1986 Act would allow grandparents (but not others) to apply to be   **18-86**
joined as parties; but it seems likely that this limited and as yet unimplemented reform—which would not permit the court to make an order giving the grandparents the care of the child—will be overtaken by the far more radical solution proposed in the White Paper. This is that anyone whose legal position could be affected by the proceedings would be entitled to party status; and the court would also be empowered to make a custody order in favour of a third party such as a grandparent if either (a) the party concerned was qualified to apply for custodianship (see paras. 17–05 to 17–06 above), or (b) the first two elements of the new grounds were satisfied and a custody order would be the most effective means of protecting the child's welfare.

However, there are—as the Review pointed out—dangers in extending the right to take part. Cases could be longer and more complicated, and discontented relatives might simply use the opportunity to make trouble. Certainly one result could be a significant increase in the number of parties before the magistrates' court (which, unlike the wardship court, would not usually be experienced in dealing with cases involving a multiplicity of parties.)

(b) *Representing the child*

At one time, parents were routinely allowed to conduct care proceed-   **18-87**
ings on the child's behalf, even if in substance the case involved allegations that they had ill-treated the child; but the court now has power to make what is called a "separation order"—*i.e.* an order that the parent be not treated as representing the child—if it considers that there is or may be a conflict of interest between parent and child.

If a court does make a separation order it will normally appoint a guardian ad litem, who will be drawn from a panel of persons with qualifications in social work together with sufficient relevant experience and whose duty is to safeguard the interests of the child in the manner prescribed by rules of court. A solicitor will usually be appointed to act for the child.

There is evidence of considerable diversity of judicial practice in the exercise of these powers: see *R. v. Plymouth Juvenile Court ex parte F and F* [1987] 1 FLR 164. The White Paper proposes that the court should be under a duty to appoint a guardian in all cases unless it appears unecessary to do so in order to safeguard the child's interests: Cm. 62, para. 57. There will thus inevitably be a considerable extension of representation and a consequent increase in the complexity of proceedings to be handled by magistrates. But the Government did not accept that the changes should be deferred until a decision had been made on the issue of a Family Court: Cm. 62, para. 12.

(4) Other White Paper proposals

18-88   The White Paper makes a number of other important recommendations for reform:

(i) *Emergency procedures and interim orders*

Place of safety orders (para. 18–59 above) are to be replaced by an "emergency protection order" which will last for 8 days only (although in exceptional circumstances this period can be extended by a further 7 days) (Cm. 62, para. 46). There are to be stricter rules for the making of interim orders; and the maximum duration of such an order is to be 8 weeks, with the possibility of 14 day extensions if there are exceptional circumstances: Cm. 62, para. 61; *cf.* para. 18–56 above.

(ii) *Discharge of care orders*

Legislation is to give the guidance now lacking (para. 18–54 above) about the weight to be attached to the child's interests in deciding whether to discharge a care order: the court will have to be satisfied that discharge is in the best interests of the child: Cm. 62, para. 65.

(iii) *Questioning decisions*

All parties are to have a right of appeal to the High Court against the making or the refusal to make an order: Cm. 62, para. 66; *cf.* para. 18–62 above. The legislation will enshrine a presumption of "reasonable access" to a child in care; and the court will be given power to define what is reasonable. Once that has been done the authority will not be able to change the arrangements without parental agreement or court order: Cm. 62, para. 64. Presumably issues about access will still be resolved by reference to the child's best interests test; so that access will be terminable where, for example, the child's interests require him to be placed for adoption. Local authorities are to be required to provide an independent complaints procedure to deal with complaints about the exercise of their powers: Cm. 62, para. 31.

Chapter 19

THE CHILD OF THE FAMILY OUTSIDE MARRIAGE

INTRODUCTION

The Common Law

9-01   Most legal systems draw a distinction between legitimate children (who are regarded as full members of the legal family) and illegitimate children (who to a greater or lesser extent are not given full legal recognition). The common law went so far as to classify the illegitimate child as *filius nullius*—the child of no-one who was therefore a stranger in law not only to his father but to his mother and all other relatives. In consequence, he had no legal right to succeed to their property or to receive maintenance, and he had no legal right to any other benefits derived from the legal relationship of parent and child.

Piecemeal reform

9-02   Over the years, the legal position of the child born illegitimate has gradually been improved. The most important reform was perhaps to enable illegitimate children to be legitimated—usually by the subsequent marriage of their parents; but children who remained illegitimate were also given more extensive legal rights. Ultimately the law adopted the policy that illegitimate children should not be penalised. For example, legislation culminating in the Family Law Reform Act 1969 greatly diminished the disadvantages of illegitimacy in relation to inheritance: an illegitimate child was given the right to succeed on the intestacy of either parent (although he still did not count as a relative for purposes of succession to his brothers or sisters or his grandparents). Again, if one of his parents was killed as a result of the negligence or other wrongful act of a third party, the illegitimate child could, like a legitimate child, sue under the Fatal Accidents legislation for loss of financial support.

Continued discrimination against the child

19-03   But there were still some areas in which discrimination against the child born outside marriage remained. For example, there were the disadvantages mentioned above in relation to succession rights; and although the illegitimate child had a right to be supported by his father, that right could be enforced only in a special form of proceedings (called affilliation proceedings) which had to be brought in the lowest court in the judicial hierarchy (the Magistrates' Court). Affiliation proceedings were surrounded by procedural and other rules which caused the illegitimate child to be treated differently from, and usually less favourably than, the legitimate child in pursuing claims for support.

The parent's position

The law came comparatively quickly to recognise the legal link between   **19–04**
the illegitimate child and the child's mother; but it has been very slow to
recognise the father. Indeed, from a strictly legal point of view the father
of an illegitimate child was perhaps put at a greater disadvantage than the
child himself: in principle the law did not recognise the legal link between
the illegitimate child and his father. Hence, the father was not entitled to
any parental authority over his illegitimate child (although he could apply
to the court for custody or access, and in such an application the court
would be obliged to follow the principle that the child's welfare was the
first and paramount consideration).

The social realities

A large number of children were affected by these legal rules. In 1985,   **19–05**
no less than 126,000 children were born illegitimate; and the proportion
of illegitimate to legitimate births has greatly increased since the end of
the Second World War. Between 1945 and 1960 about 5 per cent. of births
each year were recorded as illegitimate; but then—in spite of the
availability of abortion and reliable contraception —the rates began to
grow rapidly. By 1985 the proportion of illegitimate births had risen to 19
per cent.—twice the rate in 1975, and one of the highest rates in Western
Europe outside Scandinavia. (In Sweden, the proportion of births outside
marriage approaches 50 percent.).

But it would be wrong to assume from these figures that there has been
a corresponding increase in the number of one-parent families. The legal
rules summarised above tend to reinforce the stereotype image of the
illegitimate child as a child who has no real family; but in reality it is now
clear that many illegitimate children are the products of stable unions
outside marriage. In 1979 the Law Commission (Working Paper No 74,
para 1.4) suggested that as many as half of the illegitimate children then
born were the offspring of such unions; and there has since then been a
dramatic increase in the proportion of cases in which the birth is
registered jointly by both parents (who thus indicate at least their
acceptance of the fact of parentage). In 1985, 65 per cent. of all illegitimate
births were registered jointly; and the recent increase in the number of
illegitimate births represents almost entirely an increase in the number of
jointly registered births. It may also be the case that birth outside marriage
is more readily accepted as a social and cultural norm amongst some of
the immigrant communities than has traditionally been the case in this
country; see S. M. Poulter, *English Law and Ethnic Minority Customs* (1986)
para. 4–05. All these factors may be thought to cast doubt on the
discriminatory principles remaining in the law.

REFORM

In 1982 the Law Commission published a comprehensive and detailed   **19–0**
report (Law Com. No. 118) which concluded that discrimination against

those born outside marriage could not be justified as a general policy. This conclusion was reinforced by the fact that to preserve such discrimination would be inconsistent with this country's international obligations under the European Convention on Human Rights, and the European Convention on the Legal Status of Children Born Out of Wedlock. The Family Law Reform Bill which is before Parliament as this book is in the press will give effect (with some insignificant variations) to the policy adopted in the Law Commission's Report; and the remainder of this chapter summarises the law as it will be when the Family Law Reform Act 1987 has been implemented. The text assumes that the Bill (which is based on a draft annexed to the Law Commission's Second Report on Illegitimacy, Law Com. No 157, 1986) reaches the statute book substantially in the form in which it received a Second Reading in the House of Lords on November 27, 1986.

A PRELIMINARY ISSUE—PARENTAGE

9–07   The Family Law Reform Act 1987 adopts a general principle that the question whether a person's mother and father have been married to each other is legally irrelevant: see further para. 19–13 below. Hence, if a court has to decide whether Simon is Susan's brother, for example, the question whether their parents were ever legally married is no longer to be material. But the question of who their parents were as a matter of fact remains of crucial importance: a Court must obviously be satisfied, before making any order in proceedings where parentage is in issue—for example, an application for support for a child against his father, or an application to share in the father's estate—that the persons concerned are in fact parent and child.

No presumption of parentage where parents unmarried
9–08   The difficulty of establishing the fact of parentage will often in practice remain a serious consequence of having been born to parents who were not married. This is because the law still presumes that a child born in wedlock to a married woman is a child of her husband, but there is to be no presumption of parentage in the case of a child born to an unmarried couple. Although maternity can normally be easily proved by evidence of the fact of parturition, proof of paternity has traditionally been a much more difficult matter. However, in recent years, scientific evidence — and particularly the results of blood testing— has become increasingly useful in providing reliable evidence of parentage; and sometimes the fact that an entry has been made in the Births register will provide legally acceptable evidence of parentage:

(i) Blood test evidence
19–09   Certain characteristics are transmitted from one generation to another in accordance with recognised principles of genetics; and a comparison of the characteristics of the child's blood with that of his mother and of a

particular man may provide conclusive evidence that he cannot be the father of a child. It is because blood testing worked in this way that the emphasis has traditionally been on excluding an identified man from paternity, rather than on establishing directly who is the child's father. It remains the case that in theory blood test evidence can exclude the possibility of paternity; but can never directly and of itself provide proof that a particular individual is the child's parent. But the practical reality is that blood testing may indirectly provide effectively conclusive evidence that a particular man is the child's father. For example, suppose that a married woman has, whilst living with her husband, had intercourse with only one other person, X. The question arises as to whether H or X is the child's father. If blood tests exclude the possibility that H is the father, then X must be the father.

Even in cases where blood tests do not exclude all but one possible father, they may provide evidence about the probability of parentage. This is because the blood tests may show that the child has genetic characteristics which he is more likely to have inherited from A, rather than from B, C, or D. In practice, the value of blood testing for establishing, and not merely eliminating, the paternity of a particular man is increasing. And, more generally, rapid developments in what is sometimes called genetic finger-printing can often be of value in establishing whether or not two people are biologically related.

There have been statutory provisions governing the use of blood test evidence since 1969; and the Family Law Reform Act 1987 now gives the courts a general power to direct the use of scientific tests to ascertain whether such tests show that a party to the proceedings is or is not the father or mother of a particular person. The report of the test will indicate, first of all, whether any party to whom the report relates is excluded by the results from being the father or mother of the person concerned; and it will also state the value (if any) of the results in determining whether a person who is not so excluded is the father or mother of that person. If a person refuses to comply with a test direction, the court may draw such inferences from the refusal as seem proper.

(ii) Birth registration as evidence of parentage

The entry of a man's name as the father of a child under the Births and **19-10** Deaths Registration Act 1953 constitutes prima facie evidence that that man is the father (s.34), and registration can thus be a useful way of establishing paternity.

The normal practice is that the person registering the child's birth is asked to state the name of the child's father. If a married woman states that her husband is the father, that statement will be accepted, and the husband's name entered: see Law Commission Working Paper No. 74, para. 9.14. The name of a man other than the mother's husband can be entered (i) if the mother and father jointly so request (and, as already stated, more than 60 per cent. of extra-marital births are registered in this way), or (ii) if the mother produces a declaration by the father. The only case in which a man can insist, against the wishes of the mother, in having his paternity recorded is if the court has made an order giving the father parental rights or requiring him to make financial provision for the child. Births may be re-registered if such an order has been made, or if there has been a declaration of parentage made under the procedure discussed below.

Procedures for establishing parentage

9-11   In most cases the question of parentage will be resolved as an integral part—perhaps most frequently as a preliminary issue—in proceedings for maintenance, succession, etc. However, the Family Law Reform Act 1987 gives effect to the Law Commission's recommendation that the court should also have power to make a binding declaration that a named person is the father or mother of the applicant. This will enable the question of parentage to be settled once and for all whether or not any specific legal issue involving parentage has arisen at the time.

But what is parentage?

9-12   Until very recently it would not have been necessary to ask this question. But rapid developments in the field of human assisted reproduction have made it a very real issue. In artificial insemination, for example, a man (who will not usually be the mother's husband) provides the semen with which the mother's egg is fertilised. Is the donor of the semen, who is unquestionably the genetic father, to be treated as the legal father? Similar issues arise in egg donation (when another woman provides the egg which is fertilised), embryo donation (when both another man and another woman contribute), and in surrogacy (when a third party agrees to provide her womb to carry a foetus to birth).

It seems probable that the law would regard the genetic parentage as crucial, so that a child conceived as a result of artificial insemination of the mother with sperm provided by a third party donor (AID) would be regarded as legally the child of the donor and the mother: see Law Com. No 118, Part XII. This seemed unsatisfactory; and the Family Law Reform Act will provide that such a child born to a married woman shall be treated as the child of her marriage unless it is proved that the husband did not consent to the insemination. But the law does not deal with other cases, so that (for example) a child born by AID to an unmarried woman will be treated in law as the donor's child, and not as the child of her partner. The Report of the Committee of Inquiry into Human Fertilisation and Embryology (The Warnock Report, Cmnd. 9314, 1984) made detailed proposals to rationalise the law; but these had not been implemented when this book went to press.

THE GENERAL PRINCIPLE OF THE REFORMED LAW

9-13   The Family Law Reform Act 1976 states the general principle that references in legislation:

"to any relationship between two persons shall, unless the contrary intention appears, be construed without regard to whether or not the father and mother of either of them, or the father and mother of any persons through whom relationship is deduced, have or had been married to each other at any time."

At first sight, the adoption of this general principle would seem to make it unnecessary to go any further: a child was illegitimate if his parents were not married; the question whether or not his parents are married is now to be irrelevant in determining legal relationships; and hence (it might be thought) illegitimacy has been abolished. But this is for two reasons misleading: first, although the Act applies the new principle to any future legislation, it only affects existing legislation so far as it expressly so provides—and there are a number of areas in which the old concept of legitimacy is still relevant to a child's rights; secondly—and much more important—the Act accepts the Law Commission's conclusion that the father of a child born outside marriage should not automatically have parental authority over the child.

The position of the father

Why did the Law Commission decide to preserve the principle that the **19–14** father of a child born outside marriage should not automatically have any parental authority over him? The answer appears to be that the Commission's consultation revealed a considerable division of opinion on this issue. Influential groups thought that automatically to equate the legal position of the father with that of the mother would involve risk—first, mothers would be tempted to conceal the father's identity, so that he would not be able to exercise any authority; secondly the father's legal right might be used in a disruptive way, particularly when the mother had married a third party and established a secure family for herself and the child. An unscrupulous father might be tempted to "harass or possibly even to blackmail" the mother at a time when she could be exceptionally vulnerable to pressure.

The result is that distinctions between children based solely on their parents' marital status remain—the father of a child born outside marriage will for that reason have no parental authority over him; and to that extent children are still divided into two categories: those with a "normal" relationship with both parents, and others.

SUMMARY OF LAW UNDER FAMILY LAW REFORM ACT 1987

The Family Law Reform Act 1987 is a complex piece of legislation; and it **19–1** would not be sensible to attempt a full analysis of its provisions in a work of this character which is being written before it has been enacted. What follows is a summary of the main provisions.

(1) Parent's marital status usually irrelevant

9–16   For most purposes, the question of whether a person's parents have been married is irrelevant in determining legal relationships. Hence brother and sister have equal rights of inheritance between themselves whether or not their parents are married.

(2) Claims for financial support

9–17   A child born to parents who are not married is thus to be in the same position as the child of married parents in relation to his rights to financial support from his mother and father under the Guardianship of Minors Act 1971, and other legislation. The legislation in question has been amended accordingly; and the powers of the court to make financial orders have been considerably extended. In particular, there will be power to make orders dealing with capital as well as with income.

(3) Exceptional cases

9–18   In some cases, the existing law discriminating against the illegitimate child has been preserved. For example:

(a) Citizenship

Under the British Nationality Act 1981, the relationship of parent and child exists only between a man and his legitimate child: BNA 1981, s. 50(9)(*b*). An illegitimate child cannot therefore acquire British citizenship through his father; and there are two main factual situations in which a child of unmarried parents will not be entitled to the British citizenship which a child of married parents would take. These are, first, where a child is born in this country to a British father and a foreign mother; and secondly, where a child is born abroad to a British father and a foreign mother or a mother who is British by descent only.

The Law Commission considered that as a matter of policy a child who could prove his parentage should be entitled to British citizenship irrespective of his parents' marital status: Law Com. No 118, para 11.20. But the 1987 Act does not give effect to that recommendation.

(b) Succession to the throne, peerages, etc.

9–19   Succession to the throne of the United Kingdom is governed by the Act of Settlement 1701, the language of which restricts the right of succession to the legitimate. Because the Family Law Reform Act 1987 does not retrospectively apply the general principle set out in para. 19–13 above to the 1701 Act, the position remains unaltered. Again, hereditary peerages granted before the enactment of the Family Law Reform Act 1987 have all been limited to heirs "lawfully begotten" (see Law Com. No. 118, para 8.26) and the right of succession to such peerages, and indeed the right to take property under wills taking effect and settlements made before the implementation of the Act, will be unaffected.

The father's position

9–20   The father of a child born to a woman other than his wife has no automatic parental authority over that child. He has no right, therefore, to custody or access to the child. The father may, however, apply to the court for orders:

(a) He may apply to the court under section 4 of the Family Law Reform Act 1987 for all "the parental rights and duties with respect to the child." Unless the court directs otherwise, he will have those jointly with the mother. In practice, therefore, such an order will effectively put a father who can satisfy the court that it is in the child's interest that his legal position be recognised in the same legal position as the father of a child born in marriage. The father of a child born in marriage, in contrast, does not have to submit himself to judicial scrutiny before acquiring parental authority.

(b) He may apply to the court under the Guardianship of Minors Act 1971 (see para. 16–34 above) for access to the child, or for legal custody of the child.

Generally, if a father has an order for custody, legal or actual custody or care and control of the child under a court order then he will be recognised as the father for many legal purposes—for example he would become a person whose agreement is required to the child's adoption. The general policy is that a father who merely has a right to access under a court order does not count as a "father" for these purposes.

Proof of parentage

The child of unmarried parents cannot rely on any presumption of parentage, except that arising from the presumption that entries in the births register are correct. In certain circumstances the father of a child born to unmarried parents can insist on his name being entered as the child's father; and a child may apply for a declaration of parentage, even if he is not seeking any other relief (such as maintenance). **19-21**

CONCLUSION

Although the Family Law Reform Act 1987 removes most of the legal **19-22** disadvantages of illegitimacy so far as they discriminate against the illegitimate child, it cannot be said that in all respects the question of the parents' marital status has become irrelevant. It is an interesting question whether, in the result, the concepts of "legitimacy, and illegitimacy" have been abolished. What is clear is that this distinction will rarely be important so far as the child is concerned, and the Family Law Reform Act—following in this respect the precedent set by the Law Reform (Parent and Child) (Scotland) Act 1986: see Law Com. No. 157 (1986) para. 2.2 avoids attaching labels ((such as "illegitimate" or "non-marital") to children). But the Family Law Reform Act 1987 itself recognises that legitimacy may still be a relevant legal concept. To that end, application may be made to the Court for a declaration that a person is the legitimate child of his parents: Family Law Act 1987, s.56 (as substituted by Family Law Reform Act 1987, cl.22); and presumably demographic statistics will still distinguish between "legitimate" and "illegitimate" births since the Family Law Reform Act will not provide any alternative terminology. (The draft Bill annexed to the Law Commission's original 1982 Report would, in contrast, have embodied the terms "marital" and "non-marital" in the statute book, and would thereby have rendered unecessary the continued use of the expression "illegitimate" with its connotations of unlawfulness and illegality: Law Com. No 118, para. 4.51.)

"NET EFFECT" CALCULATOR: THE WIFE

1. **Stage 1. Calculate Wife's Taxable Income**

	ANNUAL
WIFE GROSS INCOME (employment and investments)	£
Proposed Personal maintenance from Respondent (Gross)	£
(a) Total personal income ["TPI"]	£

DEDUCT

Pensions contributions	£	
Personal allowance single person	£	
Additional personal allowance (re children)	£	
Total deductions		£
(b) "Gross Taxable" ["GT"]		£

2. **Stage 2. Calculate Her "Spendable" Income**

(c) Total personal income ["TPI"]		£

DEDUCT

Tax on GT @ %	£
Pension contributions	£
N.I. contributions	£
Travel to work	£

ADD

1. Child benefit (DHSS)	£
2. Single parent supplement (DHSS)	£
3. Maintenance for children	£

ANNUAL AVAILABLE INCOME	£

CALCULATE MONTHLY/WEEKLY—12/52=		£
DEDUCT OUTGOINGS, MONTHLY/WEEKLY		
RENT/MORTGAGE	£	
RATES	£	
Sub total	———	
GAS	£	
ELECTRICITY	£	
TELEPHONE	£	
HIRE PURCHASE	£	
SCHOOL DINNERS	£	
Sub total	———	
TOTAL OUTGOINGS		£

BALANCE AVAILABLE FOR FOOD/CLOTHING etc. FOR   £
HOUSEHOLD OF   ADULT(S)   CHILD(REN)
Aged

3. **Stage 3. Compare with "subsistence" figures**
[See Appendix Form C]

Appendix—Form B

"NET EFFECT" CALCULATOR: THE HUSBAND

1. **Stage 1. Calculate H's Taxable Income**

ANNUAL

HUSBAND GROSS INCOME (Employment and
investments ["TPI"]   £

DEDUCT
        Pension contributions   £

        Single person allowance   £
        Single person supplement   £
        (If he has children)
        Proposed Maintenance (gross)
OR   Married person allowance   £
                                                      ———

(a) "Gross Taxable" ("GT")   £

2. **Stage 2. Calculate H's "Spendable" Income**

Total personal income ["TPI"]	£

DEDUCT

Tax on GT @ %	£
Pension contributions	£
N.I. contributions	£
Travel to work	£

ADD

Child benefit (DHSS)	£
Single parent supplement (DHSS)	£
Maintenance for children	£
Net income of 2nd wife/cohabitee	£

ANNUAL AVAILABLE INCOME

CONVERT TO	MONTHLY/WEEKLY—12/52=	£
DEDUCT OUTGOINGS;	MONTHLY/WEEKLY	

RENT/MORTGAGE	£
RATES	£
MAINTENANCE	£
Subtotal	

Others:

GAS	£
ELECTRICITY	£
TELEPHONE	£
HIRE PURCHASE	£
_____	£
_____	£
Subtotal	

TOTAL OUTGOINGS	£

BALANCE AVAILABLE FOR FOOD/CLOTHING etc. FOR
HOUSEHOLD OF   ADULT(S)   CHILD(REN)
Aged   £

3. **Stage 3. Compare with "Subsistence" Figures**

[See Appendix Form C]

4. **Stage 4. Compare with One-Third Approach**

[See Appendix Form D]

Appendix—Form C

SUBSISTENCE FIGURES CALCULATION OF "NEEDS"

	Per week
SINGLE-householder	£29.80*
non Householder aged 18 or over	£23.85
MARRIED (or cohabiting) Couple	£48.40*
CHILDREN 18 and over	£23.85
16–18 (No. ×)	£18.40
11–15 (No. ×)	£15.30
Under 11 (No. ×)	£10.20

RENT PAID

RATES PAID (where not included in rent) +

MORTGAGE PAYMENTS

OTHER ALLOWABLE LIABILITIES:

TOTAL

* NB The "long-term" rates are £37.90 for a single householder and £60.65 for a married or cohabiting couple.

Appendix—Form D

CALCULATION OF PERIODICAL PAYMENTS—ONE THIRD APPROACH

HUSBAND	GROSS INCOME	£
DEDUCT		
N.H.I. contributions	£	
Pension contributions	£	
Travel to work	£	
	———	
		———
"Adjusted Gross Income" ("AGI")		£
		———
WIFE	GROSS INCOME	£
DEDUCT		
N.H.I. contributions	£	
Pension contributions	£	
Travel to work	£	
	———	
		———
"Adjusted Gross Income"		£
		———
Maintenance for Wife		
Wife's Adjusted Gross Income	£	
Husband's Adjusted Gross Income	£	
	———	
One-third thereof	£	
DEDUCT Wife's A.G.I.	£	
	———	
Wife's Maintenance	£	
	———	

INDEX

INDEX

252

INDEX

255

INDEX